"A thorough and thoughtful account of how the O. J. Simpson murder trial went awry, and its continuing negative impact on the judicial system."

—Fred Graham, Senior Editor, In Session
and former Senior Editor, Court TV

■ ■ ■

"This book absolutely redefines the meaning of the phrase 'Inside Story.' For all the people who watched the O. J. Simpson trial from the sidelines, the book presents a fascinating, up-close-and-personal history. I was a judge on the Los Angeles Superior Court at the time of the Simpson trial, and thought of myself as an insider, but I had no idea what went on behind the scenes, until now. In addition, the book provides an invaluable analysis of the nationwide impact of unprecedented media attention on the criminal justice system."

—Florence-Marie Cooper, Judge, United States
District Court, Central District of California

Anatomy of a **Trial**

Anatomy
of a Trial

Public Loss, Lessons Learned from
The People vs. O. J. Simpson

Jerrianne Hayslett

University of Missouri Press   Columbia and London

Library of Congress Cataloging-in-Publication Data

Hayslett, Jerrianne, 1941–
    Anatomy of a trial : public loss, lessons learned from The People vs. O. J. Simpson /
Jerrianne Hayslett.
        p.   cm.
    Includes bibliographical references and index.
    Summary: "This behind-the-scenes look at 'The People vs. O.J. Simpson' by the
court's media liaison gives readers an unprecedented look at the interaction of courts,
the media, and high-profile trials through interviews and quotations from her own
detailed journal and assesses the lingering impact of the trial on journalism, the justice
system, and the public"—Provided by publisher.
    ISBN 978–0-8262–1822-3 (alk. paper)
    1. Simpson, O. J., 1947—Trials, litigation, etc.   2. Trials (Murder)—California—Los
Angeles. I. Title.
    KF224.S485H39 2008
    345.73'025230979494—dc22
                                                                                    2008031786

♾ This paper meets the requirements of the
American National Standard for Permanence of Paper
for Printed Library Materials, Z39.48, 1984.

Designer: Kristie Lee
Typesetter: BookComp, Inc.
Printer and binder: Thomson-Shore, Inc.
Typefaces: Minion and Helvetica Neue

To Hilbert H. Hayslett Jr.

Contents

■ ■ ■

Contents

■ ■ ■

Literally dozens of law review articles have been written on the significance of the O. J. trial: the role played by race; the ethics of the attorneys; the meaning of jury nullification; the significance of domestic violence; and the meaning of forensic evidence. But none of that is the real legacy of O. J. It's just an attempt to find meaning in a trial that should have meant very little. The truth about O. J. is that for one brief moment, the law and the media went crazy and had a lot of sex, and gave birth to a vast sprawling beast that ate us all. With the trial over, life, law, and television returned us to our previously scheduled broadcast.

—Dahlia Lithwick, senior editor, "We Won't Get OJ-ed Again," *Slate* magazine, June 9, 2004

Reality is what the public perceives.

—National Public Radio news analyst Daniel Schorr

Those who care about the courts must intercept the more knee-jerk proposals of armchair quarterbacks that—if acted on—would undermine years of refinements that help guarantee due process and fairness for all who are involved in a court case. Those who care about the courts should use the Simpson trial as an opportunity to educate the public about the justice system and call for change that improves, not undermines, the system.

—editorial, *Judicature,* September–October 1995

Anatomy of a **Trial**

Introduction

The Reality of Perception

■ ■ ■

When former pro football player and TV pitchman O. J. Simpson was acquitted in the slashing deaths of his ex-wife, Nicole Brown Simpson, and her friend, Ronald Goldman, few foresaw the effect that trial would have on the judiciary and, consequently, on the public. Now, more than a decade after the verdicts, the Simpson trial remains a topic of debate and is cited as a major factor for an increase in such restrictive measures as gag orders, sealed documents, closed proceedings, and courtroom-camera bans. Those measures inhibit the public's access to the courts and its understanding of court proceedings and the judicial system.

No other case in recent times, not even the 2005 Michael Jackson child-molestation trial, has come close to affecting the U.S. judiciary and media access to the courts or shaping public perception as much as the Simpson trial did. Even today, judges, journalists, and lawyers across the country say *Simpson* changed everything.[1]

While hardly the first case to be called the "trial of the century," the Simpson case came to epitomize media excess and perceived judicial mismanagement. It was, and continues to be, the subject of countless news stories. It launched an industry of legal punditry and even, some say, the reality-TV phenomenon. Yet, despite an explosion of news outlets in the past decade, the media and the public now have less access to and a diminished understanding of the third branch of government, thanks in part to the Simpson trial and media coverage of it.[2]

1

Constitutional scholar Erwin Chemerinsky noted, "I think that the effect of the Simpson case was to cause judges to be much more suspicious and even hostile of media coverage of high-profile cases. This has been manifest in a reluctance to have televised proceedings and gag orders commonly being placed on attorneys in high-profile cases."[3]

Courtroom cameras were demonized by that trial, and the effects reached far beyond Los Angeles. First California and then other states revisited their procedures; at least one court system ended its camera-access pilot project, another may have decided against allowing cameras, and other countries debated the use of cameras in their courts.[4]

In addition to increased restrictions, the trial spawned a series of national conferences, became the subject of law school courses, and launched a national center for courts and the media.[5] The manifestations of the *Simpson* fallout are clear, but *why* did the trial have such an far-reaching and lasting impact?

The answer lies in the intersection of four elements: the character and approach of the trial judge, Lance A. Ito; what was happening off camera; the synergistic effect that the behind-the-scenes activities, the trial participants, the media, a number of peripheral characters, and, most significantly, the judge had on one another; and other judges' perceptions of and reactions to the trial and Ito.

Getting at the root causes of the trial's impact requires pulling back the media's Oz-like curtain and examining the behavior of everyone associated with the trial. Ito was but one of the players who emerged from relative obscurity to gain quick and lasting notoriety around the world, propelled not only by the case itself but by the attention of pundits and comedians, particularly those on the notoriously irreverent *Saturday Night Live*. Much of their commentary formed the basis for what eventually became perceived as fact.

The caricature of a weak, starstruck, incompetent judge who succumbed to the sirens of fame and even viewed himself as a celebrity persists as part of the trial's lore, which the media revisit and magnify with each new notorious case. That looms large in the minds of many judges who bristle at the mention of O. J. Simpson or Lance Ito. A review of press clippings and sound bites of the trial coverage might prompt one to wonder how such an inept person could have become a judge, much less have been entrusted with a trial guaranteed to play out on a national and, ultimately, an international stage.

But exploring now what wasn't reported then helps to shed light on how that image emerged, why the trial created such angst in other judges, and how that affected public access to subsequent court cases.

When Ito got the Simpson trial, he was considered one of the Los Angeles court's brightest rising judicial stars, destined for advancement to either a state appellate or federal judgeship. By the time the trial was over, his judicial reputation was tattered and his health battered from the stress of presiding over the very public nine-month testimony phase of the trial and the preceding six months of pretrial proceedings and jury selection.

Since that trial, a common reaction among judges who saw the media and trial attorneys as running amok has been to batten down the hatches in trials over which they preside. This retreat from public view has reduced access to courtrooms and case information, most notably as cameras have been barred from celebrity and high-profile proceedings.[6] An exception and perhaps a bellwether of reversing the trend nearly thirteen years after *Simpson* was the 2007 trial of Hollywood record producer Phil Spector, charged with murdering actress Lana Clarkson.[7]

"We have to get by [the Simpson] case," Los Angeles Superior Court Judge Larry Paul Fidler said in announcing his decision to allow camera coverage of Spector's trial. "There's going to come a time that it will be commonplace to televise trials. If it had not been for *Simpson,* we'd be there now."[8]

Ito, Fidler asserted, was wrongly blamed for and became an "unwilling celebrity" of the Simpson trial's "circus-like atmosphere."[9]

While some commended Fidler's courage for permitting cameras and publicly defending Ito, he drew criticism and declarations of skepticism not only from other judges, but also from media talking heads and self-perceived omniscient columnists. Media predictions that Spector's trial and the 2005 trial of actor Robert Blake, charged with killing his wife, would rival *Simpson* in both public interest and massive publicity proved inaccurate. Neither came close. Both were far less complex and the defendants more obscure compared to the iconic Simpson. And despite Fidler's allowing camera coverage, only Court TV televised *Spector* in full. The media contingent covering *Spector* was "minute," according to veteran Associated Press legal reporter Linda Deutsch, who was a full-time presence at all three trials.[10] Barely a dozen members of the media and a handful of other courtroom observers attended either the Spector or the Blake trial on a daily basis, Deutsch says. And the judges for those trials are not likely to retain lasting fame.

The Simpson trial, by contrast, was fourteen months of life in a fishbowl for Ito in which his every word and gesture was observed, analyzed, dissected, and scrutinized. He dealt with grandstanding attorneys, a perjuring witness, media violations, erroneous reporting, criminal investigations, charges of racism, a cross-country fight over an expert witness, worry that his chambers and phone were bugged, and pandemic problems with a largely dysfunctional jury. All of that was overlaid with the deaths of a family member, two reporters covering the case, and a popular courtroom bailiff; threats to his own life, and tabloid stories about his wife being a battered spouse and detailing a stepson's legal problems. His face became almost universally recognized, and his name endures as a frequent crossword puzzle clue.

Interestingly, although Ito was and still is trivialized as starstruck and grasping for fame, immediately after the trial he tried to return to anonymity. By contrast, the other major figures capitalized on their celebrity with book deals, speaking tours, TV shows, commentating gigs, and even acting stints. Without a doubt, Ito could have joined their ranks—publishers offered deals with two-to-three million-dollar advances and eventual five-to-six million net—but didn't. Until he agreed to cooperate for this book, he turned down interview requests and public-speaking invitations and declined to counter his critics.

"I prefer to remain in the tall grass," he said a few years ago when I proposed doing a magazine profile of him. He's done a good job of that. People generally express surprise when they learn that he's still on the bench trying felony cases and has three times since the Simpson trial been reelected to his superior court office.

While Ito's restraint and avoidance of the spotlight might be laudable, he has not necessarily done himself or the judiciary any favors. His silence has left his judicial reputation besmirched and allowed other judges' disdain for him to flourish. Some in the media, such as syndicated talk show host Larry Elder, have speculated that Ito's silence springs from embarrassment.[11] That is not the case.

While fingers have been pointed in many directions, most of the blame for the *Simpson* spectacle has been heaped on Ito. But just about everyone associated with the trial, including the vast public audience that followed it, bears some responsibility.

Ted Koppel, host of ABC's *Nightline,* said in an interview on a PBS show on the tenth-anniversary of the verdicts that although *Nightline* tried to minimize its coverage of the trial, it got a 10 percent ratings boost every time it included coverage in a broadcast.[12]

In that same show, Harvard law professor and member of Simpson's legal defense team Alan Dershowitz puzzled over the public's obsession with the trial: "I could never understand that," he said. "To me it was just another murder case."[13]

The People vs. Simpson would have been just another murder trial—Los Angeles courts are full of them—had not the public signaled its obsession even before Simpson's arrest, when hordes of people lined the streets and hung over freeway overpasses cheering and waving signs during the infamous slow-speed Bronco chase, or after he was charged, when spectators clamored for courtroom seats at the preliminary hearing and other pretrial proceedings. California's secretary of state was so worried that public interest in the Simpson case would keep voters away from the polls in November 1994, he asked Ito in August, just a few weeks after he got the case, to recess court on the day before and the day of the election.[14] The trial sent television ratings sky-high. Telecommunications companies reported a significant dip in long-distance telephone calls as the public awaited the October 1995 verdicts. And a Nielson ratings survey showed that nearly all of the Los Angeles-area residents who had turned their television sets on that October morning had them tuned to the trial.[15] Yet, almost immediately after the verdicts, people started denying having watched it or even having any interest in it; in fact, many said they were sick of the trial.

Simpson would have been just another trial had the media not stampeded the Los Angeles Criminal Courts Building in the summer of 1994; set up a camp full of trailers, satellite trucks, and microwave vans; built five-story-tall scaffolding for broadcast platforms; laid eighty miles of fiber-optic cabling,[16] and done nonstop stories on everything that moved, whether news or not. Although some members of the news media briefly looked askance at their own behavior after the trial, many soon returned to criticizing and ridiculing everyone else, most notably the judge.

Simpson prosecutors and defense attorneys also turned Simpson from just another trial into a spectacle with their outlandish and, at times unprofessional, behavior then published books and went on speaking tours blaming everybody but themselves for the excesses and outrages surrounding the case.

The trial might not have become such an aberration had the judge presiding over it not had Ito's personality, accessibility, and belief in his position as a public servant. He believed that the public had a right to see the trial, but he also thought that the initial rabid interest in the case would quickly fade and that he could with impunity do a television interview not related to the case. His expectations led him to be too gracious toward and too slow to rein in the grandstanding attorneys who were abusing his propensity to let lawyers have their full say.

Other judges, including some who succumbed to the sirens of the trial themselves, started castigating Ito and condemning the trial before it was even over, claiming they could have done a better job. Ironically, few of the judges who have smarted over the black eye they believe Ito gave the judiciary allow cameras into their own courtrooms so they can demonstrate their competence and undo the damage they say the Simpson trial created.

For well over a year, the Simpson case consumed not only the lives of the participants, their supporting staff, and journalists, but also those of government officials in California and elsewhere, entertainers of all stripes, and the general public. All focused myopically on the trial and their symbiosis with it. Few, however, stepped back to take the long view, to examine what was happening and why or what it might portend for the future of the courts and the media. And finally, despite the millions of words written and spoken about it, no one has analyzed the actions and behaviors exhibited during and after the trial to show how they altered the court-media landscape or what impact they had on the American public.

As the Los Angeles court's information officer and media liaison, I was in the courtroom and Ito's chambers daily during the Simpson trial. I worked with the news media, the judge, and other court officials and was behind the scenes at that trial as well as many other high-profile cases. I began keeping a written log of events soon after Ito got the case and started an audio journal in early March 1995.

Beyond the Simpson case and cases involving Michael Jackson, Heidi Fleiss, the Menendez brothers, and Rodney King, I continue to work in the field of court-media relations both nationally and internationally, and I continue to hear the concerns of judges, the media, and attorneys that a frequently dysfunctional relationship is depriving the country of an informed society.

From that unique vantage point, *Anatomy of a Trial* tracks how Ito went from judicial paragon to a caricature of an inept black-robed celebrity wannabe and examines not only the media's crucial role, but also Ito's and my own unwitting culpability, which contributed to the enduring negative effect. This is the untold story of a very public yet poorly understood trial watched by millions of people around the world and the tremendous impact it has had on the judiciary, the media, and the public. But more than just a captivating tale of an aberrational trial and its consequences, this account includes a blueprint for what the media and judges can do in the future to head off sideshows and to fulfill their responsibilities to the public.

Chapter 1
To Here from There

■ ■ ■

Lance Ito leaned back in the black leather chair in his chambers, propped his feet up on his cluttered desk, and clasped his hands behind his head.

"Well, Jerrianne," he asked, "what do you think I should do with the rest of my life?"

That was the first time a judge had ever asked me such a question, and it might have left me speechless had it come from any other.

It was January 1996. The abrupt and, to many people, shocking verdicts in the O. J. Simpson criminal trial had been rendered more than three months earlier. During those months, Ito had taken time off from his judicial duties to restore his health, both physical and mental, and to contemplate direction.

Lance Ito was the first judge I knew to be so profoundly affected by a trial. Sure, Stanley Weisberg of McMartin Preschool molestation, Rodney King beating, and Menendez brothers fame, and Reginald Denny–beating trial judge John Ouderkirk had endured the media glare, gotten death threats and hate mail, required heightened security, and had their personal lives invaded. Those kinds of things have become almost commonplace with trials of great media interest in contemporary culture, as Florida judge George Greer, who presided over the Terri Shiavo case, and federal judge Reggie Walton, who heard the case of I. Lewis "Scooter" Libby, can attest. But other trials in recent history pale compared to *Simpson*.

While judges on other such cases eventually fade back into obscurity, Ito's inability to do so played a part in his judicial future. He never returned to the supervising judge track, nor did he pursue appointment to a higher court, which had seemed a distinct possibility before *Simpson*. Perhaps most vexing has been the loss of public regard for his professional reputation. And other judges, regardless of their opinions of Ito's competence, quail at the thought of a similar fate befalling them.

The first loss for Ito was the possibility of a leadership role in the Los Angeles Superior Court. When he got the Simpson case in July 1994, he was the criminal division assistant supervising judge, in line to become supervising judge six months later. But after the court's judicial leaders assigned him the case, it became obvious that it would consume all of his time. When the trial's opening statements began in January 1995, new supervising and assistant supervising judges had been named. Ito never got back into the cycle.

"He never asked," says Victor Chavez, who served as the court's presiding judge and made judicial assignments in 1999 and 2000. "I would have given him any number of positions. I recognized his talent even back then. I think he himself pulled himself out of the arena."[1]

James Bascue, who served as criminal courts supervising judge during the trial and in 2001 followed Chavez as presiding judge of the entire court system, actively sought Ito out.

"I tried to see if he wanted to transfer to another assignment," Bascue says. "He would have made a great civil judge."

Security, however, had become a major concern.

"He was very concerned about the security in other court locations," Bascue says. "Because of the publicity and him being so recognizable, he was concerned about getting into the courthouse. He felt more comfortable in [the Criminal Courts Building] and [with] the judges' security for getting into and out of the courthouse."[2]

Ito's other two losses, a respected public image and judicial advancement, resulted from the synergism of the public and the media. The public's perception of Ito grew increasingly skewed in direct proportion to the burgeoning media coverage. Many reporters and producers who were providing that coverage had little knowledge of the legal system, court proceedings, judicial constraints, or of Ito himself and his judicial demeanor. Likewise, much of the criticism and ridicule in the ensuing years have come from pundits who neither attended the trial nor know their target. One column published in a Kansas newspaper ten years after Simpson's acquittal was penned by a critic who admitted to being only nine years old in 1994.[3]

In none of the many high-profile trials for which I handled press issues and logistics has the judge become news the way Ito did, not even during a Kim Basinger breach-of-contract dispute in which the judge, when not on the bench, routinely referred to the star by her first name and briefly became the subject of media speculation about bias.[4]

But in the Simpson case, not only did the judge become the story, the media morphed him into a caricature, then held him accountable for that image: The media-made Ito was starstruck, played to the cameras, didn't control his courtroom, and was alternately pro-prosecution or favoring the defense. Perceptions warped and contorted like images in carnival fun-house mirrors. What people saw depended on where they stood and the mirrors they were looking into. The conundrum is how that happened in *Simpson,* why, and what has fed the far-reaching and long-lasting repercussions.

At the outset, Ito seemed to approach *The People vs. Simpson* much like any judge would a high-profile case; he prepared, researched, and planned. He studied the problematic publicity issues and unrestrained media in *Sheppard vs. Maxwell,* which involved the sensational 1954 trial of Ohio osteopath Sam Sheppard, accused of murdering his wife. That case eventually resulted in a U.S. Supreme Court ruling that Sheppard's right to a fair trial had been violated.[5]

Yet, like other judges who had naive notions about notorious cases that befell them, Ito was caught off guard by the initial surge of media attention. He felt certain it would quickly recede and even disappear.

But this high-profile case contained differences from other cases, and one of those differences was the judge. Despite Ito's belief in the dignity of his office and the need for respectful courtroom decorum, he was more open, accessible, laid-back, witty, and bemused than other judges I had known. His courtroom style was to let lawyers have their say. Behind the scenes he invited input from many quarters, including his professional mentor, now-deceased Judge Delbert Wong, and a small, select group of other criminal court judges.[6] He also openly accommodated the press, believing it served a vital role as the public's surrogate.

At the same time, he had an almost childlike curiosity in every aspect of the case and its myriad side issues. For instance, even though he said he was leaving courtroom seating for the case up to his bailiff and me, when we started planning, Ito wandered into the courtroom from his chambers full of questions and ideas.

First, he wondered what to do about jury selection. "We're going to have a hundred jurors at a time in here," he said. "That's a lot more folks than we have seats. So maybe we can bring in a bench from the hall to add a few more."

Deputies hauled in not just one, but two backless concrete benches from the hallway, providing twelve additional seats. Then, at Ito's suggestion, they lined up six plastic chairs behind the last row of permanent wooden-bench spectator seats next to the courtroom door.[7]

Ito also took cameras into consideration. Cameras had become relatively common in California courtrooms since they were first permitted in 1981. They were generally confined to a back corner in the courtroom. That's a spot photographers and camera crews dislike because backs of heads dominate their shots. Ito, however, considered having a TV camera mounted on a side wall above and behind the jury box. His reasoning was that a camera in that position would essentially let the public see the trial from the jury's angle. It would also be out of jurors' line of vision and, consequently, less conspicuous. Also, not inconsequentially, a camera in that position would be less apt to photograph a juror, which is prohibited in California. While Ito knew the wall vantage point would yield more interesting images for the media, that was just a lucky break for them, not a factor in his reasoning.[8]

The print media wanted a wall-mounted camera too, but they had a problem. They didn't know of any high-resolution, remote-controllable still camera that could pan, zoom, and snap pictures. Ito, an accomplished photographer himself, told them about a camera he thought might work that he had read about in an outdoor sports magazine.[9] They researched and before long had something acceptable installed on the wall next to the TV camera.

While such accommodations should have endeared the judge to the media, it seemed to have the opposite effect. The wall-mounted cameras, for instance, soon became fodder for reports that Ito was pandering to the cameras and had directed that they be mounted on the wall to get better shots of him.

A contributing factor to this phenomenon was Ito's philosophy and personality, which spilled from his chambers into the courtroom and gave the media a number of toeholds in their attempt to define him. His access and common-man persona supports the "familiarity breeds contempt" cliché. He did not maintain the aloofness, distance, and, in some instances, degree of arrogance that often typifies judicial demeanor. In fact, I've come to believe that his affable nature and tolerance played as big a role in what led to the shaping of public perception as the grandstanding attorneys and manipulative media.

Members of the media learned about his interest and direct involvement in the peripheral issues of the case and about his hobbies and interests. They used comments he made during proceedings that revealed his pop-culture savvy and his propensity for instant fix-its to mechanical problems that arose during court to color in the background of the portrait they painted of him. This was unique, I believe. By comparison, how much does the public know about the pastimes and personas of the Martha Stewart, Scott Peterson, or Michael Jackson trial judges? In fact, who even remembers their names?

Commentators' and pundits' liberally ladled critiques of Ito led to his third loss: the possibility of appointment to the state appellate or the federal court.

Judicial nominations are made by politicians. In California, the governor appoints judges to state courts. Appointments to federal courts are made by the president. The collective wisdom in legal and judicial circles in Los Angeles and around the state soon after Ito's 1987 municipal-court appointment and elevation two years later to the superior court was that his intelligence, knowledge of the law, thoroughness, and low appellate-reversal rate would make him a likely candidate for eventual elevation to the state's court of appeal. But Ito's chances for advancement disappeared into the whirlpool of controversy generated by the media-spawned second-guessing and microscopic examination of the Simpson case, the courtroom proceedings, and participants' behavior. Such an appointment post-*Simpson* would have been political suicide for Governor Pete Wilson, no matter how great an appellate justice Wilson might have thought Ito would be. In fact, on the very day Simpson was acquitted, Wilson called for a permanent camera ban in all criminal cases in the state.[10]

Rather than bar cameras entirely, however, the state's judicial council eventually gave judges complete discretion over whether or not to allow cameras in their courtrooms.[11] Previously, the media could request hearings on camera coverage and could try to get denials overturned on appeal. With the revised provisions, camera coverage became much more of a rarity than it had been before *Simpson*.[12]

The reason for that, according to Steve Kindred, a longtime reporter for the Los Angeles all-news radio station KFWB, is that "judges are afraid of being Ito-ized."[13]

The term *Ito-ized* symbolizes, in part, the tremendous damage the Simpson trial inflicted on Ito's professional image. Retired San Diego Superior Court Judge William Mudd explains why. "Initially that term came about as a result of the almost overwhelming derision heaped upon Judge Ito because of his inept handling of the case," says Mudd, one of the few judges to allow camera coverage of a notable trial after *Simpson*.[14] Mudd presided over the 2002 trial of David Westerfield, which resulted in a conviction in the kidnap and murder of seven-year-old Danielle Van Dam.

Veteran broadcaster David Dow, who covered the Simpson case for CBS radio and who teaches at the University of Southern California's Annenberg School of Journalism, has a different interpretation of being Ito-ized. "When judges say that," Dow says, "I infer that they view their bench colleague as a fall guy for a volatile, overly long trial with an unpopular conclusion and nasty after-taste."[15]

Much of that perception grew out of TV spoofs by nighttime comics, like Jay Leno and his infamous "Dancing Itos" and David Letterman and his "Top Ten" list. Those routines aired on the heels of extended daily trial recaps filled with punditry, speculation, and hyperanalysis. And the comics' antics blended with daily trial recaps to become as indistinguishable in viewers' psyches as ingredients in a pot of soup.

Yet another loss for Ito was his privacy. Shopping trips, evenings out, and even gardening at home became ambush opportunities for camera crews and photographers.[16] While other judges might suffer similar deprivations, few are subjected to such invasions for long. With Ito, though, more than twelve years after the Simpson trial, his name, face, and caricatures of him remain recognizable to the masses of Americans who followed the trial.

In part, because the trial involved and attracted celebrities and notables, such as actor Richard Dreyfuss, TV show host Larry King, television news personality Geraldo Rivera, and Anita Hill, law school professor and nemesis of Supreme Court Justice Clarence Thomas, the media celebritized all of the participants. And, indeed, most became household names. Ito, however, not only emerged as a central character, he served as the primary foil, sometimes in spite of himself, and to some degree because of my own missteps. His image and persona were refracted by a prism through which the media projected him. That was the image on which the world and many of his colleagues judged him. To understand how the mutation of that image has fueled a complex court-media-public dance, it is necessary to examine the dynamics and interaction of the various entities that played a part in the trial.

Chapter 2

In the Beginning

■ ■ ■

News reporters and television producers began to filter into the cavernous nineteen-story Criminal Courts Building in Los Angeles soon after Simpson's arrest for the June 1994 murders of Nicole Brown Simpson and Ronald Goldman. They came to cover his initial arraignment and subsequent preliminary hearing, which is a sort of mini trial at which prosecutors present a summary of their case. The preliminary hearing judge must determine if the district attorney has enough evidence for the defendant to stand trial. Los Angeles Municipal Court Judge Kathleen Kennedy-Powell ruled that to be the case with O. J. Simpson.

Media coverage of Simpson's four-day preliminary hearing and some of the attorneys' behavior at that and at an evidentiary hearing that preceded it foreshadowed the media debacles and lawyers' grandstanding that were to play out for all the world during the trial.

Four months before the Simpson and Goldman murders, an article by defense attorney Robert Shapiro on how to manipulate the media to benefit a client or a case had appeared in a statewide legal magazine.[1] Whether he followed his own advice in the early stages of the Simpson case, or whether he was effective, remains debatable. He did, however, collude with what he called the "legitimate" press—which consisted of such newspapers and wire services as the *New York Times,* the *Los Angeles Times* and the Associated Press—to meet for postproceeding interviews in out-of-the-way spots on various floors of the courthouse away from the *Simpson* courtroom. If TV or tabloid crews showed up, he would duck out and scoot down the corridor to resume the interview on another floor. Then the chase was on.

The result was a Keystone Kops-type farce with people—many hauling bulky shoulder-mounted TV cameras—popping on and off elevators that rise from the building's bowels. They scurried through the grim, high-ceilinged corridors that branch to the left and right of the elevator bays. They peered around corners, then doubled back in search of the elusive Shapiro. The commotion also caused great consternation among sheriff's deputies, who tried to play catch-up, maintain order, and keep the noise below a dull roar.[2]

Shapiro's attempts to deal exclusively with the press he considered legitimate led to a discussion with Ito. Shapiro wanted to use Ito's courtroom for interviews. After all, he argued, the prosecution team could stage their interviews and press conferences in the DA's headquarters on the courthouse's eighteenth floor. Ito refused. He wouldn't be party to partiality, perceived or otherwise.

Eventually, the roving interviews stopped after other judges complained that noise in the hallway was disrupting and delaying proceedings in their courtrooms and that jurors, witnesses, and attorneys couldn't get through the throngs clogging the corridors. The building's two supervising judges jointly issued an order in September, which was amended and expanded several times during the trial, designating specific out-of-the-way spots for interviews and cameras. Everywhere else in the building was off-limits.[3]

Although it targeted the media, the order also helped disperse the crowds of curious onlookers and camp followers who milled around inside the building and skirted the fringes of the hallway interviews. Simpson's celebrity seemed to heighten the intensity of the reaction, and people orchestrated ways to grab the spotlight, to profit from or to be part of the Simpson case.

Overnight, proselytizers carrying "Jesus Saves" signs and vendors hawking T-shirts and buttons blossomed on sidewalks around the courthouse. Inside, sketch artists peddled drawings, and a woman from Washington State, apparently hoping for a very public suicide, had to be hauled in from an upper-floor ledge, not once, but twice during the course of the trial. Members of the public, lawyers, judges' spouses and relatives, judges from other states and even other countries, television actors, movie stars, yesteryear athletes, wackos, and, of course, the media clambered for courtroom seats. The daily wrangle was interrupted only by building evacuations for the increasingly frequent bomb scares called in by pranksters.

One of the first judges to attend a proceeding as a spectator was Cecil Mills. Mills, who was criminal division supervising judge at the time of the preliminary hearing, attended a lower-court hearing as a spectator before the case even got to the superior court. A few days later, he interrupted the preliminary hearing to hand Kennedy-Powell a manila envelope. That mysterious package would be widely rumored to contain either the murder weapon or a knife similar to the murder weapon. Mills's action raised an eyebrow or two. Judges didn't normally give messages or deliver packages directly to a hearing or trial judge in open court. If something was urgent enough to interrupt a proceeding, a message would be conveyed via the judge's clerk or bailiff so a meeting could take place in chambers.[4]

Mills also conducted Simpson's second arraignment, a proceeding that follows a preliminary hearing when the defendant again hears the charges against him and enters a plea. Although Mills had passed most of his courtroom duties over to the assistant supervising judge soon after becoming supervising judge, his decision to conduct Simpson's arraignment himself became understandable once the name of the trial judge was made public.

Ito, then the assistant criminal courts supervising judge, had planned to conduct that arraignment, but the day before the proceeding, the court's top judicial leadership had selected him to serve as the trial judge on the case, and in a master calendar court system like that used at the time in the Los Angeles Superior Court Criminal Division's Central District, the arraigning judge almost never served as the trial judge.

Before Ito's selection became known, a frenzy of premature reporting on who the trial judge would be set the stage for how the media would cover the trial. They speculated endlessly. They called my office repeatedly for updates, for photographs, for news of an announcement, for confirmation of their rumors, and for our best guesses. Finally, based primarily on rumors and inside tips, the press reported its best guess: Judge Paul Flynn. That speculative headline pretty much reflected court scuttlebutt.[5]

Then came the official announcement. Lance Ito would try the case. I wasn't surprised. Shortly before I learned about his selection, he had asked my opinion about a location for a change of venue because of the publicity the case had gotten in Los Angeles. I jokingly suggested Nome, Alaska, then told him about the massive coverage of the case I had seen on recent trips to northern California and the East Coast. Although a change of venue was briefly mentioned in court, the lawyers never seriously pursued it, knowing that the media blitz had saturated the entire state as thoroughly as it had Los Angeles.[6]

Knowing Ito is imperative to understanding how the trial unfolded and what shaped the media's treatment of him. My encounters with him had been few and brief before he got the Simpson case. The first was in mid-1993 when, as assistant supervising judge, he presided over the felony master calendar. That included defendants entering pleas and judges assigning cases to trial courts. I was in the hall outside the thirteenth-floor master-calendar courtroom with several television camera crews and print photographers who wanted to cover an arraignment.

As I gathered their camera-request forms, I told them they would probably have to pool. "Who was here first?" I asked. "Or do you want to pick someone?" A photographer and a camera man elbowed their way forward while the rest asked if they could all go in.

"Not likely," I said. Although judges much more routinely allowed cameras in their courtrooms in those days, seldom did they permit more than one from TV and one from the print media.

Ito was on the bench in the large dark-paneled courtroom, so I gave the requests to the bailiff, who took them to the court clerk. I sat on a wooden pewlike bench in the spectator section and waited while a dozen or more people milled about chatting with one another, the bailiff, and the court clerk. A bank of lawyers sat in seats along one wall, which in any other courtroom would have been the jury box. Others came and went, lugging heavy briefcases and armloads of files. A woman sitting at the prosecutor's table murmured into a telephone. Clerks hustled about with messages and yet more case files. The constant motion and low hubbub permeating the air didn't seem to faze the judge.

He addressed an attorney who was standing in the dock with a defendant. As I watched, the bailiff came over and said the cameras could come in but couldn't start shooting until the case they were there for got started—and they were confined to the front two rows of a side section of spectator seats.

"All of them can come in?" I asked. Surprised that they didn't have to pool, I went to fetch them, wondering when Ito had approved their requests. They padded in, set up tripods, and clicked cameras into place.

"Quiet or I'll clear the courtroom," Ito snapped, shooting them a warning glance.

The photographers froze, the lawyers paused, and Ito turned back to the defense attorney.

Several weeks after that, Ito phoned my office and instructed me to call a local TV station's news director. A cameraman in his courtroom had been clipping his fingernails while court was in session. Ito, his indignation clear, said he had tossed the miscreant out. I was to tell his supervisor that the man was banned from his courtroom for good and that no one else from that station was welcome until Ito got a written apology. It was almost funny, yet it was puzzling. Why was nail clipping, which Ito probably couldn't even hear above the stir in his courtroom, so egregious?

But what seemed like inconsistent behavior turned out to be far more complex. It involved etiquette, sensitivity rooted in a cultural upbringing that emphasized impeccable manners and graciousness, and a close-knit profession with clearly defined rules and protocols, all set against a backdrop of coming of age in a permissive, rebellious era and attending law school in the liberal environment of Berkeley.

Ito accepted the buzz of attorneys and court staff as part of the courtroom fabric. As a former deputy district attorney, he understood lawyers' tight schedules and need to get last-minute information by phone. The media, however, were without portfolio, and a cameraman clipping his nails violated acceptable courtroom decorum so far as Ito was concerned.

My next encounter with him was just four months before that fateful night in June when the bloodied bodies of Nicole Brown Simpson and Ronald Goldman were found outside the front entrance of her Bundy Drive condominium. Ito and I were fellow panelists at a California Judicial Education and Research program on the courts and media in February of 1994.

Asked what words of advice he had for the program attendees if a high-profile trial were to come their way, Ito said, "I would say, be careful because the press is a very competitive enterprise and they will create disruptions in your courtroom that essentially disrail [sic] what's going on in your courtroom." The steps he listed to minimize those and to keep the attorneys in check were measures he instituted for *Simpson.*

As to what power a judge had to rein in attorneys, Ito said he had some of the same reactions other people did when attorneys acted out, attempted to try their cases in the media, and were openly critical of judges' rulings and of judges themselves.

"I've talked to the judges involved in some of those cases," he told the CJER attendees, "and said, 'by golly if that was me, I'd hold those people in contempt and drag them in there,' and I think that's about the last—I mean, that's what you would want to do, but to do that creates a kettle of fish that has no end to the bottom."[7]

It was a kettle with which Ito became well acquainted before that year was out. He not only held the attorneys in contempt, he also levied fines against them, something the media didn't focus on or widely report. Interestingly, several months after Simpson's acquittal, a former Arizona chief justice who openly criticized Ito at a conference for court information officers expressed his outrage to me following his remarks over the way Simpson's defense team expounded to the media on the courthouse steps. "I would have had those people in front of me so fast and found them in contempt," the Arizona jurist fumed as he echoed Ito's own earlier remarks.

So, why did Ito appear unable to carry out his own resolve when on the hot seat himself? Would any judge, without benefit of learning from *Simpson*, have done better, given the pressure of being under the constant scrutiny of millions of people, including other judges, for more than a year? Or was the resultant chaos purely a function of Ito's personality and management style?

Ito is the product of an interesting combination of a national social phenomenon, an honor-imbued upbringing, a disciplined legal training, and an adult life spent in officious judicial circles. He's the second child and only son of second-generation Japanese Americans who met in a World War II internment camp in Wyoming. Ito's parents' love of and emphasis on education hadn't been wasted on him.

But Ito was also the product of the free-spirited, liberally curious, socially questioning '60s. The result is a man who reveres his parents, values family, honors commitments, applies his considerable learning, solicits input, is innately curious, thinks critically, is ever practical, and loves playing pranks. He appreciates a good joke, fine wine, classical music, classic rock, and a relaxing brewsky. He's an avid collector of fountain pens, hourglasses, and memorabilia. He reads voraciously, subscribing to several daily newspapers and a host of diverse magazines. He reads books for recreation, knowledge, entertainment, insight, information, and research. He is well versed in a variety of eclectic topics to the point of being able to offer arcane snippets that would impress certified experts on the subject.

Ito's chambers and bench were—and still are—a veritable storehouse of gadgetry, tools, mementos, and souvenirs. When his clerk was nearly buried by an avalanche of mail after Chicago syndicated columnist Mike Royko told readers to let Ito know what they thought about televising the Simpson trial, Ito gave her a little electric envelope opener he had pulled from the depths of his desk. Curious about a television crew setting up equipment on a nearby building top or about police in the courthouse parking lot who were dismantling a car that might possibly be connected to one of the countless bomb threats that cropped up during the trial, he would dig out his handy-dandy perma-focus, ten-power, wide-angle binoculars ("just $39.99 at Good Guys!") from a desk drawer to monitor the activity from the window of his ninth-floor chambers. It was, he said, one of ten or twelve pairs of binoculars he owned in addition to "this little Russian spyglass," he added, pulling out a small telescope on a tripod from under a side table.[8]

The judge's curiosity extended to people as well. During a meeting with attorneys in the early stages of the Simpson case, he stopped mid-sentence and turned up his radio, which was tuned to a rock station. The lyrics repeated over and over, "Baby, I can't please you." "Boy, that's mindless stuff," he said, then asked his research attorney to find out the name of the singer.[9]

He also seems to remember everything he reads, hears, or sees and makes references at unexpected moments. Weeks after his research attorney learned that the singer of those lyrics was Samantha Phillips, a discovery hearing deteriorated into what had become the all-too-common acrimonious and accusatory attorney wrangling. This time deputy DA Lisa Kahn and defense attorney Barry Scheck were arguing over whether the prosecution had given the defense some DNA information to which Scheck believed the defense was entitled. Kahn listed at length the documents, reports, and evidence prosecutors had already shared with the defense. But Scheck whined on about yet another report.

Kahn finally cast him a weary look and said, "We just can't seem to please you."

As Scheck started to respond, Ito cut in with "Well, they just play Sam Phillips."

Scheck stopped in mid-sentence, then said, "I'm sorry?"

"Never mind," Ito said, and the proceeding continued as he smiled at his private joke.[10]

Ito knew nearly as much about news reporters as he did news makers. When a local TV reporter, who had played a bit part in a Freddy Kruger movie, became part of the news herself for broadcasting DNA results of blood found on some socks police had retrieved from Simpson's Brentwood home before the results were even in, Ito remarked privately that part of her punishment should be to watch *Friday the 13th Part 3* "until she falls over."[11]

For all of his sophistication, knowledge, and experience, Ito held naive notions about how journalists and the news business worked. He believed that if someone misperceived or misunderstood him, he could set things straight with a friendly, informal chat. If people could just see that he was a decent sort, fair and down-to-earth, they would mellow out and get back to covering the trial instead of him. If he were nice to them, how could they not be nice to him? And they were, to his face.

But a handshake or a visit in chambers, while appreciated and even coveted by members of the media, did not remove the acid, snarkiness, or salaciousness from their reports. He didn't understand back then that not only are journalists skeptics, even cynics, by nature—and paid to be so—they also respond to peer pressure. Worse than incurring the wrath of a judge by portraying him as starstuck or incompetent would be suffering the disdain of colleagues who would consider a positive piece about the judge a sign of being weak or co-opted.

Ito's way of trying to defuse anger might have seemed like a quid pro quo to some. For example, a couple of days after *Los Angeles Times* reporter Andrea Ford, who was African American, ranted about her randomly drawn seat in the back row, what she called the "ghetto row,"[12] Ito asked what I thought about giving her some letters the public had sent him about the makeup of the jury.

"She always seems to be so angry, like she's got a chip on her shoulder," he said. "Maybe that would bring her around, placate her some." Despite his good intentions, I counseled against it. Trying to curry favor with a member of the press wasn't a good idea, I said, particularly to the exclusion of the others. It would blow up in his face one way or the other.

With the media digging in for the long term, Ito soon became as much of a story as the defendant and the crimes. It was something he couldn't understand.

As the army of reporters, producers, photographers, camera crews, engineers, and technicians grew, Ito found his ability to move about his home turf—the courthouse and environs—increasingly constrained. He had to avoid public hallways and the entire twelfth floor, where supervising judge Mills had agreed a media center could be located. He watched with disbelief the growing pack journalism, the clamor for case documents and scraps of information, and the story angles. Early on, he, half in jest, referred to members of the media as "jackals." That label tickled the imagination of at least one syndicated editorial cartoonist and stuck throughout the trial.

To the media, however, a gauntlet had been thrown down. Although a few journalists joked about it, the label set the tone for what was to become a frustrating adversarial relationship between judge and media throughout the trial. While such antagonism is not unique—trial judges in notorious cases frequently become targets of media criticism—no critiques have approached those leveled at Ito in the Simpson trial.

News of the murders and the slow-speed Bronco chase that preceded Simpson's arrest, shocking and captivating as they were to the general public, portended something else for me: another high-profile trial. I had already been through several—most notably, those involving Rodney King, Reginald Denny, and the Menendez brothers. With that experience to draw on, I, along with my boss at the time, trooped the two blocks from our Los Angeles County Courthouse office to the Criminal Courts Building, already teeming with myriad media crews and ringed by microwave vans and satellite trucks, to pay Ito a visit.

The good news was that he was no novice with high-profile trials—most notably the Charles Keating thrift fraud case. The bad news was that, despite that experience, Ito was convinced the media would have the same kind of attention span for this case as for others he had presided over. "They won't hang around long," he said, "jury selection and maybe opening statements, then they'll leave and won't be back until the verdict."

Our meeting ended with each of us convinced the other would be proven wrong. Given that the media presence had only built since the case entered the court with Simpson's initial arraignment and subsequent preliminary hearing, my boss and I believed the preponderance of evidence favored our side. Little did we know just how right we were.

Chapter 3

Careening Off Track

■ ■ ■

As mistakes go, it was a doozy. It began one October morning when I walked into Ito's chambers.

"Jerrianne, I would like for you to come up with a graceful way for me to get out of doing an interview," he said without preamble.

I found the request both puzzling and surprising. We had already discussed the pitfalls of media interviews and agreed he wouldn't do any. But this was different, he said. The TV reporter had assured him the subject would not be the Simpson case or upcoming trial but would focus on World War II Japanese American internment camps in the United States.

The interview was to be tied to the opening of an exhibit of a Heart Mountain, Wyoming, camp, a place where, coincidently, two people had met and, subsequently, married. Those two people became Ito's parents. That not only personalized the situation for him, it helped him rationalize that he was a logical choice for the interview, that the local network affiliate, KCBS, wanted to feature him in a news report about the exhibit because of his parents' experience rather than for the nouveau notoriety of his name.

Rather than say no, he had taken the interview request under submission. If he decided to do it, he would impose conditions. He would discuss only the Japanese American experience and not the Simpson case. Also, the station would have to agree to not promote the interview in advance and to air it only once, on an eleven P.M. newscast. Assured that the station would comply with his terms, he did the interview.

But those promises weren't kept. The station hyped its coup with newspaper ads and TV promos as an "in-depth interview with the judge presiding over the trial of the century."[1] The station also split the interview into six segments so it could run as a weeklong series. Although Ito didn't discuss the case, each segment implied otherwise.

Each segment had its own title. Monday: "Living in the spotlight of the trial of the century." Tuesday: "The man in the eye of a legal storm on the rights and wrongs of the system." Wednesday: "What does the future hold? Will the pressures of a big trial change his career?" Thursday: "A trial like no other in history. What does it mean to serve as a jurist?"[2] Then station officials decided to rebroadcast the entire package during an early-evening time slot.

The breaches angered and dismayed Ito. Although all of the transgressions were egregious, the plan to rerun the series, which KCBS advanced on air, was the capper.

"They've violated all the conditions," he lamented the morning after he saw a TV promo.

He asked me to call the station news director, Larry Perret, to remind him of the agreement and ask him not to re-air the interview. "Tell him I'm not happy that they have violated all of my conditions," Ito said.

I didn't feel very hopeful after talking to Perret, but at least he didn't outright refuse. Then he called back. "The judge is right," he said. "We would be overreaching if we aired the series again, so we've decided not to."

I was too elated to wait for a recess to tell Ito. I slipped through the back door of the courtroom, went up to the bench, and handed him a note. "Flash!!!" I had written. "You won. KCBS won't re-run the interview."[3]

But the elation was bittersweet. The interview not only outraged the rest of the media, most of whom had been hounding Ito for interviews since the day he got the case, they vented their anger by portraying him as hypocritical, starstruck, and a celebrity wannabe. Here's how the episode played out.

KCBS reporter Tritia Toyota didn't land her interview with Ito by being the first to ask. The instant his name was linked to the trial, his and my telephones started ringing. One call I got was from Ty Kim with *60 Minutes*. Kim proposed, on behalf of Mike Wallace, that Ito and criminal courts supervising judge Cecil Mills collaborate with Wallace on a "serious discussion" of the media coverage and help set the record straight.

"I know, we've been shocked by the saturation of coverage since the case began," Kim told me. "*60 Minutes* would be the voice of reason. Mike's concern is for a fair trial. He's looking for a window of opportunity to discuss it in an academic way, to provide perspective on how things get spun out of control. Someone has to put these inaccurate reports into some kind of perspective."[4]

Representatives of Tom Brokaw, Ted Koppel, Katie Couric, Diane Sawyer, Larry King, Barbara Walters—all the big names and many lesser ones—also called, as did local journalists and sports and entertainment writers. Ito rejected them all.

"Denied!" he barked in response to each request.

"The only interviews or appearances I would consider doing," he said weeks before the October morning he mentioned Toyota's interview request, "would be with *Rolling Stone* or as guest host on *Saturday Night Live*."

Yeah, right, I thought.

"Or," he added, almost as an afterthought, "with Howard Stern."

"Howard Stern?" My voice rose along with my eyebrows.

"That's just to show you how seriously I'm considering doing any interviews," he replied.[5]

I told everyone the same thing: Ito was not doing any interviews.

Toyota, however, was married to a lawyer who knew Ito, and she traded on that relationship to get directly to the judge. He told me weeks later that he saw doing the interview as an opportunity to honor his parents and to recognize other Americans of Japanese descent who had lost their possessions and livelihoods when they were sent to the camps. He felt it his duty, he said, to increase public awareness and improve understanding of that very dark spot in American history. KCBS's objective in wanting to interview him might have been to exploit his newly gained fame, but his was to enlighten people about the plight of World War II–era Japanese Americans. Even had I known that on that October morning, my advice would have been the same: Don't do it. In response to Ito asking about a graceful way to decline Toyota's request, I reminded him of our conversation about not doing media interviews.

"Keep thinking," he replied and turned back to his work.

I proceeded to write down every conceivable reason why he should say no, including the perception that he would be giving preferential treatment to another Japanese American.[6] I gave him the list the next morning and, hearing no more about it, I assumed he had declined. A couple of weeks later, though, my stomach lurched when a prelaw intern working for Ito asked if I knew about an interview he had taped with Toyota. Noting my distress, the intern became concerned that she might have betrayed Ito's confidence and asked that I not tell him she had mentioned it to me. Since the deed was done and nothing I could do or say would undo it, I agreed, but I remained anxious about the inevitable repercussions when the interview aired. I even fantasized that the station might somehow decide to kill it.

That wasn't to be. The morning of Friday, November 11, *Los Angeles Times* reporter Andrea Ford called. Through her sputtered outrage, I managed to glean that KCBS was promoting an interview with Ito that was to air in six parts, the first scheduled for Sunday night. Ford, after reminding me of all her requests for an interview—even claiming that she had been the first to ask—and of those from other *Times* reporters, demanded that I arrange an interview with him for her right away, before the KCBS piece aired.

More angry calls followed from reporters clamoring for interviews. Not only was KCBS hyping the interview on the airwaves, it was churning out press releases[7] and had bought a full-page ad to run in Monday's edition of the *Times*.

Ito wasn't in court that Friday, so all questions and requests had to wait, but I fretted over whether the broadcasts would lead to his removal from the case. He had, after all, been critical of how the lawyers were playing to the press and of the frenzied media coverage. Would this be grounds for the attorneys to recuse him? Since worry wouldn't change anything, I got busy with other work, including preparation for the Snoop Doggy Dogg, Heidi Fleiss, and Menendez brothers cases, all of which had trials pending. But I knew that on Monday I would have to face the inevitable barrage of criticism, renewed requests for interviews, and what I would say to Ito. He provided the opening.

The ad in that Monday's *Times* spelled out in inch-high type "Judge Lance Ito" followed by smaller type for "face to face with Tritia Toyota" popping from the center of the page. Alternating freeze-frame head shots of Ito and Toyota ran down one side, and "Tonight and all this week at 11:00" was plugged in at the bottom. November 13 through 19, I later learned, was what the TV industry calls sweeps week.

"So, what's happening with our media friends this morning?" Ito asked without looking up when I went to see him that morning.

"The question of the day is, since you've been interviewed by KCBS, everyone else wants to interview you, too—starting with Andrea Ford with the *L. A. Times*."

"No," he said without further comment.[8]

I don't know if it was mutual, but I sure felt a strain during the next few days as each night another segment of the interview aired. Although he stayed on point about Japanese American internments and the effect on his family and other Japanese Americans, he was introduced and identified throughout each segment as the judge on the Simpson case. The series sparked as many news stories about Ito and the interview as the case itself—almost all critical. Few colleagues or lawyers publicly supported him or spoke out in his defense.

The *Los Angeles Times* ran three opinion pieces about the interview on Wednesday, day four of the series. "Judge Ito Feeds the Hand He's Bitten" read the headline on TV critic Howard Rosenberg's column in the paper's entertainment section. After enumerating the times Ito had pointed out, particularly to jurors—which he was obligated to do—the pervasiveness of media coverage of the case and noting that he had excoriated the media from the bench less than two months earlier for inaccurate reporting, Rosenberg quoted a KCBS news anchor's pandering assessment of the interview:

> "I think it's wonderful to hear a little more from our judges," [11 p.m. anchor Ann] Martin said after the series debuted, in which Ito continued to speak of his roots while also modestly insisting that he was a "flash in the pan" compared to Joseph A. Wapner, the former jurist made famous by the syndicated *People's Court*.

Rosenberg went on to opine:

> One thing for sure, the impatient Wapner would have ruled Toyota out of order Monday for going back on the pledge she said she made to Ito not to broach the Simpson-Goldman proceedings with him. "So what is in this envelope?" she asked about the oft-discussed mysterious manila container that Simpson defender Robert Shapiro turned over to the court some time ago. Ito good-naturedly said he didn't know.
>
> Meanwhile, the controversy over his Channel 2 [KCBS] stardom predictably continued to swirl, with even *Nightline* weighing in Monday as a measure of just how overblown the coverage of this case has been. With [former Los Angeles District Attorney Robert] Philibosian taking Ito's side, defense attorney Leslie Abramson joined the second-guessers, saying Ito

was a bit starry-eyed and "got suckered into" the interview. "He's like all of us, a kid inside."

Although the "kid" image may fit neither Abramson nor Ito, her criticism of the judge fits perfectly. By appearing on Channel 2, he has personally reopened the door to media overkill and has only himself to blame if the door now gets ripped off its hinges.[9]

One of two views published in the *Times* Opinion section of that same Wednesday issue came from a former prosecutor-turned-law school professor. Robert C. Fellmeth, in a piece titled "Just Another Nice Guy? Phooey!" wrote,

> All along, the judge has confined his public appearances to the courtroom. Now he enters the spotlight to talk about his past, his values, his dreams. Hey, I don't want to hear that stuff. I want a neutral and detached arbiter who refuses to buy into the media extravaganza. I want someone who does not allow even the perception that media attention may be an influence.[10]

Voicing a countervailing view was then-University of Southern California law professor Erwin Chemerinsky. "It's Good to Put a Human Face on a God-Like Role," read the headline on his observation, which was published with Fellmeth's.

> The latest firestorm in the O. J. Simpson trial concerns whether Judge Lance A. Ito acted improperly in granting an interview to a local television station. This controversy is laden with ironies. After repeatedly criticizing the media's obsession with the case, Judge Ito's own cooperation with the media is, for now, the big story. At the same time, some commentators who previously criticized Ito for being media-phobic, are now lambasting him for doing the interview.
>
> Although the ironies are interesting, they mask the basic point: Ito's interview will not compromise a fair trial and is enormously important to inform the public about the human being who will be handling the most widely publicized case in American history.[11]

The news accounts, while painting Ito as antimedia, evinced primarily by his irritation at inaccurate news reports and over-the-top coverage and by his mention on the bench of an editorial cartoon portraying the media as jackals, remained silent about the unprecedented media access he had permitted. That included providing an audio feed to an overflow listening room for reporters who couldn't be in the courtroom because of space during jury selection, helping photographers with their technical problems, and allowing pretrial camera access.

The media's own hypocrisy surfaced in editorials and other opinion pieces as well as in news reports condemning the KCBS interview when reporters had been pressing Ito for interviews from the day the Simpson case was assigned to him.[12] The *Los Angeles Times,* which ran a staff columnist's piece about the interview, a news story, and an editorial on the day before the three Wednesday opinion pieces and whose reporter Andrea Ford had been particularly aggressive, seemed the most sanctimonious.

> As a newspaper that likes to publish interviews with important people in the news, we would be the last to suggest that government officials shouldn't talk to the media. But we think there's a time and a place for everything, and we'll bet we weren't the only ones left speechless when it was announced last week that Judge Lance A. Ito himself was about to appear in a six-part interview on a local television station. . . .
>
> To be sure, Ito is a newsworthy figure, and ordinarily we couldn't be more supportive of openness by public officials. But given his own impassioned concerns about the atmosphere in which the trial is being conducted, we can't help thinking it would have been more consistent and seemly for him to have waited until the trial was completed before going on camera.[13]

Yet, the *Times'* concern didn't stop the paper from accepting the advertising revenue from KCBS's full-page promotional ad.

The following Thursday morning Ito asked me to take a seat on the sofa facing his desk. He looked more haggard and drawn than I had ever seen him, even on the most grueling day in court or in the most tumultuous of controversies.

"Okay, go ahead and say 'I told you so,'" he said.

"I'm not going to say that," I replied. My main concern, I said, was that the interview would have only negative consequences for him, something he didn't need to sap his energy and attention.

"Well, I've learned my lesson," he said. "I think this borders on possibly the biggest mistake of my career."[14]

It certainly affected the media's mood. After repeatedly being told that he would do no interviews, they branded him as hypocritical, inconsistent, and lacking credibility. Thereafter, reporters, commentators, and pundits turned his every word and action into supporting evidence. In the years following the trial, the media and legal community have continued to dissect that interview and its ramifications. Most people, including many who knew him, were unaware of Ito's intention. Los Angeles defense attorney Steve Kron, at a 2005 symposium on celebrity cases, voiced the majority view:

> The thing that he did I don't think will ever be done again. He allowed the cameras to come in and interview him about his background, about his Japanese-American upbringing. He then became one of the stars of the show and I think that was totally inappropriate. He should have been sitting back and not trying to be part of the circus. He should have been controlling it more than he did.[15]

Kron's assessment of where Ito went wrong shows clearly the difference between his intention in doing the interview and others' perception of it. With his well-honed ability to compartmentalize, Ito separated the judge of a high-profile case from the loyal son of World War II Japanese American internees with his sense of obligation to help others understand what they and other internees had endured through a matter of birth. Kron gives voice to the public perception of a judge presiding over the most newsworthy case in the land using his sudden celebrity to tell the public about himself. In doing so, he shed the anonymity represented by the black robe of his office and thrust himself into the spotlight.

That interview, however, wasn't the only example of Ito's well-intentioned decisions and interaction with the media being either misunderstood or misinterpreted. Kron's comment also plays into an ongoing debate in media and legal circles over where the circus was actually playing—inside the courtroom or in the hallways and outside the courthouse.

"Despite allowing cameras in the courtroom there," said KPCC talk-show host Kitty Felde, who moderated the 2005 symposium, "the bigger circus was outside anyway, so, barring a gag order, it would have been just as wild."

Although Ito had at one time considered issuing a gag order, he believed he had no legitimate grounds once he sequestered the jury.

The court's reaction to the fallout from the KCBS interview and other controversies throughout that trial—and, indeed, those surrounding all high-profile cases—was consistent with accepted judicial thinking. The view in most judicial circles was and generally remains that, for better or worse, judges shouldn't—and shouldn't have to—explain themselves.

Some people have questioned, aside from the media's pique, why, since Ito didn't discuss the Simpson case, he shouldn't have done the interview, especially with opening statements still months away. The answer lies in the same judicial tradition as not explaining themselves and even more so in the idea of what constitutes proper judicial conduct. Ito had done the interview as a U.S. citizen of Japanese descent whose parents had been held in an internment camp. In the TV interview, however, KCBS presented him as a trial court judge presiding over a highly public case. That treaded dangerously close to the perception that he was using his position to speak out about a noncourt issue.

Refraining from public discourse, from trying to counter distorted perceptions and erroneous reports, and even from publicly defending Ito when he was under siege, whether deservedly or not, became the court's stance throughout the case and has remained so since. From the moment the case entered the court—days after the slow-speed Bronco chase past cheering, sign-waving crowds—through the ensuing parade of bizarre twists and turns and the barrage of media coverage, Ito's judicial colleagues kept their heads down and their mouths shut. It was as if weighing in would be unseemly. Although many judges sympathized in private both during the trial and after its conclusion, when Ito continued to be the brunt of criticism, few dared brave any ill wind that might blow their way by speaking up publicly.

One person who frequently comes to his defense is a member of the media. Longtime Associated Press legal reporter Linda Deutsch, a daily presence at Simpson's trial, has remarked repeatedly in speeches and at journalism and judicial conferences that she thinks Ito got a raw deal. "Judge Ito has become kind of the ultimate victim in the O. J. Simpson phenomenon," she said at a panel discussion on celebrity trials years after Simpson's acquittal.

> Judge Ito was a very fine judge who decided to let the public see what was going on in his courtroom and for that he has been held up to ridicule and criticism for it. He was in some sense the victim of huge publicity, of a group of lawyers who never stopped talking. Judge Ito's greatest failing was

that he liked to give everybody a chance to talk. He was being fair to every-one. I don't think that's something that should hold him up to the kind of criticism he's been held up to.[16]

Legal scholar Laurie Levenson acknowledges that some in the media treated Ito harshly and distorted his conduct, "By and large, his substantive rulings were good. He knows the law and is a smart guy."

At the same time, Levenson, a professor at Loyola Law School of Los Angeles, marks Ito down for what she considers "showboating" with his hourglass collection and boxes of mail prompted by a syndicated columnist.

"He tries to be friendly, but in the O.J. case, he probably would have been better off being more formal from the beginning."

On the whole, though, she says, "I don't really blame Judge Ito for what happened because I think it would have been nearly impossible for any judge to withstand the media onslaught in that case. Nonetheless, I think he and other judges learned the valuable lesson that control over the courtroom and their participants is key to managing a high-profile case."[17]

Leslie Abramson, the noted criminal defense attorney who represented Eric Menendez in his two murder trials with his brother, Lyle, offered her view of Ito and the runaway train that the trial became when she spoke at a 1996 legal symposium at Northwestern University:

What we have to start thinking about is the comparative values of the First and the Sixth Amendments. When I watched Lance Ito, who is a very bright man and one of those judges, the kind that all of us from law school admire the most, those judges who really love being judges, who have a tremendous reverence for law, who are excited by it. The fact that he has been helping first-year Harvard law students—I think there were fifty-nine students in that class—by asking them all to brief the press access issue in the O. J. case, that demonstrates not his quirkiness, but his real love for legal education and his desire to have the public understand more what the legal system at its very best is like.

When you have a judge, though, who is clearly floundering in the face of the runaway media, you know there is a serious problem. This isn't some bumbling fool. This isn't a particularly emotional person. But unless you have been on the other side of those 6,000 cameras, you don't understand how helpless and out of control you can feel. When you have an interest in a case and you are exposed to the publicity and you realize the level of falsity, it is a very frightening experience, and he is scared. He is scared that he cannot do what he has been sworn to do, which is to provide a neutral forum and a fair trial for all the parties in the case. So he floundered about, and he ran into the brick wall of the First Amendment.[18]

Ito was deeply affected by the criticism and the blow to his professional image. During the trial and in the months following it, he seemed grateful for my offers to rebut the most blatant of misperceptions. Yet, when I offered drafts of letters and op-ed pieces for his review, he would tell me not to send them.

"Just let it go," he would say.

It wasn't until I read a profile of him in a legal newspaper years later that I began to understand that aspect of his persona.

Los Angeles Daily Journal writer Don Ray, in his June 2005 article, noted that Ito "remained silent, true to the same cultural fabric that gave his parents and grandparents emotional strength during their internment."

"It's called '*shigata ga nai*,' and it's a philosophy of life that's very, very typically Japanese," Ito is quoted as saying in the profile.

"*Shigata ga nai* means it can't be helped," Japanese American pastoral counselor Cliff Ishigaki explained in the profile. "It's the deepest form of resignation. It signifies a form of victimization, where life is done without their permission."[19]

I thought it ironic that in attempting to educate the public about how "life" was done to interned Americans of Japanese descent without their permission during World War II, he had inadvertently become a victim of that very phenomenon.

Chapter 4

Pressing Issues

■ ■ ■

Press reports are wrong.
Ito feels numbed and disturbed,
What is the outcome?

I started writing daily haiku soon after the Simpson case was filed in court.[1] This one, on September 22, 1994, was inspired by a comment Ito made during a hearing about forensic testing of clothing Simpson wore the night of the murders. Both the prosecution and the defense expressed outrage over inaccurate press reports.

"There was an allegation that certain clothing items were sent to Cellmark [laboratory] for RFLP testing, and that is false, referring to the most recent report," prosecutor Marcia Clark said during the hearing. "And I would further indicate to the court that none of the parties in court were responsible for that story being disseminated and we are all very upset with it having been disseminated in that fashion."[2]

In a rare moment of unity during the trial, defense attorneys closed ranks with the prosecution.

"For the defense, Your Honor," Simpson attorney Johnnie Cochran said, "I will join in that and indicate that none of us have received any such reports and we are also very, very troubled by this, because it definitely flies in the face of our client receiving a fair trial. . . ."[3]

Echoing the lawyers' disgust, Ito remarked that the public was being saturated with irresponsible media coverage.

"I'm almost numb to it at this point," he said. "For this kind of information to come out and for it to be incorrect and for it to be so prejudicial is outrageous. . . . I'm very disturbed. I don't want to take extreme measures and I have attempted not to, but I'm sorely tempted at this point."[4]

Among the measures he was considering was a protective order, commonly called a gag order, to prevent trial participants from commenting publicly or talking to members of the media about the case. In truth, though, the erroneous reports seemed to be coming from sources who were beyond the reach of Ito's authority. As an appellate court has ruled in other cases, a gag order can only apply to those within the judge's jurisdiction, that is, the trial participants, their employees, and witnesses.

Nevertheless, the media felt unduly constrained and became increasingly critical of what they considered onerous restrictions. Finally, CNN's Larry King decided to weigh in. About the time Ito and the lawyers were grappling with bad reporting, King invited Ito and some journalists onto his show to debate the restrictions, which included requiring the media to use one pool reporter to cover jury selection and instructing the lawyers to file all motions under seal, as well as the looming threat of a gag order. Ito declined.

The spotlight swung toward me. Would I sit in for Ito and address the media's complaints? The prospect was heady—for a moment. I could certainly discuss the problems.

As I looked beyond the fifteen-minutes-of-fame lure, the shine began to fade. It would be hard to not come across as defensive or get caught up in a shouting match, neither of which I relished or thought would benefit the court. On the other hand, I was concerned about unanswered criticism reaching millions of people.

Allowing only one reporter in the courtroom during jury selection had nothing to do with restricting the media and everything to do with space limitations. Ito was already grappling with how to fit a hundred prospective jurors into a courtroom with seating for about sixty people. Understanding that most members of the media wanted to be physically present, he had agreed to let more journalists in as prospective jurors were excused.

The idea of a gag order and the requirement that motions be filed under seal stemmed from Ito's attempts to staunch the flood of erroneous media reports. He ultimately decided that a gag order wouldn't solve the problem, and he unsealed motions as soon as he could determine that they didn't contain prejudicial or confidential information that could taint potential jurors. Foremost in Ito's mind was the Sixth Amendment to the Constitution guaranteeing a defendant's right to a fair trial.

Ito's thinking, when I discussed the dilemma with him, was that if anyone went on the show, it should be a member of the court leadership, such as the presiding judge, Robert Mallano, or the criminal division supervising judge, Cecil Mills. That idea raised a different concern. Both men were certainly competent and articulate, but their knowledge of and involvement with the media issues and accommodations and the day-to-day frenzy were sketchy and would require extensive briefing. The court's assistant presiding judge, Gary Klausner, however, put an end to that worry. Klausner, with whom I spoke when I couldn't reach Mallano or Mills, said he didn't think anyone from the court should go on the program.

"It wouldn't be appropriate," he said, "because of a number of issues close to the case that are pending on which Judge Ito might have to make decisions."[5]

That thinking is not uncommon among judges, and it reflects a fervent belief on the part of judges that they should not get into the explaining game. The common rejoinder to requests for explanation or expansion of rulings is, "The decision speaks for itself."

Ultimately, Ito sent King a written statement saying simply that he had bent over backward to give the media everything they had asked for. King read the statement on the air. Left unrebutted were the media's specific lack-of-access contentions.

One significant accommodation Ito made was to permit almost unrestricted camera coverage of the proceedings, which he didn't have to do. He was also allowing more than the two-camera limit recommended in California's Rules of Court for electronic coverage of court proceedings. A third camera represented African American–owned newspapers, which wanted images that were not from what they termed the "white-owned" media perspective.

Since Ito wanted to fit as many prospective jurors in the courtroom as possible, he limited the press to one pool reporter at the beginning of jury selection. Without electronic coverage, that reporter would have to have been the eyes and ears for the rest of the media—except for an unprecedented accommodation Ito made. He allowed the media to have a not-for-broadcast and not-to-be-recorded audio feed of jury selection piped from his courtroom to my office three floors above next to the courthouse media center. My office contained two large conference room–size tables with chairs where reporters could sit and take notes. That way any member of the media who wanted to listen to jury selection could do so. He also allowed additional reporters into the courtroom as prospective jurors were excused.

The media benefited not only from Ito's decisions, but also from those made by supervising judge Mills. Mills assisted in arranging for a large courthouse media center for print and broadcast news organizations and for enabling the media to wire the center to Ito's courtroom and several other courthouse areas. Two of those areas were small offices for media use near the media center. One office housed television-signal-delay equipment, which Ito had required for the trial, and a person to monitor the signal. The other office was for an on-site or "pool" producer the media had hired.

In addition, Los Angeles County officials made extensive rental parking available for the media directly across the street from the courthouse. Quickly dubbed "Camp OJ," it became the staging area for media-equipment vehicles, such as microwave vans, satellite trucks, and mobile-home-size trailers that served a media center annex and mini TV studios. It also became the site of five-story-tall platforms from which the media did their broadcasts. One broadcast engineer commented after it was all set up that more fiber-optic cable had been laid for the Simpson trial than for the 1994 World Cup soccer tournament that had just been held at the Rose Bowl in Pasadena, California.

In fact, the media had far more access and favorable accommodations in the Simpson case than they had had for any other trial before or have had since in my experience. Although I knew that the media would never feel they had enough access—that's just the nature of the media beast—Ito couldn't understand their lack of appreciation and their ever-increasing demands for more.

I jotted down the statement he dictated to be sent to Larry King for his show:[6]

> I've bent over backwards to give the media everything they asked for. It was
> my suggestion for a remote camera over the jury box. Because of that they
> wouldn't get just the backs of heads. I arranged for an audio feed during
> jury selection for reporters unable to get into the courtroom because there's
> not enough room and state Rules of Court dictate that they can't photo-

graph, record or broadcast jury selection. I haven't imposed a gag order, although I'm tempted to after today. The media has been a burden on this case because dealing with them has taken so much time.

At that point, news reports incorrectly stated that the prosecutor had arrived at the crime scene before the search warrant and had erroneously reported lab test results on Simpson's socks, and on at least three occasions the media had photographed and attempted to interview jurors—both of which are forbidden by the state's Rules of Court. Some of the media issues resulted in time-consuming hearings. The problems, such as leaked information that could potentially prejudice prospective jurors and that arose from the crush of the burgeoning people—all stalking stories—and their equipment in the courthouse, had become daily occurrences.

And it was only September.

Chapter 5
Pack Jackalism

■ ■ ■

The media issues that dominated Ito's time and attention were largely fueled by the outsized personalities, antics, and ambitions of some members of the media. Their impact, however, affected everyone on the courthouse scene, from people massed in the parking lot to spectators gathered in the courtroom. Although many reporters conducted themselves with consummate professionalism, others left me shaking my head, like those who asked such probing questions as what the jurors did during conjugal visits.[1]

Just as the media tend to paint the anomalous with a broad brush, so did the aberrant behavior of a minority of the media affect judges' perception of all of them. While sometimes called "jackals" and "the children," another apt name for some was "characters."

Louisiana-based writer Joe Bosco, for instance, was all tweeds and elbow patches who tried mightily to present himself as a courtly southern gentleman. He even wore his white-vested "Mark Twain" suit the day he thought he might have to testify about a trial-related article he wrote that ran in *Penthouse* magazine. In truth, he came across more like a barroom brawler, albeit a likeable one.

Bosco, author of *Blood Will Tell,* about a DNA-based court case in New Orleans, arrived in my office in late August 1994 full of hand-wringing to appeal for a courtroom seat in the Simpson trial.

"Please, Miz Hayslett," he implored, bowing and bobbing and clasping his fingers as if in prayer. "I've just gotta have a seat. I've just gotta get in. Tell me what I have to do—I'll do anything. You just tell me what it is I need to do to get in."

Would letters from his publisher and others who knew his work help?

With his graying mane flopping over bushy eyebrows, he harrumphed at newspaper reporters, who were "at the bottom of the food chain," getting seats over himself, Joseph Bosco, who had paid his reporting dues and graduated to the fine art of writing books. He spewed indignation that *Fatal Vision* author Joseph McGinniss, whom Bosco called a hack, was going to get a seat and Bosco might not. The very idea was unthinkable to any rational human being with the slightest modicum of intelligence or literary knowledge.[2]

He did eventually get a seat, although he had to share it with another member of the media. And, while he pretty much behaved in the courtroom, his *Penthouse* article about Simpson's bloody socks managed to be one of myriad issues that interrupted the trial with a hearing about Bosco's source of that information.[3]

While writing about the trial, he became the walking wounded—twice. He showed up at the courthouse with his arm in a sling after a donnybrook in a bar the previous night, which had erupted when he supposedly was defending some female's honor. A couple of weeks later he arrived in court sporting a neck brace, the result, he announced without a hint of embarrassment, of a party where he had dived headfirst into the shallow end of a swimming pool.[4]

Joe McGinniss was the yin to Bosco's yang. Quiet, unpretentious, and anything but flamboyant, McGinniss washed in to my office not long after Bosco with the advent of Southern California's rainy season. Intent on learning the terrain and players, he seemed oblivious to the water dripping from his jacket and running in rivulets off the strings of his gray hair and into his eyes. He announced sometime into the trial that he wasn't talking to anyone or doing any research. His book would be from the jury's point of view and based entirely on what occurred in the courtroom.

Although Bosco beat McGinniss to Los Angeles, McGinniss had the upper hand. Within days after Ito got the Simpson case, McGinniss wrote to him requesting a seat.[5] Ito agreed, then told me. It was a done deal. Ito would not go back on his word, although in hindsight after the trial, when he learned the ultimate fate of the book McGinniss said he was going to write, he might have wished he had. At the end of the trial, McGinniss ditched his book project and reportedly took off for Europe to cover international soccer.

Dominick Dunne used a similarly successful strategy to get a courtroom seat.[6] I wasn't surprised. Dunne's letter-writing ploy had paid off a year earlier for the Menendez brothers trial.

A former Hollywood producer-turned-novelist and high-profile trial chronicler, Dunne had called on the eve of the Menendez brothers trial about getting in. *Fat chance,* I had thought. The Menendez double-parricide case had been in pretrial for months. All of the preliminary arrangements had been settled—media parking and workspace, cameras in the courtroom, interview areas, court-document availability—everything except the trial judge's final approval of my recommended media-seating plan.

To my chagrin, Dunne got in. Unbeknownst to me, he had petitioned the trial judge, Stanley Weisberg. When I told Weisberg about Dunne's request, the judge said he liked Dunne's writing and wanted him to have a seat.

The fact that McGinniss and Dunne both ended up with front-row seats in the Simpson trial drew charges from the rest of the media that the supposed random drawing to determine seating had been rigged. Dunne's seat was ideal. He was beside a Goldman-family seat. While courtroom interviews were not permitted, Dunne's position enabled him not only to overhear remarks among the Goldmans, but also to murmur exchanges with them.

As with McGinniss, I think Ito eventually rued giving Dunne a full-time seat. That was not just because of the form his book took—an amalgam of *Simpson* and *Menendez* and fact and fiction—but because Dunne later talked about a conversation that was to have been off the record.[7] Ito was particularly disappointed given that he had twice exempted Dunne from the rule that a seat would be lost if the person assigned to it was absent more than two days in a row. Dunne was out of court once because of a family crisis and later for a trip to London related to a possible interview with Princess Diana. Despite it all, Dunne was a gentleman through and through and well liked by just about everyone.

Lawrence Schiller was of a different stripe. The first time I saw him, I didn't know who he was. He was wedged between the wall and a row of Simpson relatives. Space on the bench was so tight that Schiller had to twist sideways and hang a cheek over thin air. The bench could comfortably hold six not-too-plump people. Schiller's rather wide seventh body not only crowded the others on that row, it violated fire code. The sheriff's deputies in charge of courtroom security didn't know who he was either or how he got in. Only people wearing specially issued badges were supposed to be granted entry. So the deputies told him to leave.

The next day he was back, crammed into the same spot, acting as though he were invisible. His identity and purpose were soon revealed by Simpson's so-called "dream team," starting with Simpson lawyer and friend Robert Kardashian's totally transparent probing.

"Everybody's writing books," Kardashian said, pulling me aside a couple of days before opening statements. "Someone should be writing a book about Mr. Simpson. How would I go about getting a seat for the trial for me so I can do a book?"

My domain was media, not defense, requests, so I referred him to the deputies. They were no help.[8]

Next came defense attorney Carl Douglas.

"Jerrianne," he said, whispering stridently, "we've got to get a book author in here for O. J."

"What do you mean?" I asked, feigning ignorance.

"We need someone in here who will tell O. J.'s story, who will write O. J.'s book."

Such a person would fall into the same category as the authors who were already allocated courtroom seats, I explained, and no more media seats were available. He sounded frustrated but not defeated.

"Isn't there anything you can do?" he asked.

"There really isn't," I said. "All the media seats have been assigned for some time, and there just aren't any more available to me. You might see if someone else who has a seat would be willing to work something out with you."

He snorted, knowing that would never happen.

"We've gotta come up with something," he persisted. "O. J. deserves to have his story told."

Simpson's family wasn't happy, he continued. Simpson's sisters, Carmelita Durio and Shirley Baker, would probably be talking to me about it.[9]

The "it" was Schiller.

Schiller had worked with Norman Mailer on *The Executioner's Song,* a book about condemned Utah killer Gary Gilmore, and had other writing credits. But he had no media affiliation at the Simpson trial, where he irritated many court and sheriff's staff on the Criminal Court Building's ninth floor, although no one could say exactly why.

I found Simpson attorneys' lobbying amusing because they could have pled their case directly to Ito, and, in fact, did. Twice, Cochran and Douglas brought it up with him when I was in chambers. Both times they used the historical-record argument. Ito echoed my response, and neither of us thought anymore about it until Schiller, with requisite badge, started showing up in a defense-assigned seat. It appeared as though someone on Simpson's team had ordered that someone give up a defense seat for him. At that point Carmelita Durio sought me out but didn't say exactly what Douglas wanted.

"I know Johnnie's [Cochran] been trying to get Schiller back in," she said. "I don't want him in here. I don't like him. My sister, Shirley, will tell you she wants him here. But I don't."[10]

A few days later came Shirley's pitch.

Then Cochran tried.

"O. J. wants him here," Cochran said of Schiller. "It's not for anyone's profit, but to chronicle, to record for history O. J.'s experience."[11]

I didn't see what the big deal was about getting Schiller in. He could have followed the proceedings on television, and even when he was in the courtroom I didn't see him take notes. He just watched and listened. But Schiller sitting in a defense seat caused another problem. It was like squeezing a tube of toothpaste. The toothpaste just squishes to somewhere else. In this case, whoever Schiller replaced simply shifted to a seat reserved for court or sheriff-deputy use. That ticked off the deputies. They apparently complained to Ito, because a few days later he said he wasn't going to dictate who could sit in the defense seats, but they weren't getting any additional seats. So the defense made adjustments, and Schiller made it in. Interestingly, his book, *American Tragedy*, written with the assistance of other writers, hit bookstores a year after Simpson's acquittal and received excellent reviews.

Court TV's Kristin Jeanette-Meyers swirled in the vortex of more disruptive dust devils during the trial than the rest of her colleagues combined. Most of the conflict involved skirting rules that invariably resulted in courtroom ejections and finally a permanent ban.

In a journal entry a couple of weeks before her banishment, I described her as "very attractive, beguiling, innocent blue eyes, blond hair, angelic face and kind of a prancey, cutesy, kewpie-doll figure. Her opinion of herself is she is so absolutely so special that she is just above any kind of rules and regulations and if anybody ever tries to call her hand on anything she is just like,

'Oh, well, I really didn't know,' and 'I just did this out of pure innocence,' and so forth."[12]

Clad in expensive silk suits and spike-heeled pumps, Jeanette-Meyers's sensuous mouth could curve up in a disarming smile, harden in anger, pout with pique, or turn down with chin-trembling self-pity, depending on what she thought would work most effectively. She had surfaced on the Los Angeles court scene for the 1992 Rodney King–beating trial, when she had the unenviable job of monitoring the delayed television feed for Court TV to make sure no restricted information inadvertently aired.

She later graduated to on-camera talent status. I next encountered her when she showed up at the Criminal Courts Building with dozens of other reporters to get documents for the pending trial of four defendants charged with the near-fatal beating of Reginald Denny. Denny had been pulled from his truck in a South Central Los Angeles intersection during the 1992 riots sparked by the acquittals of the police charged with beating King. The *Denny* documents were voluminous. The court's fee was fifty-seven cents a page, checks or cash only.

While her colleagues grudgingly forked over the fee, Jeanette-Meyers smiled and said she had neither money nor checkbook with her. That was a puzzling assertion, given that she had just flown in from New York. Finally, with the other reporters rolling their eyes, she stalked off empty-handed, but not before demanding the name of my boss, Court Executive Officer James Dempsey.

I soon got a message from Dempsey. Jeanette-Meyers had paid him a visit. I should give her what she wanted, Dempsey's secretary said, and send Court TV the bill. For years the media had lobbied in vain for that payment method, but Dempsey's courtesy covered only Jeanette-Meyers.

At the Simpson trial, even though she had a courtroom seat, She wasn't allowed in one morning because she showed up late. When pleading, cajoling, and tears failed, she became angry. She would be fired it she didn't get in, she yelled. She neither got in nor lost her job. In fact, it was her expertise that her employer offered to keep the courtroom TV camera from being banned after the accidental broadcast of an alternate juror. Court TV staff were supposed to be monitoring the TV signal, which, as with the Rodney King–beating trial, was delayed by several seconds to help ensure that prohibited coverage, such as confidential attorney-client conversations or jurors' faces, wasn't aired. It turns out the Court TV employee assigned to monitor the delayed signal had never been in the courtroom or seen the jurors, so wouldn't have been able to recognize them on the TV feed.[13]

Court TV officials told Ito they would have the feed monitored by a two-person team to prevent any further accidents. The team would be headed by their most experienced delay-monitor staffer, Kristin Jeanette-Meyers. Ito agreed but imposed conditions. Court TV had to put in writing measures it would take to prevent future incidents, and the camera could show only a static view of the courtroom instead of panning around and zooming in on the defendant, a lawyer, a weeping relative, or the judge. The next day an almost unrecognizable Jeanette-Meyers arrived at the CCB twelfth-floor delay-box room. Her clingy dresses, spike heels, and on-camera makeup had been replaced with slacks, flats, and swollen, red-rimmed eyes. But her new look didn't last long.

A day or two later, Court TV executive producer Steve Johnson called. They were thinking about putting someone else on the delay button, he said, and returning Jeanette-Meyers to reporting. But, I countered, Jeanette-Meyers had been represented to the judge as their most experienced delay monitor, and he expects her to fulfill that duty. What if something else happens and the judge wants to know why she wasn't monitoring the signal after Court TV had assured him that she was the most experienced person?

"Well, confidentially," Johnson said, "it might not be best to have someone responsible for the delay button who really doesn't want the job." It was a heavy responsibility and required intense concentration, he explained.

I told him if he would fax a letter outlining his proposal, I would get it to Ito.[14]

Luckily for Johnson, Jeanette-Meyers, and Court TV, when I took Johnson's letter to Ito, he was neck-deep in bickering attorneys and complicated legal issues.

"I don't have any more time for this," he said, giving the letter back to me. "But tell them they're on notice. Nothing else had better happen."[15]

Within days, replacements had arrived, and Jeanette-Meyers regained her spot in front of the camera and in the courtroom. It didn't last, though.

I was talking with a deputy sheriff in the hallway outside the courtroom one day in May when Deputy Sheriff Allison Long came out, followed closely by an enraged Jeanette-Meyers with nostrils flaring, chest heaving, and hands clenched into fists. Deputy Roland Jex was on her heels.

"You're out of your fucking mind!" she railed at Long. "You can't even see!" Her eyes flashed, and her temple veins bulged.

"Let's go back inside," Jex said to Long, "and let Jerrianne take care of her."

Jeanette-Meyers, ignoring me, spun on her spiked heel and headed for the bank of elevators. One of the two deputies staffing the security screen next to the elevators said something I didn't catch. Jeanette-Meyers, her chest beneath her form-fitting silk sheath still heaving, whirled to face them.

"You-leave-me-a-lone!" she shouted, punctuating each syllable with a backward step, as though bracing for a full-team tackle. She delivered a body blow of a punch to the elevator button, then stalked back and forth waiting for the elevator and ranting that the deputies deserved their Gestapo-like reputation.

The big surprise for me was Jeanette-Meyers's surprise at being tossed out. She had been told that would happen if she didn't wear her courtroom badge so deputies could see it. That was a requirement of all courtroom spectators, yet one Jeanette-Meyers seemed to forget. A day earlier, Jex had suggested I have a talk with her.

"She seems to think her clothes are too expensive to clip it on like everybody else in the courtroom does," Jex said. "She tries to get away with clipping it to the strap of her shoulder bag. That's not going to do it. So you might tell her that if she tries to come in here again without wearing it, she's not going to get in and if she doesn't keep it on while she's in here, she's going to have to leave."

I relayed the message.

"But it tears my clothes," Jeanette-Meyers complained, her mouth petulant and her large blue eyes wide and glittery.

"Why don't you put in on a chain around your neck with your media credentials like the other reporters do?" I asked.

"I don't have any. I-I don't know what happened to the one I had."

"It shouldn't be hard to get another one," I said. "I just don't want you to be surprised if you're told to leave the courtroom."

"I'll do my best." She averted her eyes and turned back to the mirror on the table in Court TV's small CCB media center work space to perfect her makeup for an on-camera appearance.

During the first break the morning Jeanette-Meyers was ejected, Long told me she had removed her badge in court. Long said she wasn't going to let her back in after the break if she didn't have it on.

"That's fine with me," I said. "She's been warned."

Sure enough, as everyone filed back into the courtroom, Jeanette-Meyers wore no badge. Long stopped her.

"I'll just clip it here on my bag," Jeanette-Meyers said with a smile.

"No, you have to wear it so it's in sight while you're seated in the court-room," Long said.

"You can see it here," Jeanette-Meyers said, patting her shoulder bag.

"If you're not going to wear it, you'll have to step outside," Long said without raising her voice.

Jeanette-Meyers snatched the badge off the strap, clipped it to a beaded choker around her neck, shot Long an angry look and flounced into the courtroom.

Soon after court resumed, Long, who was standing at the back of the courtroom near the door, got a call on her radio. A deputy who was monitoring a courtroom surveillance camera in the building's sheriff's command center spotted a spectator without a badge. It was Jeanette-Meyers. Long threaded through the spectators to Jeanette-Meyers on the opposite side of the courtroom, tapped her on the shoulder, and motioned for Jeanette-Meyers to follow her out. Long then worked her way back to the courtroom door. But Jeanette-Meyers didn't follow. As Long started back toward Jeanette-Meyers, Jex, who had been stationed near the defendant inside the courtroom well, converged from the front. Together, both deputies motioned for Jeanette-Meyers to leave. Long waited by the courtroom door. This time, Jeanette-Meyers, a powder keg ready to blow, stomped out. Minutes after being ejected, she was in the office of Sergeant George Smith, who supervised courthouse security.

"You're not going to let her back in!" I blurted later after he told the deputies.

"Yeah," he said, his eyes sliding sideways. "She's taken care of now. She said she'll wear the badge on her pocketbook and that's OK. That'll take care of it."

Long rolled her eyes. She and the other deputies, whose sergeant hadn't backed them, questioned why there were rules if they weren't going to be enforced. At the suggestion of the media's on-site producer, Nina Goebert, I contacted Jeanette-Meyers's boss, supervising producer Cindy Glozier. I didn't want things to get any further out of control.

Glozier, a straightforward, no-nonsense woman, snorted. "I've got a dozen of those utility chains she could have hung the badge on," she said. "She just doesn't want to wear one because it doesn't go with her ensemble."

But that wasn't the end of it. As I was preparing to leave my twelfth-floor office in CCB that afternoon, Jeanette-Meyers stopped by, smiling beguilingly.

"Oh, Jerrianne, do you have a few minutes we could talk?" she asked. "About this morning, that is all taken care of, everything is okay with that."

"I know," I said.

"But I was wondering, why did you find it necessary to call Cindy Glozier?"

"Well, Kristin, you were so angry, I was concerned about you."

"Angry?" she said, her eyes widening and her hand flying to her throat.

"Yes, Kristin. You were pretty upset and it was important to make sure that it didn't escalate from a simple incident into something bigger."

"Jerrianne, I wasn't angry. It was just a little misunderstanding that was easily taken care of, so there was no need for you to tell Cindy."[16]

The next day, she returned to the courtroom, but two weeks later she got the boot for good along with one of her compadres.

It was prompted by notes from jurors.

Ito got two in as many days. Reporters were talking, the jurors wrote, which distracted them and interfered with their ability to hear testimony. During the lunch break on the day he got the second note, Ito did some writing of his own. Everyone knew something was up when I called Court TV's Glozier to make sure I had the correct spelling of Jeanette-Meyers's name. Glozier tried to pump me for details, but Ito had sworn me to secrecy. He wanted his court order to serve as the announcement. Just before proceedings reconvened that afternoon, I distributed the order. It read:

SUPERIOR COURT OF THE STATE OF CALIFORNIA
IN AND FOR THE COUNTY OF LOS ANGELES

Date: 18 May 1995
Department 103
Hon. Lance A. Ito, Judge
D. Robertson, Deputy Clerk
People v. Orenthal James Simpson
Case #BA097211

COURT ORDER

The Court has received notes from two jurors complaining of noise created by two news reporters in the audience section of the courtroom:

"I am writing you to alert you of the two reporters sitting in seats C16 [Kristin Jeanette-Meyers/Court TV] and C17 [Gail Holland/*USA Today*] and their constant interruptions during the court session. They are constantly whispering which distracts my attention for brief moments of time. It happened yesterday and also this morning." Juror A.

"I am having trouble trying to hear the testimony at times due to the fact that a few members in the audience are whispering a ltttle [*sic*] loud. Two days in a row." Juror B.

Any unwarranted disruption of a court proceeding is a good cause for the court to take appropriate action. The court has an obligation to act where the disruption impacts upon a juror's ability to hear and see the evidence. The appellate courts have wisely conferred wide discretion upon the trial courts to control the proceedings within the courtroom. Talking or whispering amongst audience members while court is in session is never acceptable behavior, especially when it interferes with the jury's ability to hear the evidence.

The court finds good cause to bar Kristin Jeanette-Meyers/Court TV and Gail Holland/*USA Today* from admission to Department 103.

IT IS SO ORDERED.

1 The court notes her connection to the organization designated as the pool television camera. The court deems this to be an act of misconduct on the part of the television news media.

To say the order raised a ruckus with the media is an understatement. They flocked to Jeanette-Meyers's and Holland's defense. Many, including *Los Angeles Times* columnist Bill Boyarsky who had to that point used a great deal of ink castigating Ito for not being stern enough with courtroom disrupters, groused that it wasn't fair because Ito hadn't given any warning.

My concern, however, wasn't over the media's caterwauling so much as it was that the order didn't specify the time period of the ban, which left a loophole I was sure Jeanette-Meyers would try to wriggle through. She was confident she would succeed. The deputies told me that afternoon that she was already saying she would be back. A ray of hope glimmered a little later when I told Ito. "I don't think so," he said.[17]

Speculation ran rampant over the next few days about whether Holland and Jeanette-Meyers would be back. Their colleagues lobbied on their behalf. The print folks signed a letter asking the judge to reconsider. Holland called and left a message asking to talk to the judge.

Ito kept saying no.

Jeanette-Meyers maintained that her banishment was temporary. At the same time she tried to get the deputies to intercede on her behalf. They would have none of it, though. "She's burned us too many times for us to do anything for her," one told me.

Another interesting reaction came from Court TV owner and executive editor Steve Brill, who responded to a letter I faxed to him. Brill said he agreed with Ito's decision.

Next thing I knew, Brill and his network's chief anchor and managing editor, Fred Graham, arrived from New York and asked to meet with the judge. They proposed doing a public-service video and have Jeanette-Meyers visit schools and talk to students about the importance of the justice system "particularly in relation to this particular case."

Before calling Ito, though, I asked if the idea was for the video to be a condition of restoring Jeanette-Meyers's courtroom access.

Brill started off with, "Well, of course, we would love to be able to get her back into the courtroom . . . ," then hesitated and said, "Well, no, no, there wouldn't be any conditions, we will do the videotape regardless of Kristin or anything else, but, we really would love to be able to get her back in."

In Ito's chambers, Brill and Graham's community-service idea didn't get much traction until Brill finally said, "You know there are no conditions. This doesn't have anything to do with. . . . We aren't asking you to let Kristin back into the courtroom. This is not a *quid pro quo*."

"Well," Ito said, "as far as the talking in the courtroom is concerned, I'm pretty firm on my decision and I am not likely to change it."

My hands were behind my back, all fingers crossed.

After Brill and Graham had left, Ito's clerk, Deirdre Robertson showed me an envelope from Jeanette-Meyers. I asked to take it in and give it to Ito.

"Jerrianne," he said, leaving the envelope on his desk, "let me show you something."

He opened a file-cabinet drawer, pulled out a folder marked "Talkers," and showed me a fistful of other letters from her, all unopened. Then he picked up the most recent one and tossed them all back in.

"Don't you even want to open it?" I asked.

"No. Not interested," he said.

"How about if I see what she has to say?" I suggested.

"Nope, not interested," he said and closed the file drawer.

And that was that.[18]

A few weeks later, though, two more reporters followed on Jeanette-Meyers's and Holland's heels. A court order that prohibited talking, reading newspapers, chewing gum, eating, or having audible cell phones and pagers on while court was in session was posted on the courtroom door. Copies were also taped to the rail separating the counsel area from spectators and to the back of each row of seats. They were hard to miss. Yet people continued to gab, chew, and grab their ringing cell phones and chirping pagers. Ito scolded from the bench and directed deputies to confiscate offending pagers and phones. But some spectators still didn't heed the order. Even deputies making a great show of working their way through a crowded row and handing someone a wad of toilet paper into which to spit a wad of gum or escorting violators out didn't deter some. During one lunch recess Ito summoned me.

"Come here, I want to show you something," he said, beckoning me up on the bench. He played a videotape of several spectators, all in media seats, masticating. While most appeared to be chewing gum, one was obviously popping handfuls of some kind of snacks into her mouth.

Ito instructed me to have that person come to his chambers during the afternoon break. When court reconvened following that break, he announced that those who had been chewing gum and eating in court that morning were to be excluded from the courtroom. Instead of being contrite, as I expected, they and the rest of the media were aghast.

"What?" exclaimed *USA Today* reporter Sally Stewart. "Is he serious? He can't be serious! He can't do that! That is ridiculous, just for chewing gum in the courtroom. How come we don't get any warning. He can't just do that!"[19]

Stewart, one of the culprits, wondered along with others what the big deal was. I explained over and over:

(1) Judges commonly don't allow eating, drinking or gum-chewing in their courtrooms;

(2) Most courtrooms have those prohibitions posted on their doors, as did Ito's;

(3) Ito had issued a specific court order forbidding chewing gum, eating, drinking, reading newspapers, talking, and passing notes in the courtroom, and had copies of the order taped in plain sight all over his courtroom;

(4) Not a day goes by that deputies don't tell spectators not to chew gum and even hand them wads of toilet paper to spit theirs in;

(5) Everybody in the courtroom watches those little dramas, complete with the gum chewers' sheepish looks.

"It is just unbelievable," I recorded in my journal on the way home that night, "I don't know why they think they haven't had any warning or why they think they don't know the rules."[20]

But in their reports the media demeaned Ito, calling him petty and accusing him of blowing minutia out of proportion, given the serious business everyone was there for. *Los Angeles Times* columnist and future city editor Bill Boyarsky, for instance, announced a preview of his account.

"I know what my column is going to be about tomorrow," he said. "My third grade teacher, that's who Judge Ito reminds me of . . . no chewing gum in class."

That just went with the territory, so far as Ito was concerned, but what had really offended him was the media's insensitivity to what else had been occurring in the courtroom as one reporter snacked on Skittles. The Los Angeles County medical examiner was testifying about the autopsy photographs and explaining to jurors what they were looking at. I felt pretty outraged myself.

"Here is the medical examiner describing those horrendous, fatal wounds," I recorded. "Photographs that are graphic. The wounds are laid wide open. Here are jurors who are trying to look at those photographs and understand the portent of it all. Here are the relatives of the people whose loved ones were killed and whose bodies are laid out there for all to see. And here is this woman who is so insensitive that she is popping food in her mouth and chewing so casually as if this is just a leisure activity. And people were saying, 'How come the judge overreacted?' I don't call that an overreaction, I call that a compassionate human being."[21]

Although Jeanette-Meyers created more commotion than anyone else, she by no means held a monopoly. Her closest rival in number of temper tantrums was *Los Angeles Times* reporter Andrea Ford. Ford not only fumed over her back-row courtroom seat and the Tritia Toyota interview, she exploded the day she didn't get a copy of a newly filed *Simpson* document as quickly as she wanted. In those days before courts could post documents on the Internet, getting paper copies duplicated for the media was a priority and a time-consuming hassle. Soon after the district attorney filed charges against Simpson, lines of impatient media folks snaked down the hall outside my county courthouse office while my lone staff person and I monopolized photocopiers in neighboring offices (since ours had none) and cranked out copies of each new filing. We couldn't work fast enough. Everyone jockeyed to be first for everything.

The crush peaked one morning at the Criminal Courts Building when I left Ito's ninth-floor courtroom and stepped out into the middle of a mob of reporters and producers in the hallway. They all began shouting at once. It took a moment to realize they were clamoring for copies of a newly filed motion Ito's clerk had just given me.

They escalated from impatience to outrage when I said they could get copies at my office, two blocks away, as soon as I could get over there and make them. Why should they have to go all the way over there? they demanded. Why not just go to the district attorney's office on the eighteenth floor right there in CCB? They were sure the DA's folks wouldn't mind if I used their copier, they said.

Maybe not, but I sure would. As a court employee, I not only had to *be*, but had to *appear* to be, neutral in court cases. That included not marching into the office of one side or the other and using its equipment and supplies.

With my face aflame amidst a hallway full of people gawking at all of the yelling, I said no. Copies would be available in my office within half an hour.

Everyone but Ford muttered and retreated. She, however, followed me with invectives and profanities flying onto a crowded elevator and down to the ground floor. There, she finally backed off when I told her I wasn't going to deal with her until she could speak civilly.

Some, such as Dennis Schatzman, an irascible *Los Angeles Sentinel* reporter who excelled in general grousing, bubbled over only once or twice. He and syndicated columnist Tom Elias, with whom he shared a courtroom seat, nearly came to blows over who would go in first.[22] Schatzman's most notable confrontation occurred the day deputies took him down for trying to interview attorneys in the courtroom.

A smallish man in his fifties, Schatzman plowed from the back of the courtroom through people exiting during a break. He headed toward the rail that divides the spectator section from the courtroom well and called to one of the lawyers who was preparing to leave. A sheriff's deputy stopped him and said courtroom interviews weren't allowed. Schatzman first ignored and then shook off the deputy and continued to call out to the lawyer. No interviews in the courtroom, the deputy repeated. Schatzman shot back that he was exercising his First Amendment right as a journalist and would interview whomever he pleased.

Not in the courtroom, the deputy said, and told him to leave.

Although the no-interview rule had been enforced since Ito got the case, Schatzman claimed he was being singled out because he was black. A couple more deputies closed in as he began to shout "discrimination." When the deputies tried to escort him out, he struggled. In a blink his hands were cuffed behind his back.

Shortly after taking him to the sheriff's office across the hall from the courtroom, a deputy came to see if I could help calm him down. They didn't want to have to arrest him, the deputy said, but would, if necessary, not just for resisting but for his own good because he was so out of control.

I found Schatzman in the sheriff's office with the cuffs still on. Every time the deputies started to take them off, one explained, Schatzman would erupt all over again. I don't know if I had any calming effect or if he just ran out of steam. Eventually, though, after he promised he would control his temper and not try to interview anyone in the courtroom, the cuffs came off and he left.[23]

Although he could never be considered mellow, the only problem he created in court after that was dozing off. He and seatmate Elias reconciled enough to coauthor a book, *The Simpson Trial in Black and White*, in which Schatzman recounted his own version of the court's and deputies' bias against him.

Paul Pringle's problem wasn't the ban on courtroom interviews, it was having to share a courtroom seat. Pringle, the Copley News Service's Los Angeles bureau chief, didn't personally have to share a seat with anyone, but his reporters did, at least on paper. That prompted a series of increasingly sarcastic and belligerent letters and phone calls. First Pringle, then Copley's lawyer, threatened to take their case to the court's presiding judge and, if necessary, to then-governor Pete Wilson.[24] The absurdity was that Copley had exclusive use of the seat because its seatmate was United Press International. UPI, a longtime wire service that was *in extremis* at that point, had a lone Los Angeles reporter who said the only way she could cover the trial was to watch it on a TV monitor in the media center. If she sat in the courtroom, she said, she would have no staff to make phone calls or do legwork.[25]

While Ito shook his head over Pringle's and other reporters' constant bickering, it largely didn't affect him directly. Not so Kazumoto Ohno. Ohno, a writer for the Japanese magazine *Bungei Shunju,* pressed Ito not for a seat, but for an interview. His August 11, 1994, letter was courteous enough and unremarkable until the closing paragraph, which said he had Ito's home address and telephone number and might have to resort to contacting him there.

Rather than being alarmed, I was amused. The address and phone number in his letter were wrong. At Ito's direction, I sent Ohno the standard "thank you, but no thank you" letter.[26]

Ohno faded from memory for a couple of months. Then his October 9 letter arrived.

". . . I am afraid that you have failed to recognize what it means to be covered here," he wrote. "If you had been born and bred in Japan, I am 120% sure that you will not decline. If I were you, I would be tickled pink just by being approached by the magazine. . . ."

He then asked Ito to "Please be as friendly as possible when I visit your house. I cannot call you at home because I cannot obtain the phone number. Furthermore, I do not want to go to the court because I do not like to make any commotion. I am not going to ask you any questions directly related to the trial because that is not the purpose of the coverage. I believe that people in a very serious position as yours [can] have a friendly time, too."[27]

That, Ito decided, called for a more emphatic reply.

My letter to Ohno ended with, "Judge Ito also instructed me to tell you that he would consider any attempt you might make to visit him at his home a gross invasion of his personal privacy."[28]

That prompted a series of faxed letters from Ohno who became increasingly disbelieving that Ito was refusing his request. He did, however, eventually succeed in getting Ito's address.

One Monday morning a few weeks after Ohno's October 9 letter, Ito told me about his weekend: "There I was minding my own business Saturday in my own yard getting a little gardening done, when guess who showed up at my front gate."

Ito managed to shoo him off, but not before Ohno squeezed off a couple of shots with his camera.

Another reporter who surfaced briefly was someone I'd never heard of, which might speak more to my ignorance of New York City elites than to her lack of celebrity. Lucinda Franks included in her introduction when we met was that she was a Pulitzer Prize winner and the wife of New York District Attorney Robert Morgenthau. Pulitzer rang a bell with me. Morgenthau didn't. But it didn't matter. She, like so many other members of the media, pressed for a meeting with Ito. He said OK, but we set it for the end of the lunch break to ensure that it was brief. Her questions echoed those of other journalists. "How do you cope? How are you surviving?" And she praised his patience and Solomon-esque wisdom.[29]

People following news accounts of the trial knew nothing about the Kazumoto Ohnos and Lucinda Frankses skulking around the fringes and little about the court-stopping conduct inside.

Although the epitome of professional journalism, Linda Deutsch was by no means a shrinking violet and certainly projected as great a presence as anyone in the press corps. As Associated Press reporter and most senior court-beat journalist in town—her career had begun with the Charles Manson trial more than two decades earlier—she invariably lobbied for an aisle seat near the courtroom door in every case she covered.

Deutsch also felt entitled to serve as pool reporter when one was needed not only because as a veteran wire-service reporter she was fast, organized, and accurate, but because the AP served thousands of news organizations around the world. She was also frequently the first, and often the only one, to leap to her feet in a courtroom to object when she believed a judge was about to wrongfully close proceedings to the public.

While hers was a cult of professionalism as opposed to the cult of personality that imbued so much of the nouveau journalism that was emerging in the mid-1990s, Deutsch could express righteous indignation with the best of them, as she did when the Simpson trial seating plan included seats allocated to people who were writing books.

"That's unconscionable," she fumed, puffing up her five-foot-tall frame, her cloud of champagne-colored hair fairly shivering. "They're just in it for the money. They won't be reporting anything to anyone until their books come out months after the trial."

She made an even more memorable observation nearly a year later at a memorial gathering for another reporter who had been covering the trial.

No one seemed aware of the bond that had formed until that gathering. It took place four days after a Friday in August 1995 when Ito had recessed court at noon for the weekend. Because of a protracted meeting with the court's presiding judge that Friday morning, I didn't get to the courtroom until the mid-morning break. When court reconvened, a woman I hadn't seen before was sitting next to me. She wore the proper badge for the seat, so I figured she had worked a deal with *Philadelphia Inquirer* reporter Robin Clark, who normally sat there. Strange, I thought. Clark never missed a day in court.

Clark, a witty, low-key man of about forty who looked younger, wore buttoned-down plaid shirts, blue blazers, and brown loafers that gave him a Joe-college look. The twinkle in his gray-green eyes said he didn't take anyone too seriously, least of all himself. The fact that he ended up sitting next to me was pretty much his doing. He was not happy when the courtroom media-seat assignments were shuffled midway through the trial. The new assignments were based strictly on attendance. While Clark's had been perfect, he shared a seat with two other people who were frequently absent; in fact, total absences for that seat were the highest of all the media seats. That meant that with the new seating arrangement Clark and his partners got the worst spot in the room.

"It's just not fair," he said after a day or two of perching atop his satchel in the seat and craning his neck to see over the heads of those in front of him and around the Plexiglas partition shielding the bailiff's desk. "I've been penalized for the absences of other people."

Unlike the shrillness of some of his colleagues, that was the closest I had heard this soft-spoken North Carolina native come to complaining. Why not, he suggested, exchange his awful seat, which was a plastic chair just inside the courtroom door, with the one that was shared on a rotating basis by a dozen or so news organizations that were too small, too remote, or too late in requesting a seat to get a permanent assignment? Although the rotating seat was also in the back, it was on the end of the middle section of permanent benches and allowed a more direct, unobstructed view of the trial participants. Sounded reasonable, I thought. Ito agreed, and the switch was made. That put Clark next to the end of the concrete bench where I sat.

It was only after Clark and I became seat buddies that I discovered his humor and free spirit. With talking in court verboten, he occasionally jotted observations to me on his notepad, sometimes with the slight lift of an eyebrow. His comments often focused on the fashion taste—or lack thereof—of lawyers, witnesses, and spectators. For instance, when an up-scale department store's buyer of expensive custom-made Italian footwear took the witness stand sporting an eye-aching, rumpled blue suit and dull brown shoes that could have come from a secondhand thrift shop, Clark scribbled, "Not the shoes *I* would have worn with that suit."[30]

Except for the lousy courtroom seat, Clark took almost everything else in stride and soothed his colleagues with a *Leave It to Beaver*–like philosophy. He served as their sort of away-from-home counselor and social coordinator. He not only coaxed folks at a press party to join in the line dancing, he snapped Polaroid pictures and handed out instant prints.

The day before I found the unknown woman sitting in Clark's courtroom seat, he took note of a particularly humorless-looking member of the prosecution team who wore her hair in a rather nondescript pageboy. "I bet she's worn it like that since the fourth grade," he murmured.[31]

The next morning, the lawyer, as though reading his mind, had pinned her hair up into a bun and even flashed a brief smile or two. Since Clark wasn't there, I made a mental note to tell him later. But I never got the chance. Clark, his cousin, and the cousin's friend—the woman in his courtroom seat that Friday morning—who were visiting from back east, were killed that afternoon in a traffic collision on the Pacific Coast Highway.[32]

The answering machine in my office the following Monday was jammed with messages making sure I knew about Robin. Then Dominick Dunne called with a crisis of his own. His son, an experienced cyclist, hadn't returned from a weekend ride in the Arizona mountains. Dunne was frantic and planned to stay by the phone rather than come to court. He might even go to Arizona, he said. He wanted Ito to know why he wasn't there and hoped he wouldn't lose his courtroom seat.[33]

Dunne didn't lose his seat, but because he was still waiting for news about his son, he did miss the memorial service. Joe McGinniss hosted it the Tuesday after Clark's death at the Beverly Hills house he was renting. McGinniss propped up poster boards around the living room, dining room, and den displaying photographs of Clark and clippings of his news stories. Unlike the memorial for TV reporter Chris Harris, felled by a fatal heart attack months earlier, that had been attended primarily by media colleagues, the gathering for Clark included not only the trial press corps, but also members of the defense and prosecution teams and Simpson's sister and brother-in-law, Shirley and Bennie Baker.[34] Ito was also invited. He declined, suggesting that I represent him.

People hugged and mingled and talked quietly after arriving. I couldn't help but think that no one would ever have known that some of these people were on opposite sides in a double-murder trial. McGinniss talked about some of the conversations he had had with Clark, including one about the difficulty Clark had reconciling himself with his father, an educated man who became a derelict and hung out on street corners with ne'er-do-wells.

"Recently," McGinniss said, "Robin had started writing about his father and gave me the few first pages for an assessment. After reading them, I told him to keep going."

But, of course, the rest of the story died with Robin in the car crash.

McGinniss invited anyone else who want to speak to do so.

AP reporter Deutsch stepped forward. After relating several anecdotes about Clark, she surveyed the group. While most of the people present had been strangers at the beginning of the Simpson case, she observed, "Like it or not, we have become a family."[35]

But that was a brief and rare moment of unity in an otherwise distinctly dysfunctional "family," rife with bickering, rivalry, contempt, envy, and disparate philosophies, perspectives and goals.

Such behavior is generally explained as simply a clash of cultures, as judges and court staff feeling besieged by competitive, aggressive, and demanding media. The roots, however, go deeper and are far more complex. Members of the media and of the judiciary, I believe, are all struggling for survival. Yes, reporters strive to be first and want to scoop their colleagues. And, yes, part of that goes to the nature of the journalistic beast. It is in reporters' DNA to want to be first to tell the story. But members of the media are also, increasingly, scrambling to save their jobs. Failing to deliver, to produce for an editor or employer in the world of journalism, leads to irrelevance and, ultimately, pink slips or, depending on tenure, golden—or gold-plated—handshakes. Journalists, not unlike most humans, need pats on the back and kudos. The most rewarding is the lead story on the evening newscast or a newspaper page-one, above-the-fold byline. Those, of course, are career-builders, stepping stones to bigger, more significant news markets, and larger, more prestigious publications.

But there has been a seismic shift in the basic journalistic question of what is news. That has been the topic in recent years of countless books by media watchers and scholars, a plethora of judicial- and journalism-related conferences and symposia and media-industry trade publications. While perhaps not the birth of that shift, the 1995 Simpson trial certainly served as a catalyst.

An Internet blogger cut to the core of how that shift has become manifest in the news business in a September 21, 2007, posting about Simpson's Las Vegas court appearance on robbery and related charges. In "An Open Letter to the Cable News Networks," Bob Sassone writes:

> MSNBC anchor Norah O'Donnell keeps talking about how it's interesting that in 1994 we watched a slow chase with a white Bronco and now we're watching one with a grey sedan. I think somewhere along the line Norah O'Donnell took it upon herself to change the meaning of the word "interesting."
>
> And she keeps asking "why is it so fascinating?" and "why is this getting so much media attention?" as we watch a split screen that shows an aerial view of the courthouse on one side and grainy footage of O. J. in the car on the other.
>
> Maybe if the media didn't cover it so much they wouldn't have to ask why it's being covered so much.[36]

So while the media hype and sensationalize in their grasp for audience-share lifelines, judges struggle to preserve decorum, order, fairness, and even the perception of fairness in the judicial process.

Gary Hengstler, director of the Donald W. Reynolds National Center for Courts and Media at the University of Nevada, Reno, attributes these disparate objectives to professional orientations. Journalists, Hengstler says, are goal-oriented. Judges are process-oriented.

Journalists want the story, Hengstler tells attendees at center programs.[37] Of lesser importance is how they get it. Judges are steeped in process. The outcome of a trial is less important than properly and correctly following the rules and laws along the way. They want—nay, expect—the media to be equally observant and respectful of the rules. Just as journalists' careers thrive or die by getting the story, so do judges see the success of their careers on affirmation of appellate courts that they have adhered correctly to the law and legal processes.

Court staff also strive for survival, but their focus is on saving their routines and being able to do their jobs without, or at the very least with minimal, disruption. Given that in many court settings, the media are in direct contact with court employees, clashes become almost inevitable.

But do all people in the media buy in to what is becoming ever-louder clamor, shrill and breathless accounts of Paris Hilton sightings after her brushes with the law, or needle-stuck-on-the-record renditions of Simpson driving away from a Las Vegas arraignment on robbery charges?

No, says veteran NBC producer Nina Zacuto. There are serious journalists, in the traditional sense of the term, in television news who grate at bottom-line dictum often imposed at the behest of major corporate shareholders who demand ever-greater returns on their investments.

"I would like to say for my generation of journalists, are we frustrated by the fact that we can't tell the stories that sometimes we want to because we do have to care about ratings now?" Zacuto asked 2005 national high-profile conference attendees. ". . . Absolutely. Do we want to do other things? Absolutely. We have to balance this. This is reality. . . . So those of us that have stayed in the profession, stay in the profession for those moments of opportunity to inform people about the things they need to know about, even if it's through an entertainment kind of way of doing it."[38]

Chapter 6

Seeing Stars

■ ■ ■

Although Ito never wavered from his belief that the trial would amount to no more than an "Andy Warhol moment," at one point he remarked with a touch of cynicism how surprising it was that suddenly everyone wanted to be his friend. Among the minions were media stars, and some who thought they were. All jockeyed, cajoled, and pestered to meet him.

At first he was adamant. Absolutely not. Then one day, Marcia Skolnik, municipal court public affairs officer and my boss at the time, because of a brief merger of our two courts' administrations, told me to meet her late that afternoon in the elevator lobby near Ito's Criminal Courts Building court-room. Speaking in a low, conspiratorial tone, she said she had a surprise.

The surprise turned out to be then–NBC *Today Show* host Katie Couric. Skolnik escorted Couric, her editorial producer, Lori Beecher, and me through an empty courtroom to the private hallway that provides access to judges' chambers, jury rooms, and other private offices.

Destination? Ito's chambers. Court, however, was still in session, so we waited until he was off the bench.

He was cordial as he came in a few minutes later, unsnapping his robe and laying it over the back of his desk chair.

Although it sounds like a cliché, surreal best describes my sense of the scene as Couric, at Ito's invitation, dipped into the candy jar on his desk and bantered with him about the mob of media that had amassed for the case. Since I wasn't in on arranging Couric's visit, I don't know how it came about, but one motivation became apparent. As she prepared to leave, she said she hoped Ito would give her the first interview when he decided to do another one.

The most galling visit, however, was one by lawyer-turned-writer and television legal pundit Jeffrey Toobin. Before the Simpson case I had never heard of Toobin. He wrote for the *New Yorker* magazine and was going to do a book. *Well, wasn't everyone?* I thought when Toobin shared that bit of news.

Like many of his colleagues, Toobin clamored to meet Ito. Ito said no.

"He's a month behind the time," Ito said in reply to one request in mid-September of 1994. "He's too late."[1]

But Toobin persisted.[2]

"Just a few minutes with the judge," he pleaded on another occasion. "Just to say hello, to introduce myself and, as a lawyer, shake the judge's hand."

In February Ito finally relented but said to bring him in at the end of the lunch break so he could limit his time with him. As I escorted Toobin to Ito's chambers, I delivered my spiel that everything, once he crossed the threshold, was off the record. As usual, all manner of files, documents, mementos, and other paraphernalia cluttered Ito's chambers. As Toobin observed the surroundings, Ito showed him what he thought was an example of how crazy things had gotten with public interest in the trial. It was a note television personality Arsenio Hall had sent him in which he compared Ito's job to President Bill Clinton's, saying that Clinton has the second hardest job and that Ito had the hardest.[3] With a shake of his head, Ito said he found it strange that people, even celebrities, apparently wanting to be part of or to somehow relate personally with the trial, would send the court notes and photographs and souvenirs.

"You would think these people would have something better to do," he said.[4]

But that's not how Toobin told it. Nearly a year after the trial, Toobin hit the talk-show circuit to promote his book.[5] In recounting his meeting with Ito, he said the judge wanted to meet him and had "summoned" him for a visit in chambers. Toobin's tale was not only unethical because he violated the off-the-record condition, he reshaped the encounter, apparently to support his characterization of Ito as behaving like "just another celebrity-crazed resident of Los Angeles" and having "starry eyes."[6] Ito's point in showing Toobin the Arsenio Hall note was to underscore how obsessed people had become with the trial.

Toobin's account of that visit wasn't all he got wrong. In his book he described Ito as being "thrilled" by the presence of TV talk-show host Larry King when he visited the court on January 13, 1995, and said that during King's visit, Ito "started rambling about the domestic-violence ruling he had to make."

"'I know Nicole's call to the shelter is powerful evidence,' Ito told his stunned guests," Toobin writes in his book, "'but its hearsay. I can't let it in.'"[7]

The amazing irony of Toobin's account is that hearsay is what *he* had to rely on—and he provides a great example of why courts don't permit hearsay testimony. Toobin wasn't in Ito's chambers with King. I know, because I was.

It's true that after receiving repeated requests from King to either grant an interview or appear on his show, the judge did agree to meet him for what was supposed to have been a quick handshake. And Ito didn't invite King for a visit. I did. It was definitely a good intention that went awry.

Emulating Skolnik with Couric's visit, I accompanied King and his entourage of producer, staff assistant, and college-student daughter, Chaia, from the elevator lobby through another courtroom, Department 105, and down the back hallway toward Ito's chambers.

But instead of going in, King stood in the back doorway to the courtroom and waved to the press corps in the spectator seats.

With the help of Deputy Sheriff John Castro, who had accompanied us from the elevator, I finally steered everyone into Ito's chambers. There, we waited for twenty minutes while court remained in session. King, fidgeting impatiently, kept saying that his time was limited. When Ito took a break, rather than "rambling on about the case," the judge spent most of the time listening to King name-drop, boast about dating the defense team's jury consultant, Jo-Ellan Dimitrius, and compare Ito's modest chambers and small courtroom to the judges' accommodations in the grandiose federal courthouse in Miami. As Ito turned his attention to Chaia and asked about her education, King started beckoning to the defense lawyers who had gathered in the chambers' doorway to come in. The lawyers flooded in with King gladhanding and backslapping them like old friends.

At this point, Toobin portrays King as being concerned about Ito's time and even offers a quote in which King asks Ito, "Don't you have to get back to court?"[8]

Although I was standing directly behind the sofa where King was seated, I not only didn't hear King utter those words, the time didn't even seem to be on his mind. In fact, Ito apparently had slipped from his mind entirely as he continued to laugh and joke with the lawyers while Ito donned and snapped up his robe. Neither did the entourage follow Ito "through the rear door into the well of the courtroom," as Toobin relates.[9] Both Ito and I were trapped behind the gaggle of lawyers, King, and King's entourage as they squeezed through the cramped passage behind the clerk's chair. Horrified, I peered past their their heads and watched the lockup door open, the bailiff escort Simpson into the courtroom, and Cochran start to steer King toward the defendant to greet him. My repeated "Please don't do that" finally got Cochran's attention. Later Cochran told me I needn't have worried, he would never have let them shake hands.[10]

King, with his group following, proceeded into the courtroom well, where King greeted the prosecution team. Then King's daughter, who had followed him into the courtroom, drew a raised eyebrow and a "you don't want to go in there!" from Simpson and a laugh from the spectators when she turned to leave and, with the help of her famous father, tried to pull open the wrong door—the one that led into the courtroom's inmate lockup area. Finally, contrary to Toobin's account that King and his group left though the spectators' door, they returned through the back door, with me bringing up the rear. We retraced our steps down the hallway and back through Department 105, which, much to my compounded humiliation, was in session with the judge assigned there on the bench.[11]

To my chagrin, I was complicit in arranging that visit. When King's assistant, Ellen Beard, called to say he was going to be in L. A. and still wanted to interview Ito or have him on his show, I knew the judge would decline. But since he had agreed to meet Couric a couple of months earlier, I thought he might consider thanking King in person for understanding his position and accommodating his requests, not just once, but twice. First was when Ito declined to participate in the show about media complaints of restrictions in the case. King read Ito's written statement on air, with no edits or omissions, about all he had done to accommodate the media. The second occasion was when King was the only TV talk- or magazine-show host who, at Ito's request, delayed interviewing Nicole Brown Simpson's self-described best friend Faye Resnick when her "tell-all" book came out on the eve of jury selection. So I offered to see if Ito would be willing to at least say hello to King. Definitely a good intention that went south and related here to illustrate how an event is seen, perceived, remembered, and retold, particularly when hearsay forms the foundation.

Larry King was but one of many famous faces to grace the *Simpson* courtroom. Others included Barbara Walters, Diane Sawyer, Jimmy Breslin, Stone Phillips, Geraldo Rivera, Tom Brokaw, Anita Hill, actors Richard Dreyfuss and James Woods, 1976 Olympic decathlon gold medalist Bruce Jenner, former baseball star Steve Garvey, Western-stylin' lawyer Gerry Spence, and even comic Jackie Mason, sent inexplicably by the BBC to provide commentary. It inarguably became *the* place to be seen. Contrary to news reports, such luminaries didn't form a constant parade to Ito's chambers, and most of those who did were members of that very media that was criticizing Ito for allowing it. Even then he did so only after they asked for meetings themselves.

The trial also made for some strange encounters. One occurred when the former judge who had presided over the 1983 trial of the murder of Dominick Dunne's actress daughter, Dominique, showed up at the Simpson trial as a correspondent for a Malibu weekly newspaper. What made the meeting strange—or perhaps strained is a better description—was that by reducing the charge against the killer from murder to voluntary manslaughter, for which the man was sentenced to six-and-a-half years, with four years off for good behavior, the judge had set Dunne on his current course of writing about high-profile trials.[12]

Another day of a strange star alignment occurred less than a week before the trial ended. On September 27, Ito had given the two courtroom seats he held in reserve for his use, generally for visiting judges, his parents, or other relatives, to songwriter David Foster, whom he knew, and Foster's wife. The wife had previously been married to former Olympian Jenner. And there in court that same day was Jenner with his current wife, who was the ex-wife of Simpson attorney Robert Kardashian.[13] The Jenners sat with former baseball star Garvey and his wife, who, months earlier, had been a prosecution witness.

While the media didn't miss a chance to report on celebrity comings and goings, their accounts were silent on the nonstars Ito met with, often sacrificing lunch or a couple minutes of downtime to do so.

I assumed the media weren't particularly interested because those visitors weren't celebrities. It certainly wasn't because they were invisible. Well, actually, Ruth Archie was, initially.

Archie's name first cropped up when Ito took the bench on March 16 and wished her a happy birthday. He offered no reason for doing so except to say that she regularly followed the trial. That was it. Just, "Before we begin this morning's session, the court would like to take the personal opportunity to wish happy birthday to Ruth Archie . . . on her birthday today."

Archie instantly became the mystery woman everyone wanted to find out about. I hadn't a clue; I had never heard the name before. So that was my first question for Ito at the mid-morning break. Turned out she was following the court proceedings on television and had sent him an hourglass for his collection that had slowly migrated from his chambers to the courtroom in his not-so-subtle attempt to remind the lawyers to be more time-conscious.

When Ito called to thank her for it, he learned that she had cancer and wasn't doing well. Since she had been thoughtful enough to send him an hourglass, despite having problems of her own, he said, the least he could do was wish her a happy birthday on the record.

Rather than have me answer the media's questions about her and provide the correct spelling of her name, however, he said, "We are not going to tell them."

"Can we give any details at all about the circumstances and why you happened to wish her happy birthday?"

"No, we are not going to tell them anything," he said.

I was glad, I recorded in my journal. *Really, if the woman has got problems, if she is ill or whatever, I really don't think that she's clamoring for her fifteen minutes of fame so I was glad the judge made that decision. It makes it a little bit tougher. It is a nice a little story on the one hand, but some things should be kept private and I agreed with the judge on that one.*

But Ruth Archie surfaced again. Four months after her birthday, when Ito called to thank her for another hourglass she had sent, this one for his birthday, he realized how interested she was in the trial. It had, in fact, become a distraction from the harsh reality of her life. Might she like to attend it? he asked. Although still quite ill, she said she would even if she had to be carried on a gurney. She and a friend who accompanied her sat in the two seats Ito had designated to be reserved for his guests.

Archie wafted into the courtroom like a wisp of smoke, her short hair mere fuzz growing back after chemotherapy treatments. Ito invited her and her friend into chambers during recess and offered her his couch so she wouldn't have to stand in the hallway or sit on a hard concrete bench out there. Despite the media's curiosity about all the celebrities, though, no one asked me about Ruth Archie during her visit.[14]

Other visitors the media didn't quiz me about arrived less than a month after Ito's birthday greeting to Archie. A University of Southern California journalism professor had arranged for a group of former Soviet Union journalists participating in a U.S. Information Agency–sponsored program to visit the court and spend a few minutes with Ito during his lunch break. When they arrived, I started out by telling them about the case and the media covering it. I gave them a tour of the media center inside the courthouse, a lot across the street from the Criminal Courts Building where the media parked their equipment vehicles (which they had dubbed Camp OJ), and a spot within Camp OJ that I called scaffold city. Scaffold city consisted of five-story-tall rickety-looking broadcast platforms. Then we went to the courtroom to meet Ito. I had asked him earlier in the week about spending five minutes or so with them. The only time he had was during lunch, he said, but was glad to do it. I reminded him of the visit that morning. He nodded, saying he had it on his calendar.

Our timing was perfect. The visiting journalists and I arrived outside the courtroom at noon just as first the jurors, then the spectators, exited. Then we went in. With the journalists seated in the spectators' section, I went back to Ito's chambers to get him. But he was gone. One of his law school clerks speculated that he had gone down to the sixth-floor judges lounge. I flew down there and burst in on a room full of lunching judges listening to a formal program. That wasn't unusual. The noon break was often the only time judges had to conduct business, such as hold committee meetings and get information about court-related programs and issues.

I crept over to Ito and touched his sleeve. He looked startled, then contrite. He had forgotten all about the journalists' visit. I said I could extend his apologies so he could finish eating, but he said no. Leaving the remains of his lunch, we hustled up to his courtroom where he talked to the visitors about the court system, media coverage, and freedom of the press for a good fifteen minutes, then answered their questions.[15]

Also absent from media reports were visits from Scout troops, at-risk kids, and high school English-as-a-second-language students, judges from other countries, and friends and relatives of the four Pepperdine University Law School students who spent upward of twenty hours a week volunteering as law clerks for Ito.

Why, with all the pressure and rigors of the trial, did he make himself so available? Probably for the same altruistic, albeit misguided, reason he felt compelled to do the Japanese American internment camp interview. Perhaps because he felt that after the fortunate circumstances of his own upbringing, education, and career opportunities, he wanted to give back. Nowhere, from what I observed, was that more evident than in his interaction with his student clerks, whom he affectionately referred to as the "Cub Scouts."

He turned everything into a learning experience for them, understanding that they were not there just to help him, but that he had a responsibility to them.[16] At the end of each day, no matter how grueling it had been or how late the hour, he would invite them to sit on the sofa facing his desk and ask them, "Well, what did we learn today?" then quiz them on specific motions, legal issues, or attorney strategies that arose during the day's proceedings.

"He wants to make it as educational for us as possible," Pepperdine law student Paul Tyler told an ABC Los Angeles–affiliate reporter.[17]

Tyler and his three fellow clerks, Kathy Moran, Michelle Carswell, and Steve Golob, plus Claremont-McKenna College grad and prelaw student intern Tasia Scolinos spent untold hours in the judge's chambers and courtroom and recognized the media concerns that plagued him. Like almost everything else related to the trial, they, too, found themselves in the spotlight's glare and, with Ito's approval, participated in some interviews.

"The biggest problem I have with the press is their spin on the story," Scolinos said in the same interview as Tyler with the ABC affiliate. "Seeing it through the reporters' lens, seeing the judge make a decision, then seeing how it's presented to the public and how it gets twisted."[18]

"I can't speak for what's in the judge's mind," Golob told a CNN reporter in late 1994, "but I know he's concerned about violations of court rules and his orders, jury pollution, news leaks, theft of a court document that was published against his direction, and inaccurate reporting."[19]

Law clerk Tyler cropped up in a news report that illustrated Golob's point. The bespeckled young law student was sitting in the courtroom jury box one day observing a pretrial hearing that was being televised when Ito summoned him to the bench, apparently to have him research something for him. Tyler said that when he saw a tape of the proceeding, the TV commentator reported rather breathlessly, "Detective Tyler is about to testify."[20]

Chapter 7
Getting the Picture

■ ■ ■

Six months after Simpson's acquittal, U.S. Supreme Court Justice David H. Souter testified at a Congressional committee hearing about courtroom electronic media coverage.

"The day you see a camera come into our courtroom," he said, in a line now famous, "it's going to roll over my dead body."[1]

Los Angeles Superior Court Judge John J. Cheroske expressed similar sentiments at a meeting in Compton, where he was supervising judge following the *Simpson* verdicts. He said he didn't understand why any judge would ever allow a camera in the courtroom.

Souter and Cheroske voice the view of vast numbers of judges in the United States and abroad. Camera access has long sparked heated debates ranging from "the media just use trials to entertain," to "the media use only sound bites," to "televising an entire trial is boring," to "cameras sensationalize," to "cameras are no more than a silent eye."

The impact of cameras in the Simpson trial, however, changed the course of camera-access history for more than a decade afterward. Camera coverage is singled out as the biggest contributor to the derailment of that trial and the negative public perception of it and its participants. That set the stage for the future of camera access in federal and state courts across the country.

When prosecutors filed murder charges against Simpson in 1994, cameras had been a presence in California courts for more than a dozen years, and a limited three-year experiment of cameras recording federal civil cases was wrapping up with encouraging results.[2] By the end of the Simpson trial, federal officials had decided not to continue the pilot program[3] and then–California governor Pete Wilson was calling for an end of cameras in his state's courts.[4]

Although a total ban didn't ensue, the California Judicial Council revised the rule that regulates electronic-media coverage in courtrooms so judges could have complete discretion over whether to permit cameras in their courtrooms.[5]

One of the most significant effects the Simpson trial had on the judicial system was the resounding bang of courtroom doors slamming shut against camera coverage in jurisdictions where it previously had been much more the rule than the exception.

The cable television network Court TV, which got its start in 1991 and relied almost solely on being able to televise trials, felt the pinch most severely.

"The O. J. case was a disaster for Court TV access," says Fred Graham, who served as that network's senior editor until 2008, when Court TV became truTV, "especially in California but also in Texas, Virginia, Connecticut, the federal system and with individual judges elsewhere."[6]

Nowhere was that more apparent than in Los Angeles County. One of the first casualties was the retrial of the Menendez brothers in Van Nuys. With jury selection beginning in August 1995 and opening statements in October coming on the heels of the *Simpson* verdicts, Judge Stanley Weisberg, who had allowed television coverage of the first Menendez trial, banned it for the retrial.

Cameras had been permitted in California courtrooms since the approval of a temporary rule in 1981 that became permanent in 1984. Yet even some judges who had allowed cameras before *Simpson* became opponents afterward, saying that the Simpson trial indicated that cameras do, in fact, affect participants' behavior, particularly that of witnesses and lawyers. Arguments rage on both sides, but little, if any, concrete data exists. I can say, though, from my vantage point in the Simpson trial, some of the lawyers appeared to be at least aware of the cameras, however subliminally. That was generally manifested in subtle gestures, such as a glance up as the wall-mounted camera moved, sitting a little straighter, fingering a necktie, or lifting the chin slightly. But whether that factored into the outcome of the trial in any way may remain forever an unanswered question. The impact of cameras in trials, however, is a concern that continues to be voiced by judges and lawyers in this country and others. As recently as September 2007, the Simpson trial was still being cited by other states and even Canada as a consideration in courtroom-camera-coverage decisions.[7]

Souter and Cheroske have what they no doubt believe are compelling reasons to bar cameras from their courtrooms. So far as the Simpson case is concerned, though, I can say they don't know the half of it, at least so far as the media's conduct was concerned. In that case I can say categorically that in-court camera coverage most certainly affected the news media's behavior and modus operandi. While the viewing public watched *Simpson* play out on TV sets, here's what happened behind the lens.

From the beginning, Ito thought long and hard about the pros and cons of allowing camera coverage of the case. He researched the effect news media access had had on past notorious cases, including an unrestrained press in the courtroom when Ohio osteopath Samuel Sheppard stood trial for the murder of his wife. Ito also solicited advice from his judicial colleagues, lawyers, and media experts. Eventually, confident that he could keep a tight rein on the media in his courtroom, he chose the option that reflected his judicial philosophy: that he was a public official, conducting the public's business in a public place, therefore the public had a right to be there both in person and via cameras.

That doesn't mean he didn't seriously consider "pulling the plug" on cameras because of infractions. He did, several times. Once, for instance, was after the accidental airing of an alternate juror on the first day of opening statements. But to Ito, the media was a means, not an end. While he personally would just as soon have done without cameras, particularly knowing the additional work and hassle that allowing them in would create, he permitted them because he believes in public access. In the Simpson case, his consideration was for the public's benefit, not as a reward or favor to the media. Moreover, both the defense and the prosecution favored television coverage.

"Allowing cameras to remain in the courtroom would give the public the opportunity to see what the evidence actually is and to hear the truth," prosecutor Marcia Clark told Ito during a November 7, 1994, hearing on whether to televise the trial. "The best way to refute unfounded rumors and wild speculative theories is to permit everyone to see and hear the evidence that is presented in court. . . . No matter how thorough and fair reporters are, their coverage cannot equal the evidence of witnessing a trial first hand."[8]

The defense's support was qualified. Only if the jury wasn't sequestered would cameras be acceptable, defense attorney Robert Shapiro said at the same hearing.

"If your honor is so inclined to allow cameras in the courtroom at the cost of jury sequestration," he said, "we are firmly against it."

If the jury wasn't going to be sequestered, he added, he would welcome cameras,

> because we believe that the evidence or lack of evidence will show that Mr. Simpson is not guilty of these crimes. And for Mr. Simpson to have a life after this case with his children will require the American public to have an understanding that his acquittal was based on the evidence that was presented in a courtroom, not based on evidence that was in some way manipulated by lawyers, not based on evidence that was excluded based on legal technicalities.[9]

Ironically, Shapiro emphasized that, "And since just about everybody has an opinion about this case without hearing any evidence, we favor the fact that when Mr. Simpson, if he is acquitted, returns to society, that the public has a true perspective on what the real state of the evidence was in this case."[10]

So instead of excluding the cameras, Ito sought ways to control the people who operated them, such as levying fines, limiting their range and what they could shoot, and even at one time temporarily restricting the TV camera to a fixed shot with no zooming or panning.

The first infraction occurred on January 24 during the prosecution's opening statements when an alternate juror leaned into camera range. Although Ito cut camera coverage at that point, countless people have asked why he didn't keep the cameras out for the rest of the trial. He was willing, but the defense protested.

". . . [W]e would sincerely ask your honor to reconsider," Simpson attorney Shapiro said, "because of the effect this will have on Mr. Simpson, on the presumption of innocence and on his life after this case and if in fact he is rendered innocent of these charges." Shapiro asserted that it would be "tremendously unfair to have the world see the opening statements of the prosecution and not see the opening statements on behalf of Mr. Simpson."[11]

Prosecutor Clark, however, did an about-face from her previous position in which she had argued, "Keeping the camera in court will improve the accuracy of reporting."[12] Instead, apparently smelling possible advantage in the air, she thought things would be just fine without cameras.

"We have print media here. We have reporters here, all of whom will be able to print in a word-by-word basis everything that is said by counsel."

Besides, she added, "We are not playing to the world here, your honor. We are playing to the jury."[13]

Ito was caught squarely in a dilemma. He had to be fair and also be perceived as being fair.

"Well obviously, we have an unusual situation," he said. "On the one hand I've made it very clear to the news media that if there's a violation of Rule 980, that they would lose their privilege in this courtroom."

On the other was concern for the defendant. Ito continued, "There's a fundamental question of fairness too as far as his reputation is concerned. I'm very cognizant of his interest in preserving as much as he can of his reputation under the circumstances."[14]

Ito held a hearing in which Court TV officials expressed profound regret and laid out stringent measures they would take to ensure no future violations. After hearing that, plus pleas that pulling the camera plug would shut out a public that had seen everything about the case except the evidence, topped with the defense asking him to leave the camera in, Ito decided to do so. But he imposed rigid requirements.

First he had the alternate juror in question view the video footage to determine if there was a concern about continuing to serve. Then he required the cameraman to be in direct communication with the delay monitor so he could notify the monitor immediately of any violations he saw, which incredibly hadn't been included in the setup before. The person monitoring the feed was to be replaced with someone who could actually do the job, and that person had to have a backup. The media also was to install a second delay mechanism for the evidence-presentation system.

The most onerous imposition, however, was a static shot. The camera could not pan or zoom, "until further physical limitations on the camera are in place," Ito said.[15]

Rather than thanking their lucky stars that the camera wasn't booted out, the TV folks groused. The scene with a fixed shot was boring. Gone was any opportunity for camera crews, producers, and news directors to pique interest or create drama by calling for shots of different people or parts of the courtroom, picking up the reaction of victims' relatives to upsetting evidence or testimony, zooming in on a nervous witness, or peering over Simpson's shoulder at the defense table. The new conditions also pretty much idled Mary Cramer.

Hired by the media, Cramer shared on-site producer Nina Goebert's small office near the twelfth-floor media center, where she relayed requests by headset to the courtroom cameraman from news directors across the country who wanted specific shots. Using innovative camera techniques and creative editing to boost viewer interest or to be more entertaining by no means began with the Simpson trial. Broadcasters no doubt used such tools from the first time their cameras gained courtroom access. But they certainly raised the art form to a new level in the Simpson trial.

After a couple of weeks of a static shot, the media demonstrated a new robotic camera equipped with a "screen skirt" that would block any accidental shots of a juror. After seeing a demonstration, Ito allowed camera movement to resume. But he also ordered that there be no close-up or tight shots of him, the defendant, attorneys, or family members and no lingering shots on displays or gestures of emotion, and he added the caveat that any further violations would mean the camera was out.[16] Looking back, however, he thinks the camera shot should have remained static.

While TV is generally blamed for turning courtrooms into circuses, print photographers can contribute havoc of their own. In addition to the remote still camera mounted on the wall, which primarily served deadline news organizations, Ito permitted three other print positions in the courtroom. One of the other positions arose from contentions that the deadline pool excluded commercial, so-called nondeadline photo agencies. The other position went to an African American photographer who contended that the black-owned publications he represented needed shots with an African American perspective. Ito then allowed the deadline photographers to have an additional position after they complained that their wall-mounted camera didn't allow them the flexibility to get enough good shots.

Throughout the trial, the vast majority of the photographers behaved professionally and unobtrusively. A few, however, created more than enough consternation for everyone.

The most enterprising among them was Haywood Galbreath. Galbreath, a tall, imposing African American freelancer, first flashed onto my radar during the 1993 Reginald Denny–beating trial. Applying the same reasoning he used a year later for the Simpson trial, Galbreath rejected joining the existing *Denny* photo pool, arguing that its photographers were employed by white-owned newspapers and wire services, which he believed discriminated against blacks. But the *Denny* judge, while sympathetic, denied Galbreath's request because he had submitted it after the trial had begun and logistics were already in place.

Galbreath didn't make that mistake twice. Within ten days of the Simpson-Goldman murders, the National Newspaper Publishers Association, composed of black-owned publications, sent the court a "To Whom It May Concern" letter emphasizing the need for pictures of the case from an African American perspective and stating that Galbreath was the association's official photographer.[17]

When Ito became the Simpson trial judge, Galbreath pressed his case. He represented some two hundred black-owned newspapers across the country, he said, that were fed up with the distortions of the white media. Exhibit A, a *Time* magazine cover on which Simpson's mug shot had been altered, giving him a darker, and some said more sinister, look.[18]

From the outset, Galbreath irritated everyone, although despite everything, I liked him. He acted like the classroom pest who pokes and baits then, in wide-eyed "who me?" innocence, wonders why no one likes him.

Although some of the other photographers griped about Galbreath getting a separate camera position, they didn't want him in their pool any more than he wanted to be in it. The most bitter vitriol, however, spewed over the most coveted pool position of the entire trial. That was for the jury's crime-scene visits to Nicole Brown Simpson's Bundy Drive condominium and Simpson's Rockingham Avenue house, both in Brentwood.

After a dozen or so newspaper, wire and news service, and photo agency photographers wrangled for hours at the AP's Los Angeles bureau a few blocks from the courthouse over who would staff that pool, they finally decided to draw a name out of the proverbial hat.

I don't recall who drew the name, it might even have been me. But the firestorm that erupted remains indelible. The name was Haywood Galbreath.

Over Galbreath's hoots of delight, the others started demanding a do-over.

"No way!" he bellowed. "I got it fair and square!"

Someone suggested completely scrapping the drawing idea and finding another way to decide.

"No way!" Galbreath yelled again, his face flushing with rage. "Ain't no way you're going to do me outta this. This is *mine*!"

Then he and the others turned to me. They had asked me to attend the meeting as an objective bystander and to be a mediator or a calming influence, should one be needed. I could not in good conscience say that the process had been anything but fair. Nor did I want to. By their own rules, Galbreath was it. Although he could be difficult, he was tenacious. He didn't back down when he thought he was right, hadn't missed a day in the courtroom, and, I thought, by now should have earned his colleagues' respect. Amid lots of grumbling, the meeting ended. But lobbying didn't.

Several photographers contacted me later, pleading for help. They lamented that Galbreath wouldn't be up to the task, that his work wouldn't meet their professional standards, that he would somehow screw things up, that this was *the* most important photo assignment of the entire case and shouldn't be entrusted to any but the best and most experienced shooter. Resignation, however, finally settled in. Galbreath kept the position, and he did a great job, winning praise from many of the other photographers.

That wasn't the end of Galbreath-related skirmishes, however.

From the beginning, he balked at the security-screen searches outside Ito's courtroom. Things boiled over one morning when the deputies staffing the screen made him go through the metal detector twice for some reason. When he began yelling at them, they summoned me. I arrived to find Galbreath ready to tear the deputies limb from limb and them about ready to give him the boot. I'd been around Galbreath and heard him charge discrimination enough by that time to know something had to be done. Quick.

Given that, until then, the only physical contact I had ever had with members of the media covering the case had been no more than a handshake and that Galbreath towered over me, I don't know what possessed me. Nevertheless, I grabbed his arm and backed him against the wall.

Thrusting my face as close to his as I could, given that he stood nearly a foot taller than my own five feet, four inches, I said,

> Haywood, you have got to make a decision if you are going to . . . I mean, what do you want? Do you want to be in the courtroom? You worked long and hard to get into the courtroom to shoot the images that you think are important for African Americans and now here you are out here making a big stink about the security screen. Make up your mind, if you want to be in the courtroom shooting the images you think are important or if your objective is really to wage an all-out campaign about all the ills and evils that are being perpetrated against black people.

That, he replied, was exactly his intent.

"Then you go right ahead and do it," I barked back,

> and you can forget about being in the courtroom shooting pictures, because there is no way that you are going to win that battle here. . . . If you want to be in the courtroom shooting pictures, I can help you. But if your objective is to right all the ills against African Americans in this country then I can't help you shoot pictures in the courtroom.[19]

With that, he calmed down. But he didn't stay quiet for long. A few days later, a courtroom deputy of Herculean proportions said Galbreath was giving her a hard time when she told him he had to wear his press credentials on the outside of his shirt where they could be seen. That was a rule all the media had to follow if they wanted access to credentialed areas in the courthouse.

According to the deputy, Kathy Browning, Galbreath retorted that, "You talk to me the way my mama does."

Although I didn't note what Browning said to him, I'm sure she made it clear she wasn't about to take any guff from him.

"Nobody gives Kathy Browning any lip," I recorded in my journal. "She is a tough cookie and she knows it, and she just revels in it."

I do recall that when she told me about the encounter, her mouth twitched and her eyes twinkled at the thought of him trying to best her. When court reconvened after the break that morning, Galbreath, leaving his cameras in place, came over and squatted down in front of me.

"Hey," he whispered, "what's with the deputy giving me a hard time about my press credentials being outside of my shirt and then accusing me of mouthing off to her?"

"Well, Haywood, you did," I whispered back. "You better just get busy and do your job here and shoot pictures."[20]

Galbreath also had run-ins with some of his fellow photographers, most notably a freelancer named Roger Sandler on assignment for *Time* magazine.[21]

Sandler, a soft, petulant-looking man, had his own rule problems. As the case lumbered through the pretrial phase, Sandler began to show up in the nondeadline pool rotation carting more than the two camera bodies and the four lenses permitted by court rule. Thinking the extra gear was a rather petty offense to call Sandler on, I initially let it go.

Then he started hauling in two tripods, the first time I'd ever seen a photographer do that, and up to six cameras. One tripod could hold multiple cameras, something else I hadn't seen before. Since the case was still in pretrial, Ito let the photographers shoot from the jury box. But Sandler not only crowded his colleagues with all of his equipment, he set some of it up in front of them. When they complained that he was blocking their shots, I stepped in. Or tried to. No matter what I said about the camera limit and even though I showed him the court rule and gave him a copy, he continued to bring it all in, apparently thinking that once he got there, no one would say anything. Finally losing patience, I told him to either take the excess equipment out or leave.

Then came a morning in October when Sandler showed up before court convened to get a shot of the mountains of mail, estimated at more than 15,000 letters, syndicated columnist Mike Royko had generated when he urged his readers to tell Ito what they thought about the trial being televised. Ito had actually let photographers take pictures of the mail the previous day, but Sandler somehow had missed out. Ito said he could play catch-up the next day before court, but he had to be quick.

When Sandler set his bulky camera bag on a chair beside the counsel table where Ito's clerk Deirdre Robertson had already piled the stacks of letters, the courtroom was mostly empty. Only Sandler, Robertson, Ito's bailiff, Guy Magnera, and I were there. Sandler pulled out a camera, fiddled with a lens, started snapping pictures of the mail, then squeezed off a few shots of a suit of clothes hanging near the bailiff's desk that the defense team had brought for Simpson to wear in court.

Magnera told him to stop.

"But this is a chance of a lifetime," he said.

No, Magnera repeated.

"I'll give you some prints," Sandler pressed and continued to shoot as Magnera moved between the photographer and the clothes.

I finally spoke up.

"The bailiff is responsible for security," I said. "He told you not to take the pictures, so you have got to stop taking them or you will have to leave."

Sandler tried to look sheepish but couldn't hide the glee bubbling beneath his apologetic expression. As he started packing up his gear, he mumbled that he didn't see the harm. Magnera threatened to take his film but settled for a promise that the pictures wouldn't be published. Sandler, however, must have had his fingers crossed.[22]

Later that day he called to ask if he could go ahead and use the pictures since he had already taken them. After double-checking with Magnera, I reiterated that the pictures were not to be published anywhere.

But that still wasn't the end of it.

A few weeks later *Time* magazine's Los Angeles bureau picture editor, Martha Bardach, faxed a photograph to my office of Magnera with Simpson's clothes. Accompanying the photo was a request to publish it. I was really irritated. I called her and told her what Sandler had done and what we had told him. Sounding pretty irritated herself, Bardach said she didn't know that and would make sure the film and prints were destroyed so we wouldn't have to worry about it again.

But it turned out she was wrong.[23]

Before either of us knew that, though, the trial was under way with Sandler occasionally staffing the nondeadline pool position. When he did, he and Galbreath found themselves elbow to elbow in the back of the courtroom. They bickered constantly, and each complained to me about the other, sometimes about something as petty about Galbreath singing in Sandler's ear.[24]

In early March, however, Sandler committed a more egregious offense. AP Photographer Reed Saxon told me he was worried. He had seen Sandler in the hallway taking a picture of Simpson's maid and media-shy witness Rosa Lopez, who was sitting on a nearby bench. That violated a court order banning photography on the ninth floor and, in fact, in the entire courthouse, except for inside courtrooms and a few well-marked designated areas on other floors. Saxon, concerned he and the other print photographers would be punished along with Sandler, should he be caught, said he reminded Sandler about the order. When Sandler said he didn't know about the order, Saxon showed him a copy taped to the wall.

If Sandler had been a newcomer, I might have been willing to make an exception. "But he has been around forever," I recorded in my journal. "If we hadn't had so many previous incidents with him, I might be willing to recommend to the judge . . . or not say anything to the judge. But, because problems with him have just been rife, so to speak, I decided that I better let the judge know about it."

Ito told me to inform James Bascue, who was the new criminal courts supervising judge. I also notified *Time* magazine's Bardach. She said she would pass it along to her boss, photo editor Michele Stephenson in New York, who might want to lodge a protest.[25]

Sandler, Stephenson, and *Time*'s West Coast bureau chief Jordan Bon-
fontaine sent letters apologizing and appealing for reconsideration. Sandler's
bosses seemed ready to go to bat for him until they learned he had betrayed
them as well. That involved a photograph of Magnera straightening Simpson's clothes. The problem for *Time* was that it ran not in *Time* magazine, but
in *Life*. *Time, Life*. What's the difference, right? They're both owned by the
same company. Turns out it made a lot of difference to *Time*.

Sandler, much to my amazement, had actually gotten permission to use
the picture.

"Yeah," said Magnera when I showed it to him. "He went over both of our
heads. . . . He got clearance from the sheriff."

"From the sheriff? How did that happen?"

"Through Fidel Gonzales," he said, referring to a longtime sheriff's deputy
assigned to the department's information bureau. Gonzales had been the go-
to guy on other end run attempts, such as letting defense attorneys park in
the judges' lot under the courthouse after they failed to get court permission
to park there, then escorting them up to the courtroom via the judges' security elevator.

My next stop was Supervising Judge Bascue.

"Can you find out for me who gave authorization for that photograph to
be published?" he asked. "And, by the way, Roger Sandler is banned from this
building. He is not welcome in the Criminal Courts Building."

I called Gonzales. Sandler, he said, had contacted him two or three months
earlier about taking a picture of Magnera preparing Simpson's clothes for
court. Sandler had told him that Magnera had said it was fine with him but
he had to get clearance. That's why Sandler was calling Gonzales. Gonzales
said he took Sandler's request "up the line" for approval, which might have
come from the sheriff, himself, although he wasn't sure. Feeling shell-
shocked, I went back to Magnera to find out just when he had given Sandler
the okay.

"Did Roger Sandler ever come to you after that one day when he actually
took the pictures?" I asked. "Did he come back to you and ask you if it would
be all right with you if he published the pictures or took another picture or
anything like that?"

"No," Magnera replied, "I didn't have any contact with him after that one
day."

Neither Bascue nor Ito were pleased.

"The court is in control of what the media does and does not do in the Criminal Courts Building," Bascue said, "not the Sheriff's Department." Ito concurred.

Then Stephenson, *Time*'s photo editor, said the magazine was withdrawing its support of Sandler. It turned out that when he finally got approval to use the photographs, instead of telling *Time*, he apparently struck a deal with *Life*.

"I don't know if we would have actually run the picture," Stephenson said, "but we feel that we should at least have had the opportunity, since he was representing *Time* magazine when he took the photographs."

"I don't know what Roger's next step is going to be," I recorded in my journal, "but I don't think that this is the last of it."[26]

And, indeed, it wasn't.

After Sandler called several times, he showed up one morning with a lawyer, saying he had an appointment to talk to Ito, which he didn't. Bascue finally said if he or his lawyer had anything to say, they could do so on the record in a formal hearing. To initiate that, however, they would have to file papers with the court. In the meantime, Bascue issued an order:

SUPERIOR COURT OF THE STATE OF CALIFORNIA
FOR THE COUNTY OF LOS ANGELES

DENIAL OF ADMITTANCE TO	)	ORDER
THE CRIMINAL COURTS BUILDING	)	
OF ROGER E. SANDLER, PHOTOGRAPHER	)	

It is hereby ordered that Roger E. Sandler, a photographer who has been on assignment for *Time* magazine covering the pretrial proceedings and the trial of the *People of the State of California v. Orenthal James Simpson,* is to be denied access to the Criminal Courts Building for the pendency of the Simpson trial. This action is taken as a result of Mr. Sandler's violation of a Court Order restricting cameras to specifically designated interview areas in the Criminal Courts Building, and for taking or attempting to take unauthorized photographs.
Dated: March 21, 1995

James A. Bascue, Supervising Judge
Criminal Division

Sandler's lawyer eventually filed a petition, and a couple of months later Bascue assigned the hearing to Assistant Supervising Judge John Reid. Reid declared that Sandler couldn't attend the hearing because he was barred from the courthouse. Then he ruled against him.[27]

Sandler went to the state court of appeal, which bounced the matter back to the superior court for a redo, saying Sandler was entitled to a full hearing.[28]

In the midst of this, *Los Angeles Times* columnist Bill Boyarsky defended Sandler in a piece about the injustice of being punished for a "minor infraction." The column failed to mention, however, Sandler's cumulative violations and misrepresentations, even though before Boyarksy wrote his column I made sure he had the documentation detailing Sandler's offenses.[29]

Bascue presided over the rehearing, held on July 7, during which I took the stand. My testimony was brief, however, because most of what I knew was hearsay and therefore not admissible. That included deputies at the ninth-floor security screen saying that Sandler had said he was a pool photographer the day he took Rosa Lopez's picture so he could get his camera on the floor. But the deputies and Saxon had provided declarations, which pretty much sealed Sandler's fate. Bascue upheld the courtroom and courthouse bans. This time the court of appeal agreed, and that was the last we saw of Sandler.[30]

Bascue also set rules for cameras around the courthouse to contain the media rush of lawyers and high-profile witnesses, such as Faye Resnick, and to curtail impromptu news conferences.[31] It wasn't, however, the last of camera and photographer hassles.

Most memorable were incidents that involved the snapping of unauthorized test pictures of Ito with the wall-mounted print camera when court wasn't in session, the woes of a height-challenged nondeadline pool photographer, and a dustup over a close shot of Simpson taking notes. In addition, artists drew sketches of jurors that were too accurate, the media's on-site producer melted down when Ito killed TV shots of evidence being presented to the jury, and New York celebrity photo diva Annie Leibovitz showed up and took an unauthorized picture of Simpson, then ticked off the other photographers when she didn't share the photo with them.

The unauthorized test shots taken during a noon hour when Ito just happened to be in the courtroom prompted hearings that resulted in a fine and the shutting down of the remote print camera for a week, which, I daresay, the public never noticed.[32]

A rather comical incident is worth mentioning only to illustrate the petty squabbling that contributed to the never-ending nails-on-chalkboard background media din. Early in the trial, nondeadline pool photographer Lisa Rose, who was about my height, started bringing a box to stand on so she could get better shots from her position in the back of the courtroom. The problem was that violated a fire code that prohibited placing anything between the benches that could obstruct a hasty exit in case of emergency. When I told Rose, she complained about not being tall enough to shoot over the heads in front of her.

On her next turn in the courtroom, she showed up wearing shoes with thick blocks of wood glued to the bottoms and clumped around like a circus clown on short stilts. That only exacerbated a problem Ito had with the photographers popping up and down like jack-in-the-boxes as they stood to take pictures then sat between shots. But neither did the deputies want them, or anyone, standing while court was in session. Although I previously had told all of the photographers to minimize their movements because they distracted the jurors, I reminded Rose the first day she clumped to her courtroom position in her stilt shoes.

"I've already talked to the deputy about it," she said. "I've got a problem with my knees. The deputy talked to the judge and the judge said it was okay."

As Ito took the bench, I asked the deputy stationed at the courtroom door, who happened to be Kathy Browning, if she had gotten Ito's dispensation for Rose to stand because of her knees.

"Nope, she didn't say anything to me about it," Browning replied. She checked with the other deputies but found no one Rose had talked to.

At that point, Browning and I were standing in the little anteroom between the courtroom's interior and outer doors. Suddenly Rose came clomping out, surprising Browning and me—and apparently moving a little too fast. She turned an ankle and almost fell.

"Jerrianne," she said with a croak, "I have got to talk to you. This is really serious. I have *got* to talk to you." Then with her face blanching, she gasped, "I've got to go to the restroom!" And she clumped out.

Since I was headed for my twelfth-floor media-center office, I asked Browning to tell Rose she could find me there. Before long, she appeared, wound up, as I recorded in my journal, "tighter than a tick." It turned out that in addition to being height-challenged and having bad knees, she also suffered from a nervous stomach. She had dashed to the bathroom to throw up, thanks to her fellow photographer Haywood Galbreath, who, she said, was driving her nuts.

"I know he's just trying to get me tossed out," she said. "He knows all my buttons and he knows how to push them."

Part of the problem was that, unlike the pool photographers who were in the courtroom only about once a week, Galbreath had daily access. Consequently, he appointed himself chief photog-rule enforcer. The morning I reminded Rose as she arrived in the courtroom to minimize popping up and down, she told me later that Galbreath had gloated. I suggested she consider his point of view.

"Suppose you know that there is a rule in place and if someone doesn't abide by it everybody gets tossed out," I said. "Aren't you going to try to make everybody aware of it?"

"Oh," she retorted, "it's the way he does it and then when you came in and told me to not go up and down he was just so self-satisfied and smug. You didn't see the expression on his face."

Back in the courtroom later that day, I saw the deadline photographer taking pictures of Rose's block-riser shoes.

"That's probably going to be a story somewhere along the line," I recorded in my journal. "Funny, funny, I think. At least at this point it is."[33]

Another glitch involved a close-up shot of Simpson taking notes that became a flap in the midst of prosecutor Marcia Clark's closing argument and brought media attorney Kelli Sager hustling from her office a short distance away to throw her clients on the mercy of the court.

The move was actually innocent enough. When Clark mentioned cuts on Simpson's fingers, which he said he got when breaking a glass, the TV cameraman panned over for a close-up of his hands. Unfortunately, Simpson happened to be jotting something on a notepad at that moment. The defense attorneys went ballistic, claiming the media were trying to read what Simpson was writing. After viewing tapes of the shot, one at regular speed and another in slow motion, Ito declared no harm, no foul, but he fined the broadcasters $1,500 for violating his court order.[34]

Augmenting still and television images were courtroom sketches. Although camera advocates argue that cameras present unfiltered coverage that is more accurate and complete than reporters' interpretations or notes, TV stations and networks often hire artists to draw pictures, even when cameras are present. One reason is to give the public a representation of the jury, since most states bar photography of jurors.

The problem with Simpson trial artists was they were too good. People started calling the court saying they recognized a juror as a neighbor or coworker or friend based on a sketch they had seen on TV. Although the artists knew not to draw facial features, they included other characteristics, such as unique balding patterns, shapes of jowls and double chins, and distinctive hairstyles, which made some of the jurors definitely recognizable. Rather than bar the artists from the courtroom, though, Ito said I had to review and approve the drawings before they could be published or aired. That worked fine for three of the four who were courtroom regulars. If I thought a likeness was too close, I would suggest adding hair or slimming a neckline. The other artist, however, was a different story.

Whenever veteran court sketch artist Bill Robles, on assignment for CBS, was in the courtroom, I reminded him to show me his sketches after court. But when court recessed, he, unlike the others who always managed to touch base with me, disappeared, leaving me trying in vain to track him down.

One weekend in April, however, some of Robles's drawings aired that prompted Ito to summon him to court the following Monday. He was to bring all the drawings of *Simpson* jurors that "he has caused to be televised or otherwise published or that he intends to cause to be televised or otherwise published...."[35]

Ito said to the artist and his attorney, Beth Finley,

> The reason I asked Mr. Robles to appear this morning is I understand he is one of the very talented sketch artists that has been covering this case, and while watching one of the local independent television programs the other day I happened to see a rendering of our jury that was astonishing in its accuracy and depiction. And I made an inquiry into who was the artist and how it came about that that particular rendering was broadcast and I was concerned because as you know, the court has ordered the use of an anonymous jury in this case and that California Rules of Court 980 prohibits the depiction of jurors, close up of jurors, and I was concerned because the depictions were too close to what we have in the jury box.

"I think there may have been a problem," Finley replied, "because, sometimes, Mr. Robles isn't in the courtroom every day, and although he's trying to have all of his drawings cleared by your representative, he has not been able to connect with her on all occasions, and perhaps that is how one of the drawings was broadcast without someone else in the court seeing it."[36]

Ito's remedy was to issue a written order for all artists to submit their drawings to him or to me for review before releasing them for publication or broadcast.

"And Miss Hayslett is present here in the courthouse every day and this court rarely leaves the courthouse before 6:00 in the evening every day, so we will be available to in an expeditious manner review any drawings that you want to use immediately that day," Ito concluded.[37]

In addition to the order, Ito also had two stamps made—one for him and one for me—and each had a red circle on it bisected with the word **APPROVED**. "ITO" graced the top arc of the circle and "PIO" the bottom arc. He then instructed me to notify the media that all courtroom sketches had to bear that stamp before they could use them.[38]

Advanced technology also played a part in *Simpson* courtroom camera coverage in the form of an evidence-presentation system. Visual evidence, such as photographs and charts, presented to the jury electronically was aired publicly on a separate audio-visual feed from the one that broadcast the rest of the proceedings. Ito had a on-off toggle, called a kill switch, to both feeds, which he could control from the bench. Having that control was key to his approval of camera coverage, particularly for the evidence system because the exhibits placed on it included crime-scene and autopsy photographs. Ito was adamant. Out of consideration for the victims' dignity and their families' feelings, those photographs would not get out to the public. Still, a photo suspiciously similar to one shown early in the proceedings before the feed was killed, which the media agreed not to air, appeared nearly five months later in a supermarket tabloid. Ito decided not to shut down the courtroom camera only after a close examination of the photograph proved that it had not come from the system. Again, a major consideration was the perception of fairness. The prosecution had presented its case at that point, but the defense hadn't. So the camera stayed, but Ito's finger rested on the kill switch.

Barely a month later, media on-site producer Nina Goebert erupted because Ito had blocked a Simpson exercise video being shown on the evidence-presentation system. The reason was because someone had raised a copyright question.

"This is ridiculous!" Goebert stormed. "The judge can't do this! There's nobody naked in it! There aren't any dead bodies, you know."[39]

Goebert blew up again during prosecutor Marcia Clark's closing argument near the end of the trial.

"Nina was going bonkers with all of the different demands on her," I recorded in my journal. "The judge would not allow the evidence feed to be on during [the final portion of] Marcia Clark's closing, which involved a montage of photographs of the crime scene and the victims. . . . Nina had been frantically calling down saying that the evidence feed is off and she paged me to try to get me to address it."

When I told her the reason had been that photographs of the bodies were shown, she settled down some but still didn't seem to be thinking straight.

"I'll never let a judge have that kind of discretion again," she fumed.[40]

Perhaps my thinking isn't straight either, but despite dealing with the personalities, ambitions, egos, agendas, challenges, violations, and accidents, I disagree with the Justice Souters and Judge Cheroskes of the world, although not totally.

"Contrary to those who argue in favor of cameras in the courtroom, the camera is not just another courtroom spectator, at least not the way it is typically operated," I wrote in a 1997 *Court Manager* magazine article based on the first Simpson and Menendez brothers trials, which were televised, and the second Simpson and Menendez trials, which weren't. "Courtroom spectators cannot zoom their eyeballs in to peer over the defendants' or attorneys' shoulders at counsel tables, to gaze within a nose length into the faces of the witnesses or judge, or to get up close and personal with grieving victims or their relatives. Such camera work serves, not to report the trial, but to embellish and in some cases even create courtroom drama and pathos."[41]

In the wake of *Simpson*, says Gary Hengstler, Donald W. Reynolds National Center for Courts and Media director, denying cameras became exhibit A for judges attempting to prove they do, in fact, have command of their courtrooms.

"The specter of being criticized for 'losing control' prompted many judges to go to extra lengths to show they were keeping control," Hengstler says. "The most obvious was—and continues to be—the decline in the number of courts permitting cameras in the courtroom. . . . And here at the National Judicial College, you invariably encounter the judges who simply say they aren't going to take a chance on appearing badly on television."[42]

Rather than a demonstration of control, however, denying cameras is a show of power. But in exercising that power, judges hide from the public whether they are able to actually maintain control of courtrooms. Retired radio and television broadcaster David Dow says judges are afraid of being what he calls fall guys.

"One way to prevent that is to shut out the camera so their own weaknesses and courtroom irregularities can't be exposed to public view," says Dow, who, with Thomas Jefferson Law School Professor Marjorie Cohn, coauthored, *Cameras in the Courtroom: Television and the Pursuit of Justice.*[43]

Radio-Television News Directors Association president Barbara Cochran voices that common view in the broadcast industry. Although judges might "fear the kind of scrutiny and possible criticism that comes in a high-profile trial," Cochran says, "a judge who is confident about his or her ability to maintain order has nothing to fear from cameras."[44]

William Mudd, a retired San Diego Superior Court judge, is of the same opinion. Mudd presided over and allowed camera coverage of the 2002 trial of David Westerfield, convicted and sentenced to death for the kidnap, rape, and murder of seven-year-old Danielle Van Dam.

"If a judge feels competent at all," Mudd says, "he shouldn't have any problem with cameras in the courtroom. That doesn't mean you won't have problems, but you need to do what you say."[45]

Ito agrees, despite the negative consequences the Simpson trial had on his professional image and the extra work cameras generate for judges and court staff.

"Television creates so many issues you wouldn't have otherwise," he says. "You get more phone calls. You get more mail." Nevertheless, he continues to allow camera access to his courtroom. Ironically, the very camera access that Ito champions contributed to his own victimization, according to the AP's Linda Deutsch:

> I think the Simpson trial was an aberration. It's the biggest we've ever had. You have to consider that O. J. Simpson was the most famous American ever charged with murder. He was a famous football star. He was a TV star. Everyone knew him. This one [trial] touched America. Televising it made it more of a national obsession. I think TV should have been there. People had a right to see that trial. But it televised Judge Ito, too, so it made him bigger than life, bigger than he would have been had it not been televised.[46]

But not televising it would not necessarily have resulted in a more responsible media or better informed public. Court TV's Fred Graham cites the Scott Peterson, Michael Jackson, and Kobe Bryant cases, none of which were televised, as being the most circuslike in recent years.

"With no way to show the public what was actually happening, some television broadcasters resorted to reenactments, shouting matches between alleged 'legal experts,' and opinionated statements by television hosts," Graham told attendees at a University of Louisville School of Law lecture. "There are those who believe the atmosphere surrounding all three cases would have been less hyper if the public had been permitted to just watch the trials on television."[47]

Ito continues to be disappointed in the bulk of high-profile–case media coverage, including that of the nontelevised 2005 Michael Jackson child-molestation trial.

"So few are accurately reported," he said when the trial was in progress. "So few [members of the media] have the background to get it accurate, or even have the willingness or desire to cover it accurately. They're too interested in sensational aspects to be able to understand and report the proceedings and legalities."

Seeing that now, however, does not spark regrets.

"If I were to do it over," Ito says, "I would still allow cameras in *Simpson,* but with a fixed focus that I controlled."[48]

A man autographs one of many signs in support of O. J. Simpson at the front gate of Simpson's house, June 21, 1994 (Associated Press photo/Kevork Djansezian).

A man displays his opinion outside the Criminal Courts Building in Los Angeles during the Simpson murder trial, August 16, 1995 (Associated Press photo/ Nick Ut).

Judge Lance Ito addresses the court, September 1, 1995
(Associated Press photo/Mark J. Terrill, pool).

Defense lawyers and defendant (l to r) Barry Scheck, Peter Neufeld, O. J. Simpson,
Johnnie Cochran Jr., and Robert Shapiro and (background) Ito's bailiff, Deputy
Guy Magnera, watch the jury enter the courtroom, May 5, 1995 (Associated Press
photo/Reed Saxon, pool).

Prosecutor Christopher Darden points at a chart during closing arguments, September 29, 1995; standing in background, prosecutor Marcia Clark (Associated Press photo/Reed Saxon, pool).

The Victims

NICOLE BROWN SIMPSON **RON GOLDMAN**

Murder victims Nicole Brown Simpson and Ron Goldman (Associated Press photo/file).

Principals in the Simpson trial during the jury visit to Simpson's estate, February 12, 1995 (Associated Press photo/Mark Terrill).

Journalists outside the Criminal Courts Building wear Robert Shapiro masks as they await the arrival of Simpson's lawyer, October 31, 1994 (Associated Press photo/Brennan Linsley).

The Dancing Itos on *The Tonight Show,* April 6, 1995 (Margaret Norton/NBCU Photo Bank via Associated Press Images).

Robert Shapiro emerges from a group of media as he arrives at the Criminal Courts Building, October 5, 1994 (Associated Press photo/Kevork Djansezian).

A billboard bearing the message "innocent" stands before the downtown Los Angeles skyline, May 16, 1995. The billboards, some reading "guilty" and some reading "innocent," are part of a radio station's campaign to promote programming (Associated Press photo/Reed Saxon).

A billboard put up by Denver radio station KRFX-FM, shown in Denver, June 24, 1995 (Associated Press photo).

Johnnie Cochran Jr., flanked by bodyguards from the Nation of Islam, arrives at the Criminal Courts Building, September 28, 1995 (Associated Press photo/Nick Ut).

Photographers, reporters, and television cameras wait outside the gate of Simpson's estate the day after the verdicts were announced, October 4, 1995 (Associated Press photo/Paul Sakuma).

Candlelight march past the condominium of Nicole Brown Simpson, organized by the National Organization of Women, October 7, 1995 (Associated Press photo/Eric Draper).

A man looks at one of the publications featuring O. J. Simpson on sale at a
Los Angeles newstand, June 12, 1994 (Associated Press photo/Nick Ut).

British newspaper headlines on the verdicts in the Simpson trial, October 4, 1995
(Associated Press photo/Alastair Grant).

Police line up opposite crowds outside the Criminal Courts Building on the day of the *Simpson* verdicts, October 3, 1995 (Associated Press photo/Mark J. Terrill).

People on a New York street react to news of the *Simpson* verdicts shown on a portable TV carried by woman in foreground, October 3, 1995 (Associated Press photo/Adam Nadel).

In a replay of the media frenzy surrounding the Simpson murder trial, satellite trucks pack a parking lot near the Clark County Regional Justice Center for O. J. Simpson's preliminary hearing in Las Vegas, November 9, 2007 (Associated Press photo/Isaac Brekken).

Robin Clark, a journalist covering *Simpson*, died in a car accident during the trial (photo courtesy of Ann Dodge).

The business card Judge Ito had made for himself (author's collection).

RODNEY J. NAKAMURA
A.K.A. Hon. Judge Lance A. Ito

Impersonator Extraordinaire
Comic • Sage

The William Morris Agency
10 Park Avenue
New York, NY 10012   **1-800-987-6543**

The stamp Judge Ito had made for use with courtroom sketches (author's collection).

Chapter 8

Who's to Judge?

■ ■ ■

If media issues consumed a third of Ito's time during the trial, jury problems took up another huge chunk.

From secret note-taking for book deals to personality clashes, rebellions, illnesses, and psychological disorders, hardly a day went by from the time the jury was sequestered, on January 11, 1995, until it delivered the verdicts nearly nine months later that Ito didn't hold a closed session to solve one knotty juror problem or another. Jury issues became so squirrelly, Ito wondered if what he called "stealth jurors" had made it onto the panel and were trying to sabotage the case.

"Every day there would be three things I'd never seen before in my judicial career," he said years after the trial. "I consulted with other judges and they hadn't either."[1]

Steve Kindred, a veteran reporter with the Los Angeles all-news radio station KFWB, offered at least a partial explanation. "With that long a sequestration," he observed at a 2005 panel discussion on celebrity trials, "there's bound to be a blowback."[2]

No one, least of all Ito, foresaw a nearly nine-month sequestration. Right up to the completion of jury selection, the projection was a three-to-four-month trial. That expectation was evident during the selection of alternate jurors to back up the panel of twelve regulars who had already been seated.

"Because the trial, as you know, has been delayed in getting started because of the length of time we've had to spend in jury selection," Ito said

in court on December 1, 1994, "it's possible we will not start the actual presentation of evidence until sometime late in January. We may not finish until
sometime in April.

"I might have to sequester the jury for part or all of that time," he added,
asking a prospective alternate if that would be a problem.[3]

Sequestration as an option to shield jurors from media reports and casual
case-related conversation arose months before opening statements began.
Deputy District Attorney William Hodgman announced at an August 31,
1994, pretrial hearing that the prosecution intended to file a motion to
sequester. That was an idea the defense didn't like.[4]

With jury selection, which had begun in late September, continuing into
mid-October and news reports becoming increasingly pervasive, debate
heated up over how to shield jurors from the publicity. On October 20, Ito's
research attorney, John Byrne, reported that approximately 27,000 newspaper articles about the case had been published. That didn't count the tens of
thousands of broadcast and magazine stories or the daily segments on the
likes of *Good Morning America, Today, Hard Copy, Entertainment Tonight,*
Jay Leno, David Letterman, and countless radio talk shows.[5] Nor did it
include accounts of the leaked tapes of Nicole Brown Simpson's 9-1-1 calls
or the Faye Resnick interviews about her newly published book that were
beginning to flood the airwaves. At that point, attorney Robert Shapiro proposed that the trial be postponed for at least a year with Simpson released on
bail, a suggestion the prosecution vehemently opposed.

Given the suffocating blanket of media coverage, a gag order to shield
jurors from information to which they shouldn't be privy would have been
no more effective than putting a Band-Aid on a severed artery. The same
would have been true with judicial admonitions. Jurors would have had to
hide in a cave to avoid media coverage.

Allowing courtroom-camera coverage wasn't among the reasons Ito eventually decided to sequester.

"The impetus to sequester the jury in this case was overall news media
frenzy outside the courtroom in general and the computer-generated 'photograph' of a beaten Nicole Brown Simpson on the cover of the *National
Enquirer* in particular," he wrote to a Los Angeles County supervisor. "The
sequestration of the jury is not a direct consequence of the presence of the
television camera in the courtroom."[6]

The court's presiding judge at the time, Gary Klausner, supported Ito's opinion.

"[T]here is no specific indication that would lead to the conclusion that the sequestration is a result of cameras in the court," Klausner wrote in a separate letter, addressing a county task force inquiry into assessing the media covering the Simpson trial a fee to help cover the mounting costs, primarily for court security. "Without such a finding by the trial court, such assessments would be inappropriate."[7]

The media in general adamantly oppose gag orders and constantly argue for judges to take other measures, including sequestration, to shield jurors. But once the *Simpson* jury was sequestered, members of the media became vocal critics, questioning how jurors held in near imprisonment could remain functional and objective. That is but one of the "Catch 22s" Ito found himself in throughout the trial. So far as sequestration is concerned, though, he believed he had no choice.

Constitutional scholar Erwin Chemerinsky, like many legal academicians, generally opposes sequestering juries. In the Simpson case, however, he agrees that Ito would have been mistaken not to.

"I am always uncomfortable with sequestration because of the burden it places on jurors," says Chemerinsky, who in 2008 became founding dean of the University of California, Irvine, Donald Bren School of Law. "But this is a rare case where it was needed. The media coverage was so overwhelming and this was a murder trial."

But the magnitude of trying to shelter jurors from media contamination became evident before jury selection even began. Incidents such as the municipal court preliminary hearing court reporter asking defense attorney Shapiro for Simpson's autograph on a magazine cover,[8] a juror questionnaire that disappeared between the court's print shop where the questionnaires were reproduced and Ito's chambers,[9] and the juror services manager, hoping to thwart court staff-*cum*-souvenir hounds, taking home and washing a table covering containing doodling Simpson made during jury selection portended the impossibility of sheltering jurors from the very public throes of the case.[10]

Ito was vexed by the missing questionnaire, which the *Daily News of Los Angeles* published the day after it disappeared. But he eventually decided against trying to hold the newspaper accountable, except for banning *Daily*

News reporters from the courtroom during jury selection. "There are too many other things occupying my time now," he said after days of wrangling with *Daily News* editors and legal counsel, "otherwise I would love to fight."[11]

Of greater concern was the jury's exposure to the media and their reports.

The fact that jurors had to coexist in the courthouse with members of the media made exposure inevitable. There were numerous incidents early in the case of cameras shooting jurors in the hallway and through the windows of the cafeteria, which was supposed to be a camera-free zone, and of reporters trying to interview them. That, plus the broadcast of jurors entering a courtroom next to Ito's where another murder trial was in progress, resulted in a camera ban everywhere in the courthouse except for a few designated areas.

Concerns about media reports and violations were voiced in almost every pretrial hearing and in the frequently delayed jury selection. After halting proceedings on October 18, Ito apologized for the onerous new restrictions he had just placed on the prospective jurors who were about to leave the courtroom so he could hear the lawyers' concerns about the effect of Resnick's book and marathon schedule of interviews.

"... the way that this case has come up," he said, "especially the media attention, it is unlike any other case that I have personally been involved with and it presents problems to me that I don't know that any other judge in recent memory here in Los Angeles has ever had to deal with."

That included the Menendez brothers, Heidi Fleiss, McMartin Preschool, Charles Manson, Richard Ramirez (the "Night Stalker"), and the Rodney King– and Reginald Denny–beating trials.

"And I find myself in a situation," he continued, "where I need to consult with authorities before I move forward."

Ito's apology was for ordering prospective jurors to avoid not just news coverage of the case but also "not to read any newspaper, any magazine, to watch any television or listen to any radio programs, because the coverage in this case is unavoidable. Even if you try to avoid it, you cannot."[12]

This, to people who would go home and try to live normal lives, many for nearly three more months before twenty-four among them would be sequestered. That nothing short of sequestration would work became increasingly clear as selection progressed. The final decision was triggered by a trip to the supermarket.

Waiting in a checkout line, Ito found himself flanked by racks of blazing tabloid headlines and doctored photographs, including a highly prejudicial one of Nicole Brown Simpson. At that point, he knew beyond a doubt that without sequestration there was no way jurors could avoid inflammatory and damaging exposure to the case.[13]

Ito, more than any other judge I have known before or since the Simpson trial, tried to find a fair balance between the First and Sixth Amendments to the Constitution. As a judge, he was constitutionally charged with ensuring that the defendant get a fair trial. As an elected public official, he understood the people's right to know and the democratically treasured freedom of the press. Consequently, he took extraordinary measures to accomplish both. One was the unprecedented step of the not-for-broadcast audio transmission of jury selection to an auxiliary room in the courthouse where members of the media could listen when space limitations kept them out of the courtroom.[14]

No accommodation seemed to be enough, however.

My CCB office, next to the twelfth-floor media center, was large enough to set up two conference room–size tables and a large number of folding chairs and so became the listening room. To ensure that Ito's order prohibiting recording or broadcasting the audio feed was followed, the media couldn't take any electronic equipment, including laptop computers, into the room and had to hire a security guard to make sure they didn't.

The no-laptop rule rankled *New York Times* reporter David Margolick. Why, he demanded when I announced the listening-room conditions, such onerous restraints? With typing faster than longhand writing, he insisted, laptops would ensure greater accuracy.

Some had recording capability, I replied.

Reporters could promise not to record, he countered.

That's what they did in the federal Rodney King–beating trial, which federal rules prohibited from being recorded or broadcast, I reminded him. Yet one radio reporter decided to sneak a snippet onto the air.[15]

Wanting to see the listening room set up, Ito decided to check it out for himself. Although he came unannounced, word spread that he was there. That prompted a stampede of reporters and cameras from the media center. In the onslaught, an overzealous sound technician, hoping to catch an Ito sound bite, bopped him on the head with a boom mike. It became a visual that still pops up occasionally in television recounts of the case.

Another dustup erupted over who would serve as pool reporters during jury selection. The *Los Angeles Times*'s perpetually angry Andrea Ford resented being limited to rotating in once every few days with other reporters instead of getting a full-time gig like the AP's Linda Deutsch. She also complained about not being allowed to meet with Ito like Deutsch did to discuss the logistics of reporters getting to see the jurors' questionnaires.[16]

Ito's goal of questioning twelve prospective jurors a day became as unrealistic as his expectation of the trial's length. It turned out to be more like four, thanks to constant attorney wrangling that resulted in those awaiting selection spending more time outside the courtroom than in. Among the numerous disruptions during jury selection were closed hearings that resulted in the dismissal of two who had already made it onto the panel: one was a Hertz employee who was alleged to have lied about contacts with Simpson in connection with his job; the other was a woman who hadn't been truthful about an incident of domestic violence. Before the trial was over, eight more would get kicked.

A hearing was held when the defense objected to African American Christopher Darden joining the prosecution team, despite the DA's denials that it was a ploy to sway the majority African American jury.[17] Another hearing involved defense pleas for Ito to muzzle Nicole's sister, Denise Brown, whose public proclamations of Simpson's guilt permeated the airwaves.[18]

The prosecution's numerous challenges of prospective black jurors, countered by defense objections, meant even more hearings. Even though race isn't supposed to be a consideration in jury selection, the prosecution appeared to want white jurors, and the defense, black. But, according to some legal experts such as Charles Manson prosecutor Vincent Bugliosi, who wrote *Outrage: The Five Reasons Why O. J. Simpson Got Away with Murder* and *Helter Skelter,* among other books, the district attorney made a major mistake. Location of a crime normally determines a trial's location.[19] Yet Los Angeles DA Gil Garcetti filed the case in the court's downtown district, which draws jurors from communities with a higher percentage of black residents than in the whiter West District where the crimes were committed.

Even so, whites still far outnumbered blacks in the pool of approximately one thousand residents who made up the jury venire. That pool had a breakdown of 40 percent white, 28 percent black, 17 percent Hispanic, and 15 percent Asian.[20]

The racial makeup of the jurors and alternates who were eventually seated, however, didn't come close to reflecting that profile. The panel of twenty-four—twelve primary jurors, twelve alternates—consisted of fifteen African

American, five white, three Hispanic, and one half white-half American Indian.[21] Only two of the original jurors made it through the trial. With alternates replacing the other ten, the final racial composition was nine African American, two white, and one Hispanic. Of those, ten were women—eight African American, two white—and two were men—one African American, one Hispanic.[22]

Compounding the situation, according to Bugliosi, was that even though some studies indicate that women are more likely to favor the defense than men, the Simpson prosecutors seemed okay with the large number of females—ten of the twelve regulars and seven alternates—apparently under the mistaken belief that they would respond well to lead prosecutor Marcia Clark.[23] But she seemed oblivious to subtle signs emanating from the black female jurors that appeared obvious from my vantage point in the back of the courtroom.

They saw a well-paid, professional woman who, first, entreated the judge to set a later-than-normal start time each morning to accommodate her child-care situation, then, despite that accommodation, habitually arrived later than the agreed-upon time. And her entrances, at times with an entire courtroom full of people—and, indeed, the entire television-viewing world—sitting and waiting, were just that. Entrances.

Rather than trying to be unobtrusive or quiet, she would shove the courtroom door open and prance in and down the tiled aisle, the clack of her spike-heeled pumps reverberating loudly in the otherwise silent surroundings. She would push through the little swinging gates in the rail and leave them flapping behind her as she crossed the courtroom well with the eyes of spectators, defendant, fellow attorneys, bailiffs, clerk, court reporter, judge, and jurors following until she finally arrived, with no hint of apology in her body language, at her place at the counsel table, a bare arm's reach from the jury box.

The African American women sitting in the jury seats no doubt understood child-care problems but more likely from a different perspective than an affluent attorney. I detected a growing disdain among the jurors for Clark's chronic tardiness—in itself a sign of disrespect for not only them but for the entire court and its business—the haughty demeanor she projected, and her inexplicable schizophrenic alternating hostility and flirtatious posturing toward defense attorney Cochran. The black female jurors' body language included arms crossed over chests, heads lowered with chins tucked into necks, and an almost imperceptible drawing back into their seats.

Certainly, none of that was lost on arguably one of the defense team's most perceptive and incisive members in the courtroom.

Jury consultant Jo-Ellan Dimitrius provided influential input to defense decisions from jury selection straight through to verdict day. A psychologist by education and training, Dimitrius analyzed information that had been amassed about the prospective jurors from their questionnaire answers, their responses and body language during oral questioning, and from other data. That included mock or shadow juries and focus groups the defense team assembled to test reaction to the trial participants' personalities, style, and legal strategies, and to the case itself.

Although jury consultants' work focuses primarily on jury selection, Dimitrius says she is involved in everything from picking jurors, "to coaching witnesses, to fine-tuning arguments."[24]

She did a lot of that work in the Simpson case sitting next to me on the bench in the back of the courtroom during the testimony phase of the trial. There she took copious notes on jurors' facial expressions and body language in response to attorneys and witnesses. During breaks, she joined defense attorneys at their table to discuss her observations and conclusions. She even sat in on some of the attorneys' closed meetings in Ito's chambers until Ito, in his never-ending quest to stop leaks to the media, excluded everyone from those meetings who wasn't essential to the meeting topic.[25]

That, however, was after the jury and alternates had been seated and sequestered and opening statements had begun. Opening statements, as noted earlier, were delayed at the outset when an alternate juror leaned into television camera range. The lengthy hearing that ensued over how that had happened and what should be done about it was the first of countless proceedings, many sparked by the jurors' own conduct, that were held while the jurors remained cloistered elsewhere in the courthouse.

Keeping jurors occupied and as frustration-free as possible during those long, boring hours, both while excluded from the courtroom during the day and throughout endless evenings and weekends became as great a challenge as keeping the trial on track. Out were most activities that routinely fill daily life, such as catching up on the news, chatting with others about the day's events, settling on the sofa with TV remote, socializing with family and friends, doing household chores, running errands, and pursuing hobbies.

"We arranged activities for them two, three times a week for nine months," Ito said years after the trial. "We even installed a big-screen TV," donated by a local television dealer. "But they couldn't agree on what to watch, so we had to get two more."[26]

Finding ways to keep the jurors busy became the job of court intern Tasia Scolinos. She lined up entertainment for both staying in and going out. She even saw to such minutiae as bottled water, playing cards, board games, coffee and coffeemakers, cold drinks, and CDs. She ordered half a dozen newspaper and news magazine subscriptions, then helped sheriff's deputies cut out and destroy Simpson- and trial-related stories before giving jurors the riddled publications. Scolinos's work was made somewhat easier because of the celebrity of the trial, which prompted a plethora of offers from entertainers and commercial enterprises.

Aaron Spelling, for instance, provided copies of TV shows with ads deleted. Blockbuster, Music Plus, and Tower Records sent movies and recorded music. When Jay Leno said he couldn't guarantee that jurors sitting in the audience wouldn't get caught on camera if they attended a taping of *The Tonight Show*, he volunteered to stage an exclusive performance, complete with the show's orchestra, at a location of the court's choosing. The jury was also privy to exclusive performances by political satirists, "The Capitol Steps," and other entertainers.

Ito had no problem with the public's knowing about such offers and events after they occurred, but he wouldn't allow them to be used for promotional purposes. A few opportunists apparently didn't get the message. Despite the no-promotion caveat as a condition of singer Shirley Jones performing for the jury, Jones's husband-agent Marty Ingels issued a news release in advance of her gig,[27] which resulted in Ito's prompt cancellation. In the meantime, sheriff's deputies monitored television programming to ensure that the jurors saw no trial coverage.

Ito himself, however, filled their date book for the second Sunday in February. That was the day he set for the jury to be taken to Brentwood for a crime-scene visit. The trip included quick stops at the apartment complex where Ronald Goldman had lived and Mezzaluna Restaurant, where he worked, then tours of the Bundy Drive condominium crime scene and Simpson's Rockingham Avenue home two miles away.

Ito oversaw the meticulous details of the trip, from police escorts and traffic blockades along the route to restriction of airspace to pool reporters' cell phone use to unfurling curtain barricades and providing umbrellas and wide-brimmed hats at each stop to shield jurors from cameras.

The entourage, which included police motorcycles, a bus with darkened windows for the jurors, and vans for court staff, the prosecution and defense teams, and the media, created almost as much of a spectacle as had Simpson's slow-speed Bronco chase along the Los Angeles freeway system before his surrender and arrest nearly eight months earlier. Police blocked the Harbor and Santa Monica freeway ramps between downtown at the courthouse, where the session convened, and Brentwood fifteen miles to the west.

The media rented rooms with street-facing windows and stationed equipment vehicles along the route. Screaming, sign-waving mobs lined the curbs, stood on rooftops, hung out of windows, crowded overpasses, and posed for photographs as the caravan passed in the background. Kids on roller blades and skateboards raced alongside on streets and behind the bizarre parade.[28]

Ito, anticipating a spectacle based in part on reports of people already out along the route that morning, warned jurors before leaving the courthouse to ignore the crowds and signs:

> We are—the court is in a very difficult position. We will be in a formal court session. And obviously if we were in the courtroom and somebody tried to communicate with you either verbally or by signs or by gestures, that person would be removed from the courtroom and I would admonish you to ignore whatever it was they said or [had] done.
>
> The problem is we will be out—literally out in Brentwood. We cannot interfere with individual persons' right to write whatever they want on placards or banners. If they're on their own property, obviously they're entitled to do what they want to do. A man or woman's house is their castle and the court cannot interfere with that unless that person deliberately tries to disrupt our court proceeding.
>
> I am ordering you now to ignore any attempt to communicate anything to you while we are out in the field. And I'm sure you'll understand the difficulty we have in doing this. But if you see something like that, bring it to the attention of the bailiff so I can take whatever remedial measures are appropriate.[29]

He repeated his admonition after the jurors filed off the bus at the Bundy Drive crime scene. There *Los Angeles Times* lawyer Karlene Goller, along to represent the media's interests, argued that because the tour was an official proceeding, the media should be allowed to accompany the jurors onto the property and into the condominium.

Ito, having already heard protestations from the Brown family to keep the press out, denied Goller's motion on the grounds that it wasn't timely.[30]

Back aboard the buses, the jurors, along with motorcycling police and roller-blading kids, rode to Simpson's Rockingham house. Then, in a scene reminiscent of Monty Python, court convened right there in Simpson's front yard. The court reporter set up her stenographic machine and chair on the lawn. With the jurors shut away on their bus, members of the media standing in the street by their van, and Simpson asking where his dogs were, the attorneys huddled with Ito so prosecutor Marcia Clark could question anew the need for jurors to tour the house. She also protested the cozy, homey fires blazing in the fireplaces and complained that photographs of Simpson's then-girlfriend, Paula Barbieri, had been replaced with pictures of his mother and children to present a more favorable impression of Simpson.[31]

The photographs were restored to the original arrangement with as much accuracy as anyone's memory could provide. Ito admonished jurors to ignore the photos, but one apparently didn't, at least not to the satisfaction of prosecutors. That, plus allegations that Michael Knox had bet a friend during jury selection that Simpson would be acquitted, moved him off the jury on March 1.[32] Knox apparently was also keeping notes for a book. His *The Private Diary of an O. J. Juror,* published just three months later, was the first out about the trial.[33]

Knox led the parade of excused jurors and presaged the eventual epidemic dysfunctionality of the jury. Juror Tracy Kennedy was the next to go. Although excused on March 17 for allegedly not paying attention, he apparently caught enough to produce a book with three other people, including a *Los Angeles Times* reporter, Alan Abrahamson, who was contributing to his newspaper's trial coverage. That book debuted the following year.[34]

Next came Jeanette Harris. The trial had been on hold for a couple of days in early April because two of the jurors were sick with the flu. When it returned, Harris was gone. The problem, according to my journal, emerged from an investigation based on an anonymous tip, which revealed that she had lied on her questionnaire about never being involved in domestic violence.

A firestorm ensued. First a sheriff's deputy told the press that Ito had ordered an investigation of not only Harris but of other jurors. Then Harris claimed in an interview that the jurors were split over whether or not Simpson was guilty. If true, that would have been a major no-no given that they weren't supposed to be discussing the case. Harris also charged that their deputy sheriff guardians were fomenting trouble by pitting black jurors against white.

That prompted defense attorney Cochran to take a public swipe at Ito for agreeing to dismiss jurors the defense apparently thought to be favorable to its side and for investigating jurors after they had been seated. Cochran blustered that he had never heard of anything so outrageous.[35]

Then, even though Harris was obviously giving interviews, the media set out on hot pursuit of her. The problem was some of the TV stations had used an incorrect name in their broadcasts, so everyone went hightailing to where they thought she lived. Although that turned out to be the wrong address, it raised the question of whose home they had gone to. Some speculated that it must have been one of either the sitting or other dismissed jurors.

At that point ABC producer Chris Cahan tried a cornering maneuver.

"Here is the name that is not the name of the dismissed juror," he said. "We need to know if this is the name of a juror because we are going to use it this evening."

Since I didn't know any of the jurors' names, I was no help. But my sense was that if the name they had wasn't that of the juror who had been dismissed, it could easily be the name of another juror still on the panel, so I cautioned him not to use any name.

As it turned out, the media knew not only the jurors' names, but also their addresses, places of employment, and other information about them. Ito worried constantly that the media would reveal their identities. Even though he could haul out cudgels if they did, the trial would lose the juror(s) identified. That could lead to a mistrial. To their credit, and perhaps because Ito constantly reminded them of the fate awaiting them, the media refrained from disclosing identities of any jurors while they were still impaneled.[36]

In a later interview, Harris elaborated on her allegations of racism among the jurors and deputies, such as black jurors not getting as long to shop or talk on the telephone as white jurors. I found her assertions specious given that just as with the jurors, some of the deputies were black and some were white.

The sheriff's department continued to say that based on Harris's allegations, Ito had ordered an investigation into possible juror misconduct, then referred reporters to me. But all I could do was continue to say that although the judge had the authority to order investigations in anything pertaining to court matters, the court couldn't discuss juror issues or comment on investigations.

"It really puts me in an unbelievably difficult position," I carped in my journal that night. "Here I am supposed to be the spokesperson for the court, and as far as the court is concerned I can't speak, and yet the sheriff's department is saying things we can't comment on."[37]

The black-white issue continued to brew. In late April, after some of the jurors complained about three of the deputies assigned to jury care, they were removed. That sparked a revolt by other jurors who liked them. I learned about it from Ito the morning of April 21 when he said that only three of the jurors were complaining about the deputies. The rest were upset over their removal and wanted them reinstated or, at the very least, to be able to meet with Ito about it. And, by the way, they were going to "go on strike" until one or the other happened.

"I am probably going to do that this morning," he said. "That is probably going to mean that we are not going to have any testimony."

But since he wasn't certain at that point, he didn't want to tell the media yet.

Knowing that members of the media would want to know what was going on, I was to tell them only that he was going to be "meeting in chambers regarding jury issues." But when I arrived at the twelfth-floor media center, I was greeted by a horde of reporters full of questions.

"Jerrianne, what is going on? What is happening? I hear there are thirteen jurors who are refusing to listen to testimony until the judge meets with them."

I was mystified. How had they found out?

Mystery solved when I asked pool producer Nina Goebert.

Deputy John Castro, one of the two deputies assigned to liaison with the media, had come up and told them. Exasperation replaced mystification. Because of a chronic problem with sheriff's officials giving information to the media without clearing it with the judges, we had reached an agreement with the sheriff's commander of court services that anything involving the case or jurors had to come from the court via the court's information office. So why was Castro telling the media there would be no testimony that morning because the jurors were upset?[38]

It was an ongoing problem throughout the trial. Ito would say not to give out details about something, such as some sort of juror activity that they might do again, only to learn that the sheriff's department had already done so.[39]

A few days after dealing with Harris, Ito apologized yet again to the jury for making them wait while he held yet another hearing out of their presence. This time it was the lawyers wrangling about discovery violations and sanctions.

"But," he added, "we will try to make it up to you with some special entertainment this weekend."

That, of course, set the media on a quest to find out what the jurors were going to be doing. First, I started getting calls wanting us to confirm that they were going to see Leno, then that Leno was going to come and entertain them. I thought, "[D]amn, how the hell do they find these things out?"[40]

That was a question Ito and I asked each other so often that at times I wondered if the media had somehow managed to bug the fillings in my teeth. Although our musings over leaked confidential information were often infused with wry humor, it was a serious problem. It arose again later in April when the media reported that a juror was asking to be removed from the trial.

"This one complaining that her husband is sick and she is concerned about him and it is distracting and so forth," I recorded in my journal.

I showed a news report about it to Ito. He asked how they described the juror.

"A thirty-eight-year-old white woman," I said.

"Yep," he replied. "That's her."

"Well," I concluded after he assured me that the transcripts of his meetings with the lawyers and one of their consultants were sealed, "you've got some attorneys that are talking—either that or it's your court reporter and I don't think it's your court reporter."[41]

He was thinking, he said, "about requiring every single person who was in my meetings with the jurors to make a sworn affidavit statement swearing that they did not leak this information."

"Are you sure your chambers aren't bugged?" I asked.

"Yeah, they've come in and swept it," he replied.

"What about the telephones?"

"Well, you know, it could be. I was talking to Sergeant Smith earlier. He wanted my opinion about certain deputies who would get along well with the media to be on the security screen and I was talking to him about telephones that might be tapped."

"You know, you can sweep," I said. "Why don't you sweep our telephones, too, in my office. Let's make sure that nothing is tapped."[42]

The most outrageous flap, however, erupted after juror Tracy Hampton told Ito on May 1 that she couldn't take serving on the jury and being sequestered any longer.

My journal entry the next day describes what happened next:

> The juror who was excused yesterday apparently had some medical problem. The paramedics were called to her house early this morning and there were earlier reports saying that she had seizures and the press who absolutely mobbed her house yesterday completely destroying the landscaping, all the flowers, shrubs, everything, were back there in full force and worse today and it was just the most disgusting spectacle I think I have ever seen. It makes me really embarrassed to think that I used to be part of that. I guess, you know, I kept justifying it saying the ones that were really making asses of themselves were the broadcast media not the print media but nevertheless it was just absolutely disgusting. The poor woman can't even be sick.
>
> So, they hauled her away in an ambulance about noon or a little after noon. I was talking to one of the deputies, Kathy Browning, later and she was saying, "You know, we told her we would take her anyplace. Somebody should have taken her to Catalina. We told her if we took her to her house it was going to be a mob scene, it is going to be terrible, but, no, she wanted to go home."

Browning said she and the other deputies suggested that Hampton have her parents meet her somewhere. But she insisted on going home, so when they rounded the corner of her street, the mob was already there.

> Anyway she was taken to Daniel Freeman Hospital. One of the reporters made some kind of stupid remark, like, "Well, we don't need any false stories, but wouldn't it be something if she faked this and called the paramedics just to be able to get out of the house because that's the only way she is ever going to be able to get out without going through this line of reporters . . . she would never get out otherwise."
>
> [The cameras] fanned around and showed the media there, you know, they do this as if it's part of the story, which *is* part of the story but they

are *making* it the story. I just don't understand it. There is no need to do something like this to this poor woman. If she is going to be sick just let her be sick.[43]

But that wasn't the end of the Tracy Hampton story.

Two days later, the county fire department's information officer, Steve Valenzuela, got a media request for two 9-1-1 call tapes about what sounded like a suicide attempt by Hampton. When Valenzuela couldn't reach his usual legal advisors about releasing the tapes, he called me, wondering if, because Hampton had just been dismissed from the *Simpson* jury, the court might have jurisdiction.

I told Valenzuela I didn't know if the court had any official role, but I would let Ito know about his question. Ito, I thought, would be concerned not only about Hampton's medical condition but whether the call might have included any confidential information about the case, jurors, or sequestration. Knowing that people would be trying to see him after court, I snagged him in his chambers as he started taking his robe off and gave him a quick rundown of the situation.

"Oh geez! Oh geez!" he said, gripping his robe in one hand. "This is a terrible thing to have happened."

He called the lawyers in.

"Now this is just FYI," he said. "And you are all sworn to secrecy—but there has been a request for the 9-1-1 tapes and the fire department is seeking legal counsel before releasing them and I don't believe I have any jurisdiction in this—just FYI you need to know that there was a second call this afternoon."

"Another one?" Marcia Clark asked.

"Yes, and apparently she has slit her wrists."

"What!" Clark exclaimed while her colleagues joined in with, "Oh, this is really terrible!"

Then Cochran piped up. "Well, you know, judge, it wasn't us," he said. "We didn't do it to her. We didn't do it to her. The media did it to her."

I was struck with how quickly he tried to absolve the defense from blame. "Not that Cochran himself would be responsible in any way," I recorded on the way home that night.

When I told Valenzuela the court had no jurisdiction over the tapes, I suggested he talk to Fred Bennett, the court's legal counsel in the county counsel's office.[44] Bennett or someone in his office, I later learned, advised Valenzuela not to release the tapes without a court order.

The next day, the DA's spokeswoman, Suzanne Childs, called to see if I had gotten any media calls about the tapes. Amazingly, no, I said. She was equally stunned that she hadn't either.

"I know the press knew about them," I said. "Steve said they all listen to their [police] scanners, and they all knew." Yet neither Childs nor I had seen or heard a word about them in the news at that point.

The incident did eventually make it into the news, although at a much lower pitch than other trial stories. That still wasn't the end of Tracy Hampton, though.

A couple of weeks later, someone sent the court a letter saying that electronic surveillance could trigger seizures and make people act strangely, which probably accounted for Hampton's aberrant behavior. If true, that also might have explained why she agreed a few months later to pose nude for *Playboy* magazine.[45]

Despite the trampling herds that contributed so much to the chaos surrounding the trial, I saw many examples of integrity and ethical conduct by members of the media. In the midst of the Tracy Hampton fiasco, CBS radio reporter Tom Ryan told me he had seen a juror using a pen with a hotel logo on it.

"I'm from out of town—New York," Ryan said, "and I happen to be staying at the same hotel they are, and they are wearing California Pizza Kitchen T-shirts, so it doesn't take a mental giant to put two and two together to know where they're staying."[46]

Ryan sought me out again a couple of weeks later to let me know that a radio station's promotional signs, which had been showing up on billboards all over the city with the words "GUILTY" and "INNOCENT" in stark black-on-white and white-on-black lettering, had popped up overnight just outside his hotel window. Ryan said he was on the eighth floor.

"If I can see it from my window," he said, "the jurors might, in fact, be able to see it, too."[47]

Ito managed to get the sign removed, but sheriff's deputies responsible for jurors' after-hours care and feeding were told to find routes devoid of the signs when they took their wards on outings because the signs could be "prejudicial to either side of this case," defense attorney Cochran said in court.[48]

Posttrial dissections have included questions about why Ito didn't hold court on Saturdays as a way to shorten the trial. He did contemplate doing so more than once.

In response to a juror's request for Saturday sessions, he posed the question in court. That sent the media into a dither because it would cut into their weekends.

"Here we have a press corps that goes home to be with their families every night they want to, except, of course, the out-of-towners," I recorded in my journal.

> They have the freedom to associate with whom they want to, go out to lunch wherever they want to, do whatever it is they want to do.... And their complaint? "Oh, Saturdays too? I don't think I can take it! Can't we have a life?"
>
> *They're* complaining and we've got seventeen people who are literally locked up in a hotel. No free association. Can't determine what they might want to watch on TV, what they want to read in the newspaper, who they can associate with. Can't be with their families, have to have conjugal visits and everybody knows what the hell is going on. They might want to pick up and go to a movie, go to the beach for a weekend, take a little vacation, but none of that is available. You talk about not having lives. It's the jurors who don't have lives and the press corps has to whine because they can't take it. Absolutely incredible.[49]

Among the notable exceptions was the AP's Linda Deutsch. While Deutsch didn't welcome the idea of Saturday sessions, she was one of the least-vocal protesters. Yet, she probably felt the greatest pressure. Not only was she in the courtroom every day, she was on constant deadline. That meant that at every break, in that pre–cell phone proliferation era, she had to race out of the courtroom and beat everyone else to one of the few pay phones in the hallway so she could call a story in to her editors. At that time, not only was she exhausted, she was sick with the flu.

But Ito was also exhausted and had health concerns of his own, thanks to months of nonstop twelve-to-fourteen-hour days plus evenings spent with work he took home. His court staff and the lawyers were also fraying at the edges. Then there was the additional expense of an already horrendously costly trial that would be incurred by opening the courthouse on nonbusiness days and paying security and court staff overtime without any indication that doing so would significantly shorten the trial. Those were some of the considerations that kept the trial on a five-day schedule.[50]

But jury problems only got worse. The thirty-eight-year-old white woman who had worried a month earlier about her husband's illness finally got the boot on May 25, but not for anything to do with her husband. It was over a note.

An omen surfaced one afternoon with a sheriff's message about a jury problem. Ito left the press and spectators to languish in the courtroom while he closeted himself with the lawyers, court reporter, court clerk, law clerks, and a single-file parade of jurors.

The situation indicated just how much subterfuge, factionalization, and personal agendas were plaguing the panel. A deputy had heard that thirty-eight-year-old Francine Florio-Bunten had somehow managed to land a book deal. Whether it was rumor or fact, that information, plus other disruptive issues, led Ito to interview each juror individually. Apparently, another juror, Farran Chavarria, who preceded Florio-Bunten into Ito's chambers, tipped Florio-Bunten off about the subject of the interviews by scribbling a note to Florio-Bunten in the margin of a newspaper. Some jurors who saw Chavarria write the note ratted on her. That led to Ito's clerk, Deirdre Robertson, and research attorney, John Byrne, gathering up all the newspapers in the jury room and taking them to Ito's chambers where they, Ito, the lawyers, and law clerks sifted through them and found the note. That led to another round of interviews with some of the jurors, including Florio-Bunten, who still refused to fess up about the note despite Ito giving her several opportunities.

Chavarria, too, first denied that she had written the note, then relenting when pressed. Ito believed he had no choice but to dismiss Florio-Bunten. He was torn, however, about Chavarria and a black male juror, Willie Craven, whom some of the other jurors claimed was disruptive, intimidating, and bullying.

After seeking counsel from two other judges, he decided to keep them. Dismissing them would have left only two alternate jurors, and the prosecution hadn't even rested its case yet (and wouldn't until six weeks later). Still on tap was the defense's case in chief, both sides' rebuttals, and closing arguments. In other words, with several weeks, if not months, to go, Ito didn't want to run out of jurors.

After everyone else left his chambers, Ito was sitting at his desk, I recorded in my journal, "looking wasted, just wasted."

"Well," I asked, "what should I tell the press?"

At first he said to just say there wouldn't be anything until the next day. He reconsidered after I pointed out that when the jurors were escorted from the courtroom and through the public hallway to the elevator that would take them down to the bus for the ride back to their hotel, the reporters would count heads and know that someone was missing.

"All right," he said. "We'll say, 'after a lengthy hearing the court has dismissed one juror and will make a court order to replace that juror with an alternate at nine a.m. tomorrow.'"

Fed that crumb, the media could only speculate and milk their sources, which included the lawyers, whom Ito had ordered not to "say anything to the press at all. Nothing."[51]

He might as well have dumped Chavarria and Craven right then and there, too, because less than two weeks later they both were gone. Before that happened though, Florio-Bunten, like her fellow former jurors, did not go gentle into that good night. Within a day, even though she had been spirited off to Las Vegas to elude the media melee, she turned up on ubiquitous Los Angeles lawyer Gloria Allred's ABC radio program, denying that she had a book deal. There wasn't any real reason for her dismissal, she insisted, and she was really upset. She complained about how terrible it was that all anybody had to do to get somebody off a jury is write an anonymous note.

"I think we did things right this time," I noted in my journal. "We gave the sheriff's department enough time to get her where she was going to be, which was not home ... so nobody knew where to find her."[52] How Allred got to her remained a mystery, at least to me, but I wasn't surprised that she had.

Florio-Bunten surfaced again in mid-July when Ito learned that she had been sending letters to juror 1290, later identified as Anise Aschenbach, who was one of the two remaining white jurors. After weighing several options, Ito finally decided to talk to Aschenbach about it.

"It's a delicate balance on the jury," he said after settling on his decision. "I don't want to lose 1290, but I have to caution her about 353's misconduct."[53]

While neither Aschenbach nor any other jurors were dismissed after Chavarria and Craven, juror and ex-juror problems continued to plague the trial, and scads of motions and issues the jurors couldn't be privy to had to be heard while they cooled their heels out of sight and earshot. The media initiated some of those hearings by filing motions asking that transcripts of hearings and meetings that led to the dismissal of the ten jurors be unsealed and that the autopsy photos be released.[54]

The jurors' own problems, which involved illnesses and medical and dental appointments, caused other delays.[55]

Dismissed juror Michael Knox bobbed up again when the book he wrote was to debut on June 5—right in the thick of the trial. Although a recently enacted law barred former jurors from profiting from their jury experience until ninety days after they had served, Ito's concern focused primarily on the identities of the jurors still in service and the sequestration site. Although he and I both knew that the major news organizations already had extensive information about all of the jurors, including where they were sequestered, none had made it public. An investigation to ensure that Knox's book hadn't compromised the jury and preparing for a hearing about it also took time away from the trial.[56]

In almost every lengthy trial, some jurors eventually begin to feel a financial pinch. Amazingly, that didn't seem to be problematic for most of the *Simpson* jurors. Toward the end of the trial, however, one woman ran into trouble with some rental property she owned. Just as it had spawned bids to entertain the jurors, the trial's high visibility helped in this situation, too. Offers to assist poured in. Some were of outright cash gifts, others involved temporarily renting the woman's property. Her juror status was saved by a benefactor Ito described as "a friend of the court," but not before at least one unsolicited donation arrived. Six hundred seventy dollars. In cash. Interestingly, it was from a local sports-oriented radio station, raised from listeners by an on-air host. Altruism, however, was not the primary motivation. Shortly after making the delivery, station staff started calling: "We need to know what the status of the money is," one said, "because we have a show going on at ten o'clock, so we need to be able to say what happened to it."

The reply of "thanks, but no thanks," the court is returning the cash to the station deflated that attempt at promotional puffery.[57]

As the trial finally seemed about to be handed to the jury, Ito issued a couple of rather atypical orders. One discontinued conjugal visits. The other initiated the monitoring of their telephone calls.[58]

The stunningly quick "not-guilty" verdicts are well known. Another possible record is the number of jurors who perpetuated—or sought to perpetuate—their fame. At least seven, four of whom made it to the end and three who were dismissed, collaborated with professional writers, including at least

two *Los Angeles Times* staffers who were involved in covering the trial, to produce books.

"All of the *Simpson* jurors participated in books in one way or another,"
Ito says. "They saw it as a money-making opportunity. That was very disap-
pointing."

In constitutional scholar Chemerinsky's opinion the lengthy sequestration might not have influenced the verdicts, but many experts say the jurors
were caught up by the lure of celebrity and possible fortune.

"I say this, given what jurors and excused jurors ended up doing in the
case—from TV interviews, to *Playboy* centerfolds, to a party at O. J.'s house,"
Loyola Law School Professor Laurie Levenson says, "the jurors definitely got
caught up in the fame."[59]

Court TV senior editor Fred Graham says that's a phenomenon that has
been obvious in post-*Simpson* high-profile trials, whether televised or not.

"Celebrity cases sometimes . . . attract jurors who are so starstruck they
behave in bizarre ways," Graham said in a 2005 speech at the University of
Louisville (Kentucky) Law School.

"One of Michael Jackson's jurors smuggled a videotape of a Court TV
broadcast into the jury room to make a point," he said. "After the jury unan-
imously acquitted Jackson of all counts, two jurors declared he was in fact
guilty and they plan to write a book about the case."[60]

Excessive media coverage and possible fame can certainly affect jury selection. Defense attorney Mark Geragos, who has represented Winona Ryder,
Susan McDougal, Michael Jackson, and Scott Peterson, says that sixteen hundred questionnaires were used as an initial screening of prospective jurors in
the Peterson case to weed out those with experiences, knowledge, or opinions
that might indicate bias or conflict of interest.

"The prejudgment rate for [Peterson's] guilt was the highest my experts
had received, exceeded anything they had tested in thirty years," Geragos told
attendees of a 2005 conference on high-profile trials.[61]

He explained further in a 2006 Loyola Law Review article:

> Due to the spectacular amount of pretrial publicity surrounding the case,
> I expected some juror taint. However, nobody could have imagined the
> extent to which pretrial publicity had polluted the jury pool, and in my
> opinion, effectively preordained a guilty verdict. Prospective jurors came to
> jury selection not only with a presumption of Scott Peterson's guilt, but

actually convinced of it . . . one of the most notable [questionnaires] was filled out by an illiterate man. Although he could barely write his own name, he was able to scratch out a single word on the 23-page form—"g-u-t-y." The other questionnaires revealed equally committed convictions of guilt. Two practicing Buddhists who opposed the death penalty were willing to make an exception for Scott Peterson and three potential jurors actually volunteered to pull the switch. It bears reemphasis that this was all before one iota of evidence had been presented in a court of law.[62]

More insidious, in his opinion, are what he and Ito refer to as stealth jurors.

"Literally, there were three separate jurors during the [*Peterson*] jury selection process I was able to demonstrate were lying to get onto the jury so that they could fry him," Geragos said.[63]

Speaking at the same conference as Geragos in 2005, College of Charleston president emeritus Alexander Sanders Jr. said he believes lawyers and judges have to question prospective jurors more closely. He gave as an example asking about media reports of a defendant's supposed confession. The questioner should not only probe prospective jurors' ability to be impartial despite such media reports, Sanders said, but specifically ask if they could keep an open mind if evidence were presented that proved the defendant not guilty. Answering yes would disqualify the person as a juror, because the juror admitted that he had already "reached the conclusion of guilt," which would shift the burden of proof from the prosecution to the defense."[64]

Chapter 9

If It Please the Court

■ ■ ■

Dealing with the lawyers in the Simpson case seemed at times like trying to contain a roomful of two-year-olds. Ito fined them, sanctioned them, admonished them from the bench, chided them in chambers, and issued written orders about their conduct. Still, they cavorted, pouted, postured, quarreled, delayed proceedings, defied the judge, ridiculed one another and at least one witness, and often behaved as if everything was all about them.

Even lawyers not on the case got in on the act. In addition to the camera-homing Gloria Allred, who represented Nicole Brown Simpson's family,[1] issued press releases about them[2] and even appeared in court on their behalf,[3] other attorneys cashed in on the emerging cottage industry of TV legal punditry, regardless of whether they had any firsthand knowledge of what was going on with the case.[4]

"There probably aren't two lawyers in all of Los Angeles who haven't been on TV about this trial," Ito said in May of 1995. KNBC news director Bill Lord confirmed that, saying lawyers were constantly calling him about serving as commentators.[5]

Eventually joining their ranks was Eric Menendez's lawyer Leslie Abramson, a tightly wound woman with a steel-wool mop of blonde hair who was known during the Menendez brothers trial to repeatedly throw angry barbs at the broadcast media and even to raise a strategic finger at camera crews trying to get shots of her as she walked to and from the courthouse.

Interestingly, Marcia Clark had asked at least one prospective juror during jury selection if he thought Simpson should be treated differently because he was a celebrity.[6] And an outraged Cochran blustered in a pretrial hearing that it was "preposterous to say that Mr. Simpson expects any special kind of treatment. He's not getting any special treatment. . . . He's being treated like any other defendant."[7] Yet, here the attorneys themselves, particularly defense attorneys, were treating him differently and arranging for others to do the same.

Defendants who are in custody during trial, as Simpson was, are customarily held in a small locked cell, called lockup, off the courtroom when proceedings are in recess during the court day. Simpson's attorneys, however, made a case for him to remain in the courtroom when court wasn't in session, particularly during the lunch break. They contended that they wanted to confer with him on issues on which they needed his input.[8] Ordinarily, lawyers confer with in-custody clients in lockup. The nearly dozen lawyers on Simpson's defense team, however, made meeting in the close confines of a cell nearly impossible.

Lunch became the next issue. Lockup fare consisted of a sandwich of baloney, jokingly referred to as "mystery meat," and perhaps cheese and an apple. The food that Simpson's lawyers brought in for him was a definite improvement over that. Before long, however, courtroom deputies reported that instead of working, Simpson was bantering and playing solitaire on a computer his defense team had installed on the counsel table. Ito promptly ended the privilege and ordered him held in lockup when court wasn't in session and directed that he have the same lunches as other in-custody defendants.

Simpson's lawyers also gave him candy from a jar that sat on the clerk's desk and doughnuts Ito brought in on Fridays for court staff. Ito's bailiff eventually put the doughnuts out of sight on a little table in the back hallway behind the courtroom.[9]

The immature, snippy, frat-house behavior some of the lawyers engaged in included little episodes such as Shapiro pointing at Deputy District Attorney Christopher Darden's necktie one day as they came out of Ito's chambers. When Darden looked down, Shapiro chucked him sharply under his chin and made a remark I didn't catch. From the look on Darden's face, though, I doubted it was collegial.[10]

While the vitriol that flew between the two sides in court was thinly glazed with such preambles as, "my esteemed colleague," "my good friend," and "my opponent, whom I highly respect," behind-the-scenes confrontations were more bare-knuckled. During one meeting in Ito's chambers in early May, defense attorney Cochran accused one of the prosecuting attorneys, Hank Goldberg, of being defensive.

"You should be a defense attorney," Cochran taunted. "You would win hands down. You could write the book on how to be defensive."

The meeting, which included other lawyers for both sides, then deteriorated into what had become one of their inevitable shouting matches of "you did this" and "well, you did that," until Ito had to break it up.[11]

The lawyers didn't confine themselves to denigrating one another. One day during a break in defense attorney Barry Scheck's withering cross-examination of Los Angeles Police Department criminalist Dennis Fung, Shapiro handed out Chinese restaurant fortune cookies to his colleagues, saying they were "compliments of the Hang Fung restaurant," for which he later apologized in court.[12] The next day, at the conclusion of Fung's testimony, during which he made concessions about mistakes he had made handling evidence, Cochran cavorted in the hallway, singing, "We're having Fung! Oh, we're having Fung!"

For his part, Fung also did something that raised eyebrows. After stepping down from the witness stand at the end of his testimony, he crossed the courtroom to the defense table to shake hands with Simpson's attorneys. The next day, newspapers carried a photograph of the lawyers grinning and gripping Fung's hand and slapping him on the back.[13]

It was puzzling. The defense had attacked and humiliated the guy for days on the stand during which time Scheck had skewered him with his infamous, "How about *that*, Mr. Fung!" over evidence that Scheck believed proved Fung wrong.[14] Yet when Fung left the stand, they all greeted one another like old friends. Granted, he had done them a great favor; his testimony had damaged the prosecution's case. But their behavior made it look like the attack had been staged or like Fung was in cahoots with them.[15]

Some of the fun was just flat-out silly, harmless, and, no doubt, tension-relieving, such as the day one of the lawyers gave the others samples of dental floss he had gotten at a recent trip to the dentist. During a break, a bunch of them pranced around the courtroom flossing their teeth in an exaggerated manner.

The short skirts worn by the particularly leggy female lawyers and staff drew comments. Some courtroom regulars swore the feminine attire was a contest to see who could show up in the shortest skirt. Some in the courtroom prayed none of them would bend over. Others hoped they would.

Famed lawyer F. Lee Bailey, whose frequent trips to clerk Deirdre Robertson's candy jar prompted cracks about alcoholics' sugar cravings, was soon being routinely referred to as Flee Bailey.

Adding to an almost farcical atmosphere was the defense team's invasion of the courtroom. First, their sheer number—a dozen or more, counting all the lawyers and supporting experts—crowded the well. Second, unlike the prosecutors, whose offices were in the same building as the courtroom, Simpson's lawyers were itinerant. Even though some had cell phones, their batteries were constantly dying, so, much to the consternation of Robertson, they frequently tied up the courtroom phone, all the while dipping into her candy jar and looking for the doughnuts.

The equipment they hauled in, which included desktop computers and a fax machine, crowded the courtroom to the point that court staff quipped that Shapiro had probably secreted a tanning bed and boxing ring under the skirted defense counsel table so he could maintain his perpetual tan and workout routine during the trial.[16]

Even the defense's jury consultant, Jo-Ellan Dimitrius, got in on the fun. When the assistant U.S. attorney general in Los Angeles requested that two defense witnesses who apparently were FBI informants not be televised, recorded, photographed, or sketched, the media's attorneys marched in to protest. The men were not in the federal witness protection program. They had given interviews, had been photographed, and had appeared on TV.

"It was just too funny," I recorded in my journal. "These two characters were right out of central casting, with shiny silver pants and wide shoulder-padded jackets. They were just incredible. Tony 'The Animal' [Fiato] in particular."

Dimitrius, who often sat next to me in the courtroom, said she thought we should all have mafia names and that mine could be Jerrianne "The Muscle" Hayslett, which I figured referred to my role as media enforcer.[17]

Most of the jocularity remained out of public view, but a marathon of lawyer issues, antics, and delays gobbled up vast quantities of time that could have been devoted to the trial. First there was the fact that Marcia Clark and her children's schedule resulted in court starting half an hour later each morning than Ito wanted. No matter what he ended up deciding when Clark asked in open court for a later start time, he knew he would get grief. Denying her request would incur the wrath of women's rights advocates. Granting it would draw disapproval from a world full of Monday-morning critics. He opted for the latter, not necessarily because he feared the scorn of assertive women more than condescending colleagues, but because, much as he hated starting later, he believed it was the right thing to do out of consideration for Clark's circumstances.

"I can't get Marcia Clark in here before nine a.m. because of her child-care situation," Ito said in response to Court TV anchor and attorney Fred Graham's comment about the relatively short court day a couple of months after opening statements. "And all the attorneys are begging me to end at three p.m."

Graham agreed when Ito said trials shouldn't be run for the convenience of the attorneys.

"That's right," he said, "but I'm one of the attorneys and I'm beat."[18]

The lawyers also took up court time wrangling over the number of courtroom seats each side could get. Initially, the defense wanted twenty-eight and the prosecution slightly fewer in a courtroom with sixty-two seats. Ito initially allocated six for the defense and ten for the prosecution. That represented five for each victim's family. But Clark lobbied for more.

"I think that there is no one of greater importance who has a greater right to have a presence in this courtroom than the family of the victims," she argued. "The media then is occupying more than two times what the prosecution and the defense are occupying, and that seems way out of balance, your honor."[19]

Ito finally settled on seven seats for each family, but added the same conditions he set for the media; everyone must be in his or her seat before court convened, no one could enter while court was in session, any assigned seat not occupied when court convened would be reassigned for the day, and any seat not occupied by the party it was assigned to for two days in a row would be permanently lost.

Robert Shapiro wasn't satisfied. He wanted the Brown and Goldman family seats to be far enough away from the defense tables and computers that they couldn't read or overhear anything that might be confidential. He also didn't want them too close to the jury.[20]

Other delays resulted from contentious hearings over witness lists and evidence, called discovery, that the law required each side to share with the other. Discovery disagreements started flying almost immediately after Ito got the case. When Deputy District Attorney Bill Hodgman declared on August 29, 1994, that the discovery process was proceeding well, Shapiro disagreed. He pointed out a six-to-eight-week lapse between the prosecution's receiving evidence and their sharing it with the defense.[21]

Disputes, accusations of violations, and countercharges continued for months after testimony began, despite a court order setting a date in December 1994 for compliance and Ito imposing sanctions for violations. Much of the wrangling led to hearings that had to be conducted without the jurors present. That meant that they had to be escorted out of the courtroom and cloistered while the lawyers hashed out their differences.

Other causes for delay abounded.

January 23, the day scheduled for opening statements, was fraught with interruptions. The defense objected to ten prosecution exhibits, which sparked an argument. The defense presented a surprise supplemental witness list (Ito having required an exchange of witness lists weeks earlier). In the midst of that squabble, Marcia Clark tried, unsuccessfully, for an eight-week delay in the trial so she could prepare for the new witnesses. Then everyone was thrown off stride when security had to deal with a bomb threat.[22]

Three days later, Clark again requested a delay so she could investigate the status of both the discovery process, which was being handled by Hodgman, and so she could evaluate the status of Hodgman himself, who suddenly had been hospitalized. Although the exact nature of his illness wasn't made public, he ended up in a cardiac unit and didn't make it back to court until mid-February.[23]

When Hodgman did reappear, Ito expressed concern about the stress and physical toll the trial was taking on the participants and discussed modifying the court day, especially considering that the trial was, at that point, still in the early stages. That fueled increasingly acerbic criticism by pundits and other judges across the country, who carped about how Ito was observing "bankers' hours."

Despite Ito's ongoing efforts to keep the proceedings moving, fate seemed eternally against him. One morning in June, the prosecution found itself at 11 a.m. out of witnesses for the day.[24] On another occasion in September, the deputy district attorney who was supposed to appear for the prosecution in a hearing didn't show up because she overslept, an infraction for which Ito fined the DA's office.[25] On yet another day, when a prosecution witness in the midst of testimony said he needed to attend his mother-in-law's funeral the next day in Northern California, Ito suggested going as long into the evening as needed so he could finish testifying. But the witness replied that he had to leave right away so he could attend a Rosary that night.[26]

The antics, invective, and arguments became so pervasive, despite repeated admonitions, Ito issued a formal court order that spelled out in detail conduct that should have been routine for experienced lawyers in litigation:

SUPERIOR COURT OF THE STATE OF CALIFORNIA
IN AND FOR THE COUNTY OF LOS ANGELES

Date: 26 April 1995
Department 103
Hon. Lance A. Ito, Judge
Deirdre Robertson, Deputy Clerk
People v. Orenthal James Simpson
Case #BA097211

COURT ORDER:
ATTORNEY CONDUCT

In addition to the rules of professional conduct embodied in the Business and Professions Code, all trial counsel will adhere to the following rules of professional conduct at all times during all court proceedings:

1. Only one counsel per side may address the court during the course of any motion, objection, or other proceeding, unless permission is sought and granted by the court.

2. While counsel is addressing the court, opposing counsel may not interrupt except to advise the court of an emergency or other similar good cause.

3. While court is in session, counsel shall address their comments to the court and not to opposing counsel unless permission is sought and granted by the court.

4. Speaking objections are forbidden. The proper procedure is to notify the court of the objection by standing and stating, "Objection." The court will then ask for a statement of the specific legal ground(s). Coun-

sel may not expand beyond that specific and precise statement without leave of the court.

5. While court is in session, counsel shall not indicate any reaction to any of the proceedings. This includes gestures, eye rolling, head nodding, laughter, stage-whispered comments, or any other conduct of reaction which is visible and/or audible to the jury.

6. Counsel shall not engage in gratuitous, personal attacks upon each other.

7. Court hours begin at 9:00 a.m. and again at 1:00 p.m. Counsel shall be present in court, seated and prepared to proceed with all necessary documents, exhibits and witnesses when the court takes the bench. Any exhibits which require viewing by the court prior to being used before the jury shall be presented to the court and opposing counsel at the close of business the prior court day.

8. Motions will be heard on Wednesday at 4:00 p.m. Counsel shall abide by California Rules of Court Rule 313(d) as to page limitations. Oral argument will be allowed as to those points not addressed in any written motion or response. Each side will be accorded 15 minutes for oral argument, of which up to 5 may be reserved for rebuttal.

8. [*sic*] Failure to abide by these specific orders or the rules of professional conduct embodied in the Business and Professions Code will be deemed the failure to abide by a court order pursuant to Code of Civil Procedure Sections 177.5 and 1209.

IT IS SO ORDERED

Despite fines and sanctions, however, problems persisted. Among the many penalties and admonitions was an incident on June 21 when Ito assessed Darden and Cochran a hundred dollars each for baiting each other.[27]

"The prosecution is supposed to be concluding its case and yet it's like the corpse that wouldn't really die or something," I recorded in my journal on June 28. "It ended up with a hearing [with the defense] asking for sanctions for the prosecution harassing defense witnesses and all kinds of crap and then the prosecution ends up bringing in a huge stack of photographs that the defense has never seen and so they had to adjourn early to allow the defense an opportunity to look at the photographs, confer with their client and decide what they are going to do."[28]

Then Ito held a hearing on a defense request to sanction the prosecution for harassing the defense expert witnesses. Less than a month later, Ito imposed a two-hundred-fifty-dollar fine on Clark for "improper conduct," which basically amounted to belittling defense witnesses. Later, in chambers, sounding like he might relent, he said, "I will probably have every female activist group in the country on my case for it."

"What are you talking about?" I asked. "This is the first time you've fined her. The first time you fined a female attorney in this case, yet look at all the times you've dinged Darden and Cochran."[29]

He came down on all the lawyers again in the final week of the trial when they still wouldn't behave.

"I'm going to admonish counsel on both sides not to make any head shakes, gestures [or] grimaces," Ito told them on September 29, just four days before the trial ended with Simpson's acquittal. "I have seen it on both sides, and if I see it again, I'm going to stop you in front of the jury and I'm going to upbraid you in front of the jury."[30]

Yet, while Ito cut off the attorneys' endless soliloquies and counterarguments that had early on erupted with every objection by holding them to the "no-speaking objections" commandment in his April 26 order, he wasn't preemptively dismissive or imperious, for which his more authoritarian colleagues and legal pundits publicly criticized him. He took the lawyers' protestations over such things as wearing symbolic jewelry in court seriously. Rather than just tell them to sit down, shut up, and leave such stuff at home, Ito let them hash it out. When Cochran objected to a small angel-shaped pin Clark wore on her suit jacket, Ito heard his argument and permitted Clark's countercharges about a cross-shaped lapel pin Cochran routinely wore. The back-and-forth lasted a good half an hour. While on the record, it occurred after the jurors had been dismissed at the end of the court day.[31]

Such situations provide fodder for critics who contend that Ito didn't control his courtroom. Some observers, however, such as the AP's Linda Deutsch and CBS radio reporter David Dow, both of whom covered proceedings daily from pretrial to verdicts, have a different view.

"I think [Ito] became something of a scapegoat for the trial's excesses," Dow says. "I'm not sure any judge could have gracefully and firmly controlled the crowd of high-octane lawyers that marched into court each day with their seemingly endless witness lists and bombardment of motions."[32]

While Ito tried to corral lawyers' behavior inside the courtroom, Supervising Judge James Bascue worked on it outside. But the lawyers must have had a lot more money than fear of judicial wrath because they repeatedly flouted both written and oral orders from both judges. Despite Bascue ordering the lawyers to not stop en route between the courtroom and their cars to give interviews, hold press conferences, or even to just chat—they could talk as long as they kept moving—the temptation was apparently too great for Cochran and Shapiro, as they were repeatedly reported to Bascue for violations.[33]

Once Shapiro stood in the hallway outside of the courtroom and briefed reporters about a hearing most had not known about. That incident ended up in a hearing before Bascue during which Shapiro admitted he had violated the "keep moving" court order.[34] Then Shapiro, claiming Bascue's order violated his First Amendment rights, announced that he was going to take legal action against the court. I met with the court's attorney, Fred Bennett, who apparently smoothed Shapiro's feathers sufficiently because, so far as I know, nothing more came of his threat.[35]

In the midst of this kind of acting out, the media's onsite producer, Nina Goebert, asked me about a motion Carl Douglas, an attorney with Cochran's law firm, told her was being filed. When I asked Ito about it, he confirmed that the motion had been filed but was under seal. I relayed that to Goebert.

"Then we've got trouble," she said. "Carl Douglas's office has faxed the motion to me to distribute."

Although Ito repeatedly told the lawyers not to give case documents to the media, they would do it anyway. The problem was the media would get wind of something, get antsy, and not want to wait for an official release. They would start pressuring the lawyers, and the next thing you know one attorney or another would decide to be helpful and let it out. This time, though, I was lucky. Goebert gave me her copy of the sealed motion, and we both called Douglas and told him not to send it to anybody else.[36]

The trial was replete with other violations, so many, in fact, that in April, Ito grouped several together to be heard at the same time and to levy sanctions. While Ito fined lawyers on both sides repeatedly—for a total of four thousand seven hundred dollars—he kept most of the assessments to just below the one thousand-dollar threshold that was reportable to the state bar. He did so not out of compassion for the lawyers but in the interests of self-preservation. A fine large enough to be reported to the state bar required the judge to submit paperwork that Ito, in the midst of the stress, all the trial-related balls he was juggling, and the already long work hours, decided not to add to the heap.[37]

Although the defense attorneys repeatedly denied playing the so-called race card, one day they all showed up in court wearing yellow neckties and sashes with an unusual pattern. Even Simpson's sister, Carmelita Durio, had a strip of yellow fabric with a similar design braided into her hair. It was "Kunta Kinte cloth," they explained when asked about it and just coincidentally they all happened to wear accessories with that design on the same day. Ito mused over the possibility of a sale Target must have had. It seemed to me, though, to be some sort of display of unity, which also wasn't lost on the viewing public.

"We got lots of faxes about the neckties," I recorded in my journal that night. "People being upset, saying that if Marcia Clark couldn't wear her angel pin then the defense team shouldn't be able to wear matching neckties and especially ones that were apparently symbolic of something."[38]

The public also saw such indelible scenes as the comical sight of Cochran, dressed in his beautifully tailored purple suit as he tried to make a point with the jury by wearing a black watch cap pulled down low on his brow, and Deputy District Attorney Christopher Darden inexplicably having Simpson try to tug the shrunken leather "bloody glove" on over his latex-clad arthritis-gnarled fingers, which set the stage for Cochran's infamous "if it doesn't fit, you must acquit" command to the jury in his closing arguments.

Some of those scenes also made an indelible mark on the judiciary, a negative one that many judges vowed would never be repeated in their court-rooms—or at least, if it was, no one outside of their courtrooms would witness it. But there were some scenes surrounding the Simpson trial that neither the public nor other judges ever saw. One was in mid-September, just a couple of weeks before the verdicts. Cochran arrived at the courthouse accompanied by about six men who looked like Nation of Islam bodyguards. They said nothing to anyone that I know of and did nothing more than walk the hallways and stand sentinel at what they apparently considered to be strategic spots. I couldn't help but think, though, that the show of force and attempt at intimidation must have been Cochran's way of handling the death threats that he, like Ito, had received.

Although, obviously, none of the death threats Ito got preceded actual attempts, at least one legal and journalism expert considers him a Simpson trial casualty.

"Overwhelmingly," says Gary Hengstler, "he was perceived by both the media and the judiciary to have lost control of the trial. Media commentators still refer back to the trial. Judges still say the don't want to be the next Judge Ito."

Hengstler, a lawyer and journalist, who was editor of *ABA Journal* before becoming director of the Reynolds Center for Courts and Media Center, has watched a bulk of the footage of the trial and believes criticism of Ito is both fair and unfair.

> [It is] fair in the sense that I sometimes found myself talking to the television, asking Judge Ito why he was letting the lawyers on both sides go on and on. I wanted him to simply say, "Enough, Counsel." But in his effort to be fair and [to] appear to be fair, he didn't clamp down on the lawyers as soon as I would have liked.
>
> But the criticisms are also unfair because . . . we never had a trial with this many issues, this many dynamics and this much spotlight on it. So I am not convinced that any other judge necessarily would have coped any better under the circumstances.[39]

Chapter 10
Judges Judging Judges

■ ■ ■

The judiciary in every state and at the federal level is subject to an official code of conduct.[1] The codes vary somewhat state to state, but they generally cover such areas as independence, impartiality, integrity, impropriety—and equally important, the *appearance* of impropriety—diligence, quasijudicial and extrajudicial activities, conflict—and the *appearance* of conflict—of interest, and inappropriate political activity. Of particular note for California judges so far as high-profile cases is concerned is a section of that state's code that says, in part,

> A judge shall not make any public comment about a pending or impending proceeding in any court, and shall not make any nonpublic comment that might substantially interfere with a fair trial or hearing....[2]

Another section of the code that became significant during the Simpson case, says,

> A judge shall not participate in, nor permit the judge's name to be used in connection with, any business venture or commercial advertising that indicates the judge's title or affiliation with the judiciary or otherwise lend the power or prestige of his or her office to promote a business or any commercial venture.[3]

Although the vast majority of judges observe the code religiously, some had to be reminded during the Simpson case, and a few, apparently wanting a piece of the spotlight, seemed to just ignore one section or another altogether. The name of one, whose courtroom was right down the hall from Ito's, became connected with a spoof that might have affected the public's perception of the judiciary, had it not been foiled at the last minute.

Before that, though, a federal judge in a courthouse a few blocks from the Criminal Courts Building started taking potshots. One flew in from left field when a *USA Today* reporter wanted the L. A. court's reaction to criticism the judge had leveled in a speech that was reported by the Associated Press.

With *Simpson* opening statements still three months away and before Ito's Japanese internment camp interview on KCBS aired, the AP story said U.S. District Judge Edward Rafeedie, based in Los Angeles, asserted in an address in Idaho that Ito wasn't handling the case very well.[4]

"One of the biggest pressures on him [Ito]," I wrote after court the day I learned about the story, "must be being second-guessed by colleagues."[5]

That apparently was happening enough within the Los Angeles Superior Court for the court's presiding judge, Gary Klausner, to send a memo to "All Active and Retired Superior Court Judges." The month after becoming presiding judge on January 1, 1995, Klausner reminded his colleagues that they should keep their opinions to themselves. Citing California Code of Judicial Conduct, Canon 3B(9) (noted above) he wrote,

> Each of you knows the tremendous additional pressure media presence in a trial puts on the officiating judicial officer. It is surprising that we continue to find judges who are willing to preside over such cases. The least we can do is not undercut them.
>
> . . . Certainly I would not expect us all to be in agreement as to a number of the issues that gain media attention. Nevertheless, I would hate to think that any of us would make statements criticizing a sitting Judge just for our own personal recognition.[6]

Klausner issued the memo about two months after the planned spoof that appeared to have the tacit, if not the actual, approval of one of Ito's superior court brethren.

George W. Trammell III, a longtime judge and techno-whiz, reveled in showing off a revolutionary real-time court-reporting system he had recently had installed in his courtroom, which was on the same floor as Ito's. The system created an instant electronic transcript that trial participants could read on computer screens as the trial progressed. The equipment was similar to the system Ito's court reporters planned to use in the Simpson trial. When Ito turned down the media's requests for a demonstration of the system in his courtroom, Trammell gladly agreed to show them his. Ito's loss, so far as endearing himself to the media was concerned, was Trammell's gain. They flocked to Trammell's courtroom and quoted him extensively as he held forth about the wonders of his new system.[7]

One December morning, a local ABC-affiliate cameraman contacted me about getting additional video footage of Trammell's system that day during the noon break. No problem, Trammell's bailiff said when I checked with him. He was already planning to be there with a friend of his—a professional photographer who ran a celebrity look-alike business. The friend was bringing an Ito look-alike so he could take pictures of him sitting on Trammell's bench.

I was stunned. Generally, any commercial use of court facilities went through the county's film office. Curious about this favor the bailiff was doing for his friend, I trolled for details.

"What's he doing for a robe?" I asked.

"Judge Trammell's going to let him use his," the bailiff, whom I knew only as Deputy Peal, replied, sounding pleased.

"Does Judge Ito know about it?"

Peal said he didn't think so, then, to my surprise, asked if I thought Ito might like to come and watch.

"I don't think he can," I replied, wondering about the deputy's judgment. "He has to attend a meeting."

Although Peal obviously saw nothing problematic about what he was up to, what about Trammell? I decided to let Ito know. It was nearly noon when he took a break and I could talk to him.

"What?" he exclaimed. "Absolutely not! Does Judge Trammell know about this?"

I had assumed he did since Peal had indicated that his bench and robe were primary props, but I realized I needed to find out for sure. I scooted down the back hall to Trammell's courtroom but found it empty, and the judge didn't answer when I knocked on his closed chambers door or called his private phone line.

"I have no authority to say what can or can't happen in another courtroom," Ito said when I reported back to him, but he thought criminal division supervising judge Cecil Mills might.

I found Mills eating lunch three floors down in the sixth-floor judges' lounge. "You find Sergeant Smith," he ordered, referring to the sheriff's sergeant in charge of CCB security. "You tell him that if he doesn't put a stop to it, I'm going to have his ass."

Given that the photographer and look-alike were due any minute, if, in fact, they hadn't already arrived, I raced back up to the ninth-floor security screen in hopes of intercepting them and finding Smith.

Standing next to the screen when I hustled up was a man wearing a shiny gray suit and carrying a camera bag. Standing with him was a short, heavy, profusely sweating Asian man in a dark suit. He looked more like a pudgy Charlie Chan than he did Ito. One of the deputies on duty there was asking a fellow deputy where Peal was.

"Wait!" I said. "Don't let Deputy Peal take them to the courtroom until I talk to Sergeant Smith."

At that moment, Smith emerged from his nearby office. After filling him in and getting assurance that the photo shoot wouldn't happen, I hurried off to let Ito know, then told the TV cameraman I would arrange for him to get additional footage a little later. As I went down to the first floor to go to my county courthouse office, I was relieved to see Peal's photographer friend and the Asian man on their way out, too.[8]

Trammell still lurked on the *Simpson* fringes, however. He wrote an article that appeared while the trial was still in progress for a publication called *Court Technology Bulletin*. In it, he referred to the trial as "Cirque du O. J." He also took Ito to task for shunning his advice to use the kind of court-reporting system he had in his courtroom, instead allowing the attorneys to use an electronic system of their choice. That, he predicted, would cause trouble.[9] To my knowledge, it never did.

Trammell's name ended up in print again barely a year later, although not in connection with the Simpson case. The fifty-nine-year-old judge, who had been on the bench for more than twenty-five years, began a sexual liaison in February of 1996 with a female defendant in a case before him. That ultimately cost him his job, although he hastily retired before he could be forced from the bench. He also lost his pension and eventually was convicted on two counts of criminal fraud for which he served two years in federal prison.[10]

Although moving quickly to douse the Ito-double spoof, Mills tangled briefly with Ito when Ito wanted cameras barred from the CCB ninth floor. A camera in the hallway had caught a juror entering the courtroom next to his. The juror saw herself on TV that night and asked to be released from the trial because she feared for her safety, she told the trial judge. The multiple-defendant death-penalty case involved gang members accused of killing a police officer, and some of the suspects were still at large. At first Mills wasn't aware of the severity of the situation, and he wasn't inclined to go along with a ban. Ito did prevail, but not before I got embroiled in a shouting match with some members of the media who thought the prohibition on photographing jurors was "silly."[11]

Although getting caught in the middle goes with the territory of a court information officer's job, it can get a little dicey when judges expect to get seats in an already overcrowded courtroom. Soon after the Simpson case entered the court, requests started coming in. Judges asked for seats for themselves, their clerks, their friends, their relatives, their wives, and their wives' friends.[12] Judges from other states and even other countries, some from as far away as Great Britain, Albania, and Australia, traveled to Los Angeles, wanting to sit in on the Simpson trial. My out was that I had no say over any seats except those assigned to the media. Most of the others were divided between the defense and prosecution, neither of which was apt to give up any. So judges could either take potluck with the daily morning drawing for a public seat, which had dismal odds, or try for one of the two seats Ito had reserved for special guests. Ito's clerk, Deirdre Robertson, was the gatekeeper for those seats, but some judges, no matter how often I referred them to her, continued to call me.[13]

Then there was the much-publicized pickle Simpson defense attorney Peter J. Neufeld got himself into with New York jurist Harold Rothwax. Neufeld was defense counsel in a murder trial scheduled to start in Rothwax's court on December 1, 1994. At the time, he was one of only a few attorneys in the country who were also top DNA experts. Neufeld had been hired by Simpson's defense team and was needed in Los Angeles for a crucial hearing scheduled for mid-December. The timing, however, almost guaranteed it would conflict with the New York trial.[14] Despite pleas from Simpson's lead counsel and a telephone conversation with Ito, Rothwax refused to delay his trial so Neufeld could prepare for and attend the hearing in Los Angeles.

Things turned nasty in Rothwax's courtroom on November 28 when Neufeld said he had never promised Rothwax he would be available for a December 1 trial date. According to news accounts, Rothwax accused Neufeld of misrepresenting the facts. That prompted Neufeld to call Rothwax "shameful." Rothwax then ordered Neufeld out of the courtroom. Neufeld refused to leave. Rothwax charged that all Neufeld cared about was making his fame and fortune in the Simpson trial. Neufeld, in essence, then called Rothwax a liar. Rothwax retaliated by threatening to hold Neufeld in contempt and said if the lawyer wasn't in his courtroom on December 1 ready to start trial, he would have him jailed.[15]

Although Ito ordered Neufeld to be in L. A. for the DNA hearing, which created the rather unseemly appearance of two judges engaging in a bicoastal tug of war and test of judicial wills,[16] it was more a case of judicial collaboration to put pressure on Neufeld for double-booking himself. The impasse finally cracked when Ito granted a defense request to delay the DNA hearing until January 5.[17]

Envy flared a couple of times with another judge during the trial. Once was in July 1995. I was going over responses I had drafted for Paul Flynn—the same Paul Flynn who nearly had nearly gotten the Simpson case the previous summer—to requests Flynn had received from Court TV and the local broadcasters' association to televise an upcoming murder trial over which he was presiding. The defendant was Calvin Broadus, better known as the gangsta rapper Snoop Doggy Dogg. While discussing the draft letters to Court TV and the broadcasters' association, Flynn brought up the Simpson trial.

That evening, I recorded in my diary,

> I think he's resentful of Judge Ito. He really takes issue with the way Judge Ito is handling things, particularly with regard to the media and cameras in the courtroom, saying that, boy, he would have taken that camera out. He would have allowed them in to begin with, he said. But the first infraction and they would have been out of there, like when they showed that juror. Then he was talking about how Judge Ito really likes the media attention, really likes to be on camera, loves to be on camera. He had said something the other day about him having a big ego, Judge Ito having a big ego.[18]

Interestingly, for all of Flynn's and others' perceptions that Ito loved the cameras and played to them, Ito had repeatedly tried to keep them on the trial itself. In addition to ordering no close-up shots of himself as a condition of reverting from a static shot, he repeatedly asked the camera operators not to focus on him. "I'm not the story here," he told them.

A CBS producer from New York confirmed that midway through the trial during a discussion concerning another local television report that portrayed Ito as starstruck and gaining too much fame too fast.

"Oh, no," the New York producer, Tim Tyson said, "he keeps asking over and over again, 'Please don't have me on camera' and he was constantly told, 'Judge, we can't do that. We've gotta have you on camera.' So he says, 'Well, don't do close-ups, keep it at a wide angle and don't linger on me.' He truly does not want to be on camera."[19]

Time apparently wasn't much of a salve for Flynn's feelings. A couple of months later he was telling me about a trip to England he planning.

"Oh," I said, "we just happen to have an English judge down in [Department] 103."

Flynn said he would like to meet him. No problem, I said. I could bring him over after he met with Ito, which was going to happen in just a few minutes.

"Oh, yes, of course," Flynn said, not even trying to hide his sarcasm. "He *is* more important."

"It is so interesting how Judge Flynn's jealousy is so apparent," I noted in my journal. "It's like he doesn't even try to veil it from me. In fact, he even made some remarks to the English judge, which was pretty much a giveaway about how he felt."

I felt awkward, to say the least.

"He would kind of say things and look at me for confirmation or something," I recorded.

> He said something like, "Oh, Judge Ito just eats up the publicity. He just loves being in the spotlight." And he looked at me as if I should be agreeing with him and I couldn't do that. I would have liked to somehow have made a little explanation, like I don't think he loves the publicity. I think he is trying to do the best he can by everybody involved and he doesn't write the media off as being nonessential or non-participants, not having some kind of a right to be there. The media do have a right to be there because it is a public proceeding.[20]

Flynn also told the British judge about the upcoming Snoop Doggy Dogg trial and what a big trial it was going to be. "He's the biggest, biggest rap star in the world," he said. "Kids all over world are going to be clamoring to know about it."[21]

Nevertheless, as the Broadus trial drew closer, Flynn said he wasn't going to allow cameras in, even though the only reason he gave for keeping them out was that he didn't want the same kind of circus he had seen in the Simpson case. In other words, despite criticizing Ito earlier, he was now blaming cameras in the courtroom for what he perceived had become a circus and was conceding that he would be no better at maintaining control than Ito if he let them in. It didn't make much sense to me. I noted his comments in a notebook I carried with me during the day:

> Lance loves all this publicity. I'm embarrassed about what it's done to the court system. I'm not going to allow cameras in the Snoop trial. Media attorney [Kelli] Sager was in on Monday, arguing for gavel-to-gavel coverage. I'm going to deny it. I'm not going to do this trial what's happening down there [in Dept. 103].

Flynn, I noted with my own touch of sarcasm, no doubt would have conducted it entirely differently.[22]

He apparently outdid himself in scaring off the media. The trial, which started several weeks after the Simpson verdicts, got little coverage compared to other high-profile and celebrity trials in Los Angeles, both televised and not. The coverage was so sparse, in fact, that my office had to do little in the way of media arrangements or worry about a shortage of courtroom seats, and the rapper came and went with no media gaggle laying in wait. The same was true in the county courthouse a few months later when Broadus was embroiled in a wrongful-death civil lawsuit over the same case. In fact, I happened to be in the hallway near the courthouse main entrance one day and watched him walk in alone—no entourage and not a camera in sight.

Another incident in the Simpson case that turned out to have a judicial connection was the missing juror questionnaire that showed up in the *Daily News of Los Angeles* on the eve of jury selection. Years after the trial, Ito said he had learned that, inexplicably, another judge, who has since died, had purloined the questionnaire for the newspaper. Although Ito had been convinced from the beginning that the questionnaire had been stolen somewhere between the court's reproduction office and delivery to his chambers, both he and I were left to wonder what possibly could have been the judge's motivation. That remains a mystery.

Equally puzzling is the ongoing plethora of judges who pillory Ito, particularly those who learned what they know about the trial from the media. A former Arizona Supreme Court chief justice, addressing a 1999 Court Information Officers national forum, said that if he were going to approve a television network's request to follow a jury from selection through deliberations he would make sure the case didn't have an "O. J. judge." Later, when I asked him about that comment, he listed the things he would have done differently. Primarily, he said, he would have hauled the attorneys who spouted off to the media on the courthouse steps into his courtroom and admonished and perhaps even sanctioned them. Everything he listed, Ito had done, including fining and sanctioning lawyers on both sides for their misbehavior inside and outside the courtroom. Although totals aren't kept as statistics, the Simpson trial was reputed to have been one of the most heavily attorney-fined criminal cases in California history. The Arizona justice, a bit chagrined when I told him that, admitted he hadn't known. That was my point, I said. His perception was media-induced and not founded on fact.

The same is true of a Massachusetts judge who has repeatedly disparaged Ito for holding what he calls bankers' hours, a Canadian Supreme Court justice who took a poke at Ito in a speech to an 1998 international conference on courthouse design, and countless others. That includes some who have presided over high-profile trials themselves and have decried the distortions and inaccuracies related to their cases that are reported in and perpetuated by the media.

To me, such judges appear to be, like Pontius Pilate, trying to wash any possible taint of the *Simpson* spectacle from their reputations. But their attempts require that people not do to them what they, in fact, do to the media, which is paint the entire profession with a broad brush based on the behavior of a few.

Government watchdog attorney Terry Franke questions what those jurists base their opinions on. "Most judges never encounter a personal, direct clash between their judicial routine and First Amendment pressures," says Francke, general counsel for Californians Aware and previously with the California First Amendment Coalition. "They form their views of press rights based on others' experience, or, ironically, press accounts of others' experience. Those who do see the lightning strike their courtrooms have to learn the case law the hard way—from media lawyers."[23]

Some who do have direct experience and thought they had also learned from *Simpson* about how to avoid the media quicksand, still encounter problems and surprises. Santa Barbara, California, Superior Court Judge Rodney Melville had more than fifteen years on the superior court and a number of trials of significant interest under his belt when he got the Michael Jackson child-molestation case in 2004. Although he had never denied a camera request or imposed a gag order, he did both in the Jackson case based in large part on the Simpson trial. Although many with the media gave the soft-spoken, white-haired grandfatherly looking judge high marks for keeping a firm grip on the trial and short leash on the flamboyant, melodramatic defendant, others thought he went too far.

The AP's Linda Deutsch, in the 2005 high-profile trial conference, called the trial a "nightmare" to cover, primarily because of the onerous rulings and conditions Melville imposed. In addition to sealing the indictment and grand jury proceeding transcripts, some of which had yet to be unsealed, Deutsch said, courtroom rules forbade all communication, including saying hello, between members of the media and other spectators even when court wasn't in session.[24] Despite allowing no cameras in the courtroom, television coverage of the trial still looked for all the world like a circus. That wasn't helped by a ridiculous reenactment with actors and a spoofy puppet theater that a couple of cable TV networks resorted to in the absence of camera coverage.[25]

William Mudd is one judge whose experience does include not only presiding over some trials of significant interest, but dealing with courtroom-camera coverage. Before retiring from the San Diego Superior Court, the twenty-two-year-veteran jurist allowed camera access for the highly emotional 2002 trial involving the murder of seven-year-old Danielle Van Dam.

"Without a doubt, the handling of [the Simpson] case, in all aspects, from a judicial point of view, had a devastating impact on the credibility and integrity of the criminal bench," says Mudd, a rare Simpson-trial critic who does not blame cameras for what he sees as a trial run amok.

"Since Judge Ito presided over the trial, it exposed him, personally, to scrutiny from his peers in all states, as to how he handled his courtroom, the attorneys, staff and media. On a wider level," Mudd adds, "it had a catastrophic impact on the willingness of judges to opening their courtrooms to television."[26]

But Mudd and his judicial colleagues across the country were most likely presiding over cases in their own courtrooms during much of the time the Simpson trial was in progress. Only Court TV aired complete gavel-to-gavel coverage of the entire trial. CNN devoted six hours daily, and the major networks interrupted regular programming with live coverage only on what they considered important days of the trial.[27] Consequently, without any firsthand knowledge, examination of the transcript, or discussion with Ito, they, like the rest of the public, formed their opinions from recaps overlaid with commentary and punditry. Unfortunately, by making judgments from second- third- and fourthhand reports instead of getting the facts for themselves, judges display their own failings even as they criticize Ito for what they perceive to be his. How much better to read the trial transcript, to discuss their perceptions with Ito and get his side of the story. Isn't that their jobs as judges, to get or allow in both sides of a story?

Every judge who feels that he or she has been "burned" by the media might want to keep in mind the purported old Indian saying of not judging someone else until you walk a mile in his moccasins. Or as a more sympathetic judge observed at a court-media relations workshop, "There but for the grace of God go I."

Gary Hengstler says he has often wondered what some of Ito's judicial critics would have done had any of them been the trial judge and Johnnie Cochran had criticized them on national television for not letting the defense present its full case.

"In other words, those judges whose hindsight would have had them act differently still would have had their own set of problems and equally would be second-guessed, only over different issues," Hengstler says. "Such was the volatility of that unique trial."[28]

Chapter 11
More Craziness

■ ■ ■

Judges weren't the only officials smearing on clown paint during the trial. When New York radio shock jock Don Imus argued with U.S. Senator Alfonse D'Amato, R-NY, on an April 1995 "Imus in the Morning" program about delaying the Whitewater hearings until the Simpson trial was over, D'Amato cavorted, feigned an exaggerated Japanese persona, and referred to Ito as "little Judge Ito."

"D'Amato went into this mock Japanese kind of accent," I recorded in my journal, "mocking Judge Ito's handling of the trial, saying things to the effect that he just wants the limelight and is dragging the trial out because he likes the limelight and it is a disgrace to the judicial system and so forth and so, of course, everybody in the world was calling and trying to get a response to that."[1]

But the story grew legs. The next day, D'Amato, amid a flurry of criticism, issued a statement, which I considered a "pseudoapology." "If I offended anyone," his statement read, "I'm sorry. I was making fun of the pomposity of the judge and the manner in which he's dragging the trial out."[2]

The day after that, he tried again, this time in the Senate. Although he spoke to a nearly empty chamber, it still made the news.

"In barely audible tones, a chastened and visibly nervous Senator Alfonse M. D'Amato delivered a rare apology on the Senate floor today, calling his heavily accented remarks about the Japanese-American judge in the O. J. Simpson case 'totally wrong and inappropriate,'" the *New York Times* reported. "... [T]he Senator stumbled through his opening lines, nervously handling the text of his remarks, and spoke for about two minutes in a stiff, halting style completely out of character for the freewheeling and frequently outrageous Senator.

"'What I did was a poor attempt at humor,' he said. 'I am deeply sorry for the pain that I have caused Judge Ito and others.'"[3]

Next, he groveled on the *Today* show when Katie Couric asked him why he took so long to offer a real apology. His Italian immigrant father had always taught him, he replied, that when someone makes a mistake they need to own up to it, to be a man and apologize, so that's what he was doing.

Ito asked me what I thought he should do about these highly publicized apologies.

"I think you should just let it die," I said.

He said he had also asked a couple of other people the same thing, and they said they thought he should accept D'Amato's apology privately, perhaps by personal letter.

I disagreed. "I know how important apologies are to you," I said. "And if someone is gracious enough to apologize, you pride yourself on being gracious enough to accept the apology. I know that's very important to you, but even a private acceptance is something you have no control over once you have extended it. You don't know what the ramifications will be. Here is a man who has soiled himself publicly and your accepting his apology dignifies what he did and he can make political hay out of it."

I was particularly concerned because Japanese Americans across the country were expressing outrage and demanding that D'Amato also apologize to them. Should anything from Ito become known, other Japanese Americans might infer that he was trying to speak for them.

"I am just concerned that the repercussions would be negative for you," I said. "You'll just open yourself up for criticism all over again. You maintain your dignity by not saying anything. Let it die," I said. "Just let it die. You know if you send any kind of private communication it won't remain private. The man is a politician, and a politician in trouble."[4]

Ito never indicated whether he contacted D'Amato. If he did, though, he proved me wrong, as the controversy quickly faded.

Although the media covered practically everything that moved, sanity did seem to prevail every once in a while. One such occasion was when a personal tragedy befell Ito and his wife, Margaret York.

One of York's grandchildren, a boy in his teens, had cystic fibrosis, for which he was frequently hospitalized. When that happened, she would call Ito and update him on the teen's condition. In mid-August of 1995, however, the boy lost the battle. Even though the defense's blood-spatter expert, Dr. Henry Lee, told the media one afternoon that court would be dark the next day because Ito would be attending a relative's funeral, they, to their credit, respected the judge's privacy and didn't report on it or show up at the cemetery.

They also didn't do stories on some of the odd occurrences, and odd people, in the courtroom, which often surfaced when the camera was off but nonetheless registered on Ito's radar. Some of those included

A spectator who seemed to have a lucky charm for winning a public seat in each morning's lottery. He was a tall, fortyish, balding man remarkable for his garb. It never varied: a dark T-shirt, combat boots, and full skirt. Despite the feminine attire, his posture was anything but ladylike. Perpetually stone-faced, he sat leaning forward, his elbows propped on splayed knees, his long, hairy arms dangling between his legs. Since he came and went quietly, spoke to no one, and sat silently in an unobtrusive back-row seat, the deputies decided that barring him might create more commotion than the odd looks he got as he lumbered in and out.

Yet another odd dresser seemed more partial to mismatched ensembles, such as plaid pants with a striped shirt, flowered tie, and shoes of different colors. He showed up lugging two large briefcases, which he said contained his divorce papers, but he was ejected after urinating in a courtroom seat.[5]

Another one-session attendee was a man in a wheelchair who sat at the end of a row of spectator seats. He was accompanied by a guide dog who lay in the aisle beside him and jumped up with a little "woof" every time someone stepped over him, which was frequently.[6]

Another spectator in court one day had some type of disability that required him to be encased in a brace with a steel rod that ran from his shoulders to his ankles. He sat, or rather propped himself straight as a board, in his seat by hooking his head on the back of the bench and sticking his feet under the seat in front of him, looking, as I noted in my journal, "horribly uncomfortable."[7]

As Ito called a break in proceedings on the day LAPD Detective Mark Fuhrman testified, a woman spectator stood as Ito rose from the bench and walked down the aisle toward the rail, saying she had a message from God. When a couple of deputies grabbed her arms to escort her out, she implored the judge to release the tapes of Fuhrman's interview in which he used an epithet in referring to African Americans. She then tossed an envelope into the bailiff's chair.[8]

The arresting sight of more than half-a-dozen television cameramen on the front steps of the Criminal Courts Building on Halloween wearing Robert Shapiro masks—all appearing to be looking heavenward—was captured by an enterprising photographer and shot around the world via the Associated Press.[9]

An amateur sketch artist who would loved to have gotten some media coverage and, like the skirted and combat-booted spectator, got into the courtroom so often I thought he must have been buying passes from people who won the public-seating drawing deputies conducted each morning. He generally ended up sitting next me, frequently poking sketches at me and pestering me to show them to Ito and even asking me to give him some. Years later I read about an art exhibit in Claremont, California, of *Simpson* courtroom sketches which the artist, who was not one of the four hired by the media, claimed Ito wanted him to do.

Those sketches were not the only things people wanted to give Ito. Memorabilia in the form of coffee mugs and T-shirts with all manner of logos, hourglasses, editorial cartoons, *Simpson*-themed board games and wristwatches, bags of candy with caricatures of the trial principals, and macabre souvenirs such as a red leather, sand-filled hand-shaped paperweight with the label "Your Own Bloody Glove (Shrunken Of Course)," arrived by the basketsful, as did cards and hundreds of faxes and letters that fell decidedly into two camps: those that lavished praise on the judge for the great job he was doing, and those that condemned him for being biased toward one side or the other.

Most enterprising, though, was the TV station technician who lampooned every phase of the case and trial-related personality along with events and holidays with laminated, commemorative, fake press credentials—eighty dollars for a complete set of thirty-nine.

Less enterprising and more expensive was the idea that the judge as well as the courtroom and everyone in it would look ever so much better, especially on TV, if only there were better lighting. Pulling me aside one day, Los

Angeles District Attorney Gil Garcetti's director of communications, Suzanne Childs, said that since the whole world was watching and forming an impression of the court and judge, she thought we should change out the standard florescent bulbs in the ceiling—used throughout the Criminal Courts Building—and put in less-harsh pink-tinted ones. Those, she asserted, would give the courtroom and everyone in it a softer look. Childs, an elegant blonde and former television broadcaster, said that had been done in the press-conference area of her boss's headquarters on the eighteenth floor of CCB, which she thought made a world of difference.[10]

I thanked her for the suggestion then deep-sixed it, having no desire for the drubbing I could just imagine the court and Ito getting for being so vain and for incurring such an expense.

Of greater concern to me and, eventually, to him than all the people who wanted to get in on the act was what their motives might be. Some of those people with hidden agendas actually came from my office. During the months leading up to the trial, an administrative merger with a municipal court put the public information office under the supervision of a woman who ingratiated herself with members of the media by having journalism students or other aspiring journalists work in our office as unpaid interns. Most were recommended by members of the media covering the trial. I didn't like the arrangement, given the nature of our work.

"I feel uncomfortable having people so closely associated with the media working where they hear our conversations, see sealed documents and are privy to our opinions," I jotted in my notebook.[11]

The office supervisor, however, saw it as a win-win situation: a great experience for the interns and additional help for the office, which was swamped with trial-related phone calls, faxes, and mail, all while trying to keep up with the media coverage and the office's other duties. Almost immediately, the interns started asking to go to CCB and attend the *Simpson* proceedings. The supervisor suggested I take them with me on occasion. It would be a nice reward, she said, for working for us for free.

Although that was awkward, too, given the shortage of courtroom seats, I usually got them in. But it turned out that some were more interested in catching the eye of male TV reporters and finding scoops to pass on to the media. I eventually learned that one particularly leggy young lady who wore skirts the lengths of which vied with those of Marcia Clark and Jo-Ellan Dimitrius actually worked for the *Los Angeles Times*. Even the deputies noticed that she spent a great deal of time on a hallway pay phone outside Ito's court-room after chatting people up. I finally decided to talk to the judge about the situation. He said that he had noticed the interns, too, and wasn't happy. "You let them know I don't want them in here again," he said.[12]

Perhaps a harbinger of the public's obsession with the case—with its grandstanding lawyers, spoiled and demanding defendant, swarms of fre-netic media, leaks to reporters, and frequent bomb scares—arrived in August before jury selection had even begun. That was the California secretary of state's unique request that Ito cancel court not just on election day, but also the day before, because he feared voters would stay home to watch the pro-ceedings on TV instead of going to the polls.

The craziness spilled over from the courthouse into Ito's personal life. Because he had become so recognizable, Ito, an avid shopper who even liked to buy his own groceries, resorted to finding stores that were open at mid-night on weekends, when few other shoppers—and autograph seekers—were around.

"Because of the judicial canons of ethics," he said a couple of months into the trial, "I can't do anything that would demean the office. That would include giving autographs."

It often got unpleasant, he said.

"People follow me through the supermarket, cursing [because he wouldn't give them autographs]. When I'm driving on the freeway, they start honking and try to get closer."

He vowed that when the trial was over, ". . . this beard is going to go and I'm going to get a new hairstyle."[13]

The notoriety even dogged him on trips. One weekend in April, while driving in Arizona, he and his wife, a high-ranking LAPD officer, stopped at a restaurant in Flagstaff. "There I was minding my own business," he said the next Monday morning. "When we came out, the parking lot was full of cam-eras. We jumped in the car, with my wife driving, taking evasive tactics she learned as a police officer. I'm in the back seat, yelling at her." Next day, he said, the *Arizona Daily Sun* had a story and a photograph.[14]

Although he still read his usual daily fare of five newspapers, he foreswore television soon after the trial got under way.

"I'm not watching," he said in mid-March. "Friends are watching for me. It was driving me crazy. Life has been a lot more sane since I stopped."[15]

But while he wasn't watching, others were. Things got so bad that Ito decided, while his humor was still pretty much intact, to have some business cards made. They included the familiar comedy/tragedy masks logo and the name Rodney J. Nakamura with "A.K.A. Hon. Lance A. Ito" beneath it along with the identifier "Impersonator Extraordinaire • Comic • Sage." The cards included a fake address and phone number.

Crazily, at least one real impersonator actually was misidentified as the real Ito. A supermarket tabloid ran photographs in July 1995 of the impersonator, whom the paper said was the judge, dancing at a party.

Late-night entertainment included myriad Ito TV spoofs, most notably those on *Saturday Night Live, The Tonight Show,* with its "Dancing Itos," and David Letterman's "Top Ten Lists." Although Ito found all of the tomfoolery amazing, he didn't share the outrage of some of his colleagues. Mostly he just shook his head and laughed. "Twenty years ago when I was sitting in law school at Berkeley, watching *Saturday Night Live,*" he said at one point, "little did I know that I would ever be lampooned on that show, and it wasn't even funny. I was disappointed."[16]

Then one day in July, the courtroom spectators included New York comic Jackie Mason. Word was BBC had hired him to do commentary.

"What a weird looking character," I recorded in my journal. "His hair weave was so tight and what looked like the results of a face peel or face lifts gave him the appearance of someone who had suffered first-degree burns. He had this real slick smooth, almost wrinkle-free kind of skin."

His behavior was also kind of bizarre. "He looked and acted as if he were not really with it, kind of spaced out or something," I recorded.

The session he sat in on concerned a motion to exclude the testimony of an expert witness during closing arguments and lasted less than an hour. Even so he appeared to doze off several times, and when he was not snoozing, he just gazed around.

"He took no notes," I observed. "All in all a very strange-looking guy, and you wonder what the heck his commentary for BBC will be like."[17]

Despite the chaos and oddball shenanigans, however, Ito never seemed at a loss for a quip. One November morning in 1994 when he was up to his eyeballs in jury selection, I told him I had to go to the courtroom where the Heidi Fleiss case was being heard. "When you talk to Heidi," Ito said, "thank her for me for removing that certain page from her 'book.'"[18]

He even managed to find fun in the black hole created by his KCBS interview with Tritia Toyota. After my office next to the media center was set up with the closed feed for the media who couldn't get into the courtroom for jury selection, Ito decided one evening after everyone else had left for the day to check it out. There, taped to the walls of the so-called listening room, were a half-dozen copies of the *Los Angeles Times*'s full-page ad of the KCBS interview. The ad included several freeze-frame pictures of Ito and Toyota supposedly engaged in the interview. The cynical media folks had drawn speech bubbles beside some of the photos and filled them with such wisecracks as

Toyota: "Thanks, Judge. I'll be network in no time. You made my career."
Ito: "It's sweeps week!"

Instead of getting angry or taking offense, Ito decided to judge the graffiti and award prizes for those he thought exhibited the most "wit, bite, originality, charm and just the right ring of truth."[19]

This exemplifies, probably better than any other incident, Ito's guilelessness and how it was so easily and widely misread. Knowing Ito is to understand how he tried to turn the snarkiness of the graffitied ads into good-natured repartee.

That good nature had apparently worn a little thin by the following May when I let him know about a Long Beach newspaper photographer who wanted to bring his camera into the courtroom, but not as a member of the photo pool. I almost told the photographer no without checking but decided against it. I'd seen too many end runs.

So there I was in Ito's chambers, probably for the hundredth time that week, letting him know about the Long Beach photographer.

"I am hoping your answer is no," I said. "That is what I would tell him."

"You know, Jerrianne," he said without looking up, obviously irritated, "you make those decisions. Don't bother me with that. I don't have time to worry about it."

"That's what I would like to do, judge, but they don't want my answer. I will tell them the answer is no and they won't take that. They will find other people to ask and other people will come to you, and you won't know the background and you may not understand fully because it is not explained fully or whatever, and they may get a different answer."

"Yeah," he said with a sigh. "We should be making sure that we get out the same message."

"That is my point exactly. It's not that I can't make a decision, but I think it's good that you know about the requests that come in. Not for you to make the decision necessarily but that you know that I've already gotten the request and this is the answer so that you are not saying yes to something that I've already said no to."

I told him I would let his clerk know about the photographer in case he called her, so she would know the scoop "and that there is no other inroad here."[20]

I wasn't quite as agile with an ABC producer who wanted to get file footage of the deliberations room before the jury got the case. I relayed Ito's *no*. Next thing I knew, the guy was saying that Supervising Judge Bascue had given the green light. Baffled that Bascue would be making decisions about media access to Ito's jury room, I contacted him. Turns out, he had done no such thing but had told them the producer had to talk to me.

That, in my experience, was one of the most difficult aspects of being the court's liaison with the media on the Simpson case—and is a hazard with just about any high-profile trial. The media tried every route they could think of to get the answer they wanted. Having been a journalist, I understood that they had a job to do and that not only was the competition fierce, but pressure from their bosses was tremendous and perhaps their jobs might be at risk. I also understood that some of the thousands of court and security employees were fascinated by the celebrity of the case and tried to ingratiate themselves or help one of the media stars as a way of getting a little piece of the action. My understanding of that, though, didn't mean I could just throw my hands up and say, "Oh, well, that's just the way they work."

"It is especially difficult when there are different agendas," I recorded on my way home the night after talking to Ito about the Long Beach photographer. "I don't know what the sheriff's deputies and the sheriff's sergeant's agenda is, but as much as I request, 'will you please leave courtroom information, court information, scheduling, documents, things of that nature, to me, and you handle the security, the movement of the defendant and taking care of the jurors, . . . I don't get the same kind of courtesy in return. That is just one more difficult issue."[21]

Another thing I didn't understand about the folks in the sheriff's department was why they credentialed George Reedy Jr. Reedy showed up in the early stages of a case wearing a sheriff-issued media credential and saying he worked for the *Post Gazette Chronicle*. I often spotted Reedy, a large African American man who occasionally got one of the first-come, first-serve media seats before the trial seating plan was finalized. He generally hung out near other members of the media in the courthouse corridors. One day, after the Tracy Hampton flap, he showed up with an armload of papers. They turned out to be copies of an unpublished three-page story about the alternate juror who had replaced Hampton. He was handing copies out to anyone who would take them. The story was not only poorly written, it contained unattributed allegations that the replacement juror was pro-prosecution and had been overheard at a restaurant telling her coworkers that she thought Simpson was guilty.

"I want you to know that I didn't go seeking this out," Reedy told me. "It literally fell right into my lap."

Although Southern California was rife with all kinds of weekly and community newspapers and newsletters, I hadn't heard of the *Post Gazette Chronicle* and had never seen or heard of Reedy before he started showing up for the Simpson case. At that point, I began to quiz him about his publication: Where was it located? What area or areas did it cover? Who owned it? and so forth. After being evasive, he said that it wasn't really a newspaper yet, that he was just in the process of trying to get it started.[22]

Interestingly, most of the high-profile trials I have worked on have had some variation of a George Reedy. At the Simpson civil trial, which would get under way nearly two years later in Santa Monica, a man hoping to get into the courtroom as a member of the media presented a Writers Union card that had expired six years earlier. Reedy, however, had managed to fly under the radar longer than any of his fellow would-be journalists.

Although I was sure the story he gave me was baseless, I took a copy to Ito, saying I thought it was a bunch of tripe. I feel sure, though, that Ito passed it along to the two undercover sheriff's detectives assigned to investigate such allegations.[23]

Chapter 12
Aftermath

■ ■ ■

It's history now

Jurors were unanimous

The public is not

It was over so fast.[1]

The day after the verdicts, everyone was pulling up stakes. Trash littered the courthouse media center. Broadcast equipment left for future trials, in vain as it turned out, sat idle like ghosts wondering who to haunt. The place resembled a postwar battlefield—except the only dead soldier was Ito. And, indeed, more than a decade later, he remains the primary casualty—he and a public that has become more shut out from objective, unadulterated court proceedings via what could be a great medium. Television.[2]

Television could have informed and educated, could have brought people unable to physically attend the trial into the courtroom. Instead it used the trial for entertainment and unabashed commercial promotion. Reporters, commentators, pundits, and comedians used it to advance careers and agendas and to create cartoon caricatures.

Los Angeles Times television critic Howard Rosenberg passed judgment in his column the day after Simpson's acquittal:

> The Simpsonizing of TV news in the mid-90s affirms that the people going into the business are dumber and dumber, the people directing them

are dumber and dumber and, as a consequence, the public is dumber and dumber.

Except about the O. J. Simpson case. We know everything about that.

If these protectors of the airwaves would invest in their coverage of other news the same energy, resources and commitment they continue to apply to the Simpson case, we'd be much smarter about ourselves and the world around us. Instead we are getting telecoptered, skycammed, team covered, live stand-upped and exclusived into a state of mental numbness. TV news having found a way to shrink the brain as if it were a malignant tumor. . . .

It couldn't get worse. Yet it gnaws at you that it will, that 20 years from now things will have gotten so bad that Americans will recall the Simpson period of 1994–95 as the golden age of journalism, as many now look back with misty nostalgia at the era of Edward R. Murrow.[3]

Many of the judges in Los Angeles—including Reginald Denny–beating trial judge John Ouderkirk and Presiding Judge Gary Klausner—were predicting weeks before the *Simpson* verdicts that his trial more than any other single factor would spell the demise of televised trials.

"We are going to see more and more instances in which judges are not going to allow cameras in the courtroom," Ouderkirk said. Not because of Ito, necessarily, but because of the way cameras were used or, from the judges' perspective, misused.

About three weeks before the *Simpson* verdicts, Ouderkirk said that as he watched the trial, he reflected on his decision two years earlier to allow camera coverage of the Denny case.

"I did it at the time because of the mood of the community," he said, recalling the racially charged riots that devastated Los Angeles the previous year after the acquittals of four white police officers in the Rodney King–beating trial. Four African American men arrested at the height of the riots were charged in the near-fatal beating of white trucker Reginald Denny, who unwittingly drove into a South-Central L.A intersection at the wrong time.

"I didn't want anyone claiming that I was trying to cover up or hide anything," Ouderkirk told me. "I didn't want anybody to be able to charge that anyone got railroaded. I wanted it to be open so people in the community could see that it was being handled as fairly as possible."

Ouderkirk conceded that the presence of cameras probably did affect some trial participants' behavior. Both pilot/reporter Bob Tur, who shot footage of the beating from his helicopter, and Denny himself, for instance, were perhaps more dramatic on the witness stand and after testifying than they would have been had cameras not been rolling, he said.

"Like, maybe Denny wouldn't have gone over and hugged [defendant] Damian Williams's mother in the courtroom when he left the stand?" I suggested.

"Right," Ouderkirk said. "I doubt that he would have done that."

The lawyers in that trial, however, seemed oblivious to the cameras. That almost certainly would not have been true had Ouderkirk not ordered a separate trial for one of the defendants, Antoine Miller, who had a much smaller role in the beating than did Williams and codefendant Henry Keith Watson. Knowing Miller's attorneys and their penchant for courtroom antics, Ouderkirk said that had Miller been tried with Williams and Watson, "it would have been an absolute disaster."

That comment prompted me to think about the Simpson trial lawyers.

Ouderkirk believed that letting the Denny trial be televised had been good for the community as a whole. He found it interesting, however, that a small faction still claimed, more than two years later, that the trial was unfair and the guilty verdicts unjust, even though the defendants were convicted of less serious charges than the district attorney had filed. So in that sense, he didn't think televising the trial made much difference. But overall, he said, letting cameras cover the trial had been the right decision.[4]

A few hours after the *Simpson* verdicts had been read on the morning of October 3 and the media-related cacophony had begun to subside, I finally found a moment to touch base with Ito. I went to his chambers to find Ouderkirk and William Pounders, who handled the two-and-a-half-year first McMartin Preschool child-molestation trial in 1987–1990, visiting with him. Ouderkirk and Pounders had both presided over difficult, emotion-charged trials in the glare of intense, often negative, media coverage. Those trials had ended controversially, one in mistrial, the other in a publicly polarizing verdict. They felt empathetic and wanted to offer Ito their support. I couldn't help but marvel at the judicial history represented in the room by those three judges. But it was clear even then that *Denny* and *McMartin* would never be as historically enduring, or carry such long-lasting baggage, as *Simpson* would. What I didn't foresee, though, was just how deep, persistent, and far-reaching the *Simpson* consequences would be. My visit to Ito's chambers that October afternoon was the first opportunity I had had to ask about his reaction to the jury's verdicts.

"Stunned," he said, explaining that he had believed when the jurors got the case that they would not be able to agree on a verdict.

I told him about a conversation I had with a deputy sheriff who had been assigned to the jurors the previous night and that morning before court convened. The deputy had said some of the jurors were "die-hards" for guilty but had caved in to the pressure of everyone wanting to go home. That and the possibility of things getting bogged down with questions some had about the exact meaning of "reasonable doubt" swayed them.

"So, they just plain long gave up," I told Ito. "They all just wanted to go home."

The deputy sheriff, Ito's clerk, Deirdre Robertson, and I had speculated about the difference it might have made had jurors not been sequestered or whether sequestration favored the defense. It seemed pretty clear that the more than seven months of near-imprisonment had narrowed jurors' focus to the single goal of ending their misery and getting home, even if it meant voting for something they didn't believe was true.

Yet, if they hadn't been sequestered, without question they would never have been able to cloister themselves sufficiently to have remained unaffected by the pervasive and all-invasive publicity or to be sheltered from exposure to the issues and questions they legally could not have considered. It would have been impossible for jurors to have remained truly impartial and independent of outside influences.

"Well, there you have it," Ito said when I told him about my conversation with the deputy and Robertson.

"It really is a conundrum," I said.

"It's much more than a conundrum," he replied.[5]

Media requests to interview Ito had dropped off after the Tritia Toyota debacle of the previous fall. But they started back up in September 1995 as the case wound down. They began as a flurry then escalated to a blizzard the day the jury got the case. Lucinda Franks Morgenthau had returned and was padding around the media center, hoping to get an interview.

"She is one of many media types almost like flies flocking to a carcass," I recorded in my journal. "Mark Robinson, who works for Diane Sawyer, has put in a couple of desperate pleas, telephone calls saying, 'I know you are very busy, Jerrianne, but if you could just take a couple seconds to give me a call.' Larry King apparently has somebody new working for him, not Ellen Beard any longer, and that person has called two or three times. Larry King wants to take Judge Ito out for a private dinner. They are just all flocking."[6]

Staffers for King, Katie Couric, and Barbara Walters called several times, each within a span of just a few hours, even though they had already caught me in person in the courthouse hallway. Walters's assistant, Kay Thomas, dangled the lure that Walters wanted to feature Ito either on her *20/20* show or on a special she planned to do on the ten most fascinating people in America. Others included John F. Kennedy Jr., paralyzed actor Christopher Reeve, and tennis star Monica Seles. "And we want very much to include Judge Ito."[7]

Calls also swamped Ito's clerk and other staff. He finally told me to issue a media advisory saying he wasn't giving any interviews and, since a civil trial was in the offing, to cite (California judicial ethical) Canon 3(b)9, which prohibits judges from commenting publicly about pending cases.[8] Even though Simpson had been acquitted, which meant the criminal case was no longer pending, a civil lawsuit had been filed and the issue of custody of Simpson's children remained in an Orange County court.

"Well, that will take care of those who want to talk to you about the case," I said, "but what about those who just want to talk about the personal toll the trial has taken on you and your family, the stress, or the law in general?"

"It's too easy to cross over the line, so I am not doing anything," he said.[9]

So all the clamor was for naught. Ito refused everyone—well, almost everyone.

About three weeks after the verdicts, the *Daily News of Los Angeles* ran a story about a California State University, Northridge, journalism student who had copped the coup of the century—an exclusive interview with Judge Lance Ito. The story gave few details, such as when, where, or under what circumstances the interview had occurred, except that the lucky—or enterprising, or both—student was majoring in broadcast journalism and that the interview was going to air that evening on a local cable television channel. As the blood, which had drained from my brain, began to flow back, shock turned to anger. What was he thinking? Why had he done it? And why hadn't he told me about it? I headed for his chambers.

Yes, he said, he had talked to the student. She had shown up the previous Friday with camera in hand doing a class project.

I should have known. He was such a sucker for helping kids. I thought of all the groups of Scouts and students he had talked to during the trial, and how he had held class in chambers with his law clerks at the end of most days, asking them as they sat, lined up on the couch in front of his desk, "Well, what did we learn today?"

But he had laid down conditions with the Northridge student, he said. Hmmm, did *that* sound familiar.

He had limited her to only three questions, he said. The interview could not be used for anything except her class project, and nothing about it could be made public. After all he had been through, I found this naivety astounding. Going into a rant, however, wouldn't change anything. What was done was done, so I asked how the *Daily News* knew about it.

"That's what *I* would like to know," he said. "I am not happy about that. In fact, tell them that because it was in the *Daily News* I withdraw my permission for it to air."

With the specter of prior restraint hanging over my head, I called the student's professor. He hemmed and hawed then said he needed to check with the department chairman, who, in turn, called me. He carried on about how we were making a mountain out of a molehill and making the situation a lot worse and how Ito would end up looking like a fool because the student had said the interview would be on television and on and on and on.

Given Ito's intelligence, urbanity, and insightfulness at so many levels and in so many respects, his not foreseeing the ramifications of doing that interview puzzled me. Even though he wanted to help the kid out on her class project and it was going to air on a noncommercial channel and wouldn't be released to the general media, didn't he realize that all someone had to do was tape the cable program with a VCR and, boom, it would be all over the place? I could only think that now after the verdicts, as when he got the case, he thought media attention would be short-lived and things would return to normal. Or perhaps he hoped it so fervently that he was blind to reality.

I ended up telling the department chair that I would convey his message to the judge. "Too late," Ito said when I told him. "Unequivocally, they do not have my permission to air it now. They have lied to me."[10]

At that point, Ito's clerk said the student's professor was on the line. I took the call. He gave the same rationale as the department chair for why they couldn't pull the interview.

"What would it do to this kid?" he asked. "Here she has got the interview of lifetime and we can't do that to her. Even if we tried, that would be censoring and we can't censor."

As I hung up, Robertson said the student had also called. When I called her back, she told a different story from her professor's. She was just sick over the whole thing, she said. She hadn't been able to sleep after it came out in the *Daily News*. She was so upset, she didn't want it to air and had asked her professor to kill it, but he said he couldn't.

"Wait a minute," I said. "That's not what they are saying. Both your professor and the department chair are saying that it has to air because of you, that they can't kill it because they couldn't do that to you. And you are telling me that you don't want it to run, but they are telling me that it has to out of consideration for you?"

When I called the professor back, he wouldn't discuss the student's version, but he reasserted that Ito's lack of permission notwithstanding, the interview would air. It would, however, carry a disclaimer to the effect that it was being aired over Ito's objection because of the *Daily News* story. He also said that the university wasn't responsible for the newspaper story and that the university was within its rights because no one had done anything wrong. He also denied that either he or anyone else at the university had contacted other media outlets, which were calling us about the interview and Ito's not wanting it to air.

"Well, the only people who know about this," I told the professor, "are Judge Ito, myself, his clerk and my assistant and then all of you people."

"Oh," he countered, "I can tell you it is not us. It is not getting out from any of us."

In the end I told him that the whole department there needed a lesson in ethics and that I would be glad to give a lecture on that topic whenever they wished. I never heard back from him.[11]

The media's hypocrisy reached new heights a few days later with a *Daily News of Los Angeles* editorial decrying the media's continuing *Simpson* addiction. The first of a series of examples it cited was the Northridge student being "catapulted into the spotlight after she managed by chance to land a very brief—and thoroughly unrevealing—interview with Judge Lance Ito."[12] Not mentioned in the editorial was a page-one story the paper had run the previous day that dwarfed the student's actual interview. The story package, which jumped to an inside page, included two photographs—one of the student, the other a grainy video freeze-frame of Ito—and a sidebar containing a transcript of the interview.[13]

So here was the *Daily News* saying to the rest of the news media, enough is enough. Lay off. It's time to quit. The trial is over. Get on with life. The hypocrisy of it was that the *Daily News* made the student's interview a news story in the first place, then the very next day said, *Okay, we've got our scoop, now you other guys lay off. Everybody is sick of the whole thing. You are all giving something legs that should have died three weeks ago.*

When I told Ito about my offer to the professor to teach a class in ethics, he showed me a newspaper cartoon he had taped to his chambers door. It depicted students registering for journalism classes. Hordes were clamoring to sign up for courses on how to apply pancake makeup and how to keep hair in place on a windy day in an outdoor live shot, but the line for a class in ethics was empty. What a commentary on the Northridge incident, although I thought in this case it applied to the faculty, not the student. Gazing at the cartoon, Ito commented, "I would have to say that it's true. A picture is worth a thousand words."[14]

I reminded him that as much as he liked helping people—especially students—until he could return to some degree of obscurity, I didn't think it would be to his benefit. He agreed.

"If I ever talk to anybody again," he said wryly, "would you please just shoot me."[15]

And he hasn't. Other than addressing a few private association gatherings, he's remained "in the tall grass," where he said years after the trial he prefers to stay. No interviews, no television guest spots, no public speeches, no statements to the media—except for universally declining the myriad interview requests that flooded in on the tenth anniversaries of first the murders and then the trial verdicts—no Wapneresque TV show, no book deals. He continues to sit in a criminal courtroom in Los Angeles where he tries murder cases as heinous, if not more so, than that of Nicole Brown Simpson and Ronald Goldman, and some with multiple juries. His courtroom is easily identifiable. It's the one with no nameplate on the door. Although a nameplate was affixed to it when he moved in from the courtroom down the hall where the Simpson trial took place, it disappeared, apparently taken by a souvenir seeker. Two replacement nameplates suffered similar fates. Finally, he told the building administrator to just forget about it.

Although Ito's name remained in the headlines, the flare-up over the Northridge student's interview was quickly buried in the avalanche of universal criticism and castigation that consumed the posttrial landscape. Although the trial was over, with no appeals or any other official proceedings to come, controversy over the case continued to consume me as well. As my office monitored posttrial coverage, I saw story after story full of distortions, inaccuracies, mis-perceptions, mischaracterizations, and erroneous assumptions. One report claimed Ito was considering an offer to be the judge on *The People's Court,* the popular show that for years featured Judge Joseph Wapner. Although the pay reportedly was a million dollars a year, the cases on that show involved petty little municipal court–level spats, which Ito would have found boring and a giant step backward to his earlier days as a municipal court judge.

One of the more improbable reports, apparently based on a *New York Daily News* story and repeated by other news outlets, said that immediately after the verdicts, Ito shut himself in his chambers with his wife, police cap-tain Margaret York, where they sobbed so loudly they could be heard out in the hallway.[16] Ito's reaction when I told him about it the next day was, "Pure fabrication, absolutely asinine."[17]

One account said, "There was no immediate comment from Ito. He was reported to be vacationing Tuesday."[18] Since I was standing face to face with him in his chambers asking him about the crying story, obviously the media had gotten the vacation part wrong, too. Ito had told me right after the trial that much as he would like to get away for a while, his wife was unable to take time off from work just then.

In the ensuing days and weeks, I frequently offered to send op-ed pieces and letters to stations and publications to counter the more egregious reports. Initially, Ito would agree, only to change his mind once I had drafted something. It wasn't because of the writing. He had no problem with the writing, but I think in mulling it over, he decided it would be futile, and he just wanted to put the whole affair behind him.

The effect of the ongoing bashing had to have been devastating, particu-larly given his pre-*Simpson* reputation as a legally brilliant, thoughtful, seldom-reversed judge with the brightest of judicial futures ahead of him. Although we never discussed it, I don't see how it could have been possible that, in trying to ignore the almost universally negative press, the dearth of public support from colleagues, and the perception that he was, as he later described it, "everybody's worst example," he was not affected by depression.

The stress of the case itself certainly affected his health in other ways, although few people knew about that. In addition to nonstop work at all hours, he persevered through bouts of the flu during the trial, and as early as June he began suffering debilitating headaches. Those turned out to be a symptom of high blood pressure, which became chronic.

It is often said that history is written by the victors. That might or might not be true, but in the Simpson case, everybody had a story to tell. So many did so that it launched a cottage industry of books about the trial, the defendant, the crimes, the victims, and the jurors. Each book, of course, conveyed a specific point of view, and all of the authors needed a scapegoat to absolve themselves of their own faults, missteps, and questionable behavior. Despite rampant rumors during and immediately after the trial that Ito, too, had signed a multimillion-dollar book deal, he's the only major figure in the trial not to have written a book. Many other books were published by people who never set foot inside the courtroom or had any firsthand knowledge of the trial but took Ito to task based primarily on media coverage.

The AP's Linda Deutsch blames the bashing, in large part, on the verdicts. "People wanted Simpson to be convicted," she says. "When he wasn't they figured it was the judge's fault. If [Simpson] had been convicted I don't think the fallout would have been so bad."[19]

But the flurry of unrebutted criticism made Ito an increasingly easy target. The lack of push-back or of any semblance of a public defense has turned perception into a perverse universal truth, which could easily be interpreted either subconsciously or consciously as Ito's acknowledgment of his own failings. It's reminiscent of the public's denigrated perception of the title character in Harriet Beecher Stowe's *Uncle Tom's Cabin*. Even blacks have come to equate the name with an epithet, yet I dare say that none who does so has read the book.

The dismal public perception of Ito continues more than a decade later as a second generation of pundits, most with no knowledge of what they are talking about, perpetuates the distorted views of those who have gone before them. A self-described sports fanatic boasted in a 2005 free-lanced opinion piece in a Kansas newspaper of being only nine years old at the time of the trial, which means he was all of nineteen when he opined about Ito's performance: "The trial itself was a circus," he wrote. "Judge Lance Ito transformed into Court Jester Ito as he lost his courtroom and let it evolve into a circus.... There are those who criticize the media for creating a circus. However, Ito opened the courtroom for everyone and as a judge, he could have stopped that."[20]

One can only wonder where he heard such words or how he thought limiting access to public proceedings could contribute to trust in, or a positive perception of, a court system.

Cameras, probably as much as Ito, were demonized for what was perceived to be a trial run amok, and, initially, they were victimized almost as much. On the day Simpson was acquitted, a harbinger of the fate of courtroom-camera coverage in California emerged in the form of the governor calling for a total ban on cameras in criminal cases in the state.[21]

Chapter 13
From There to Here

■ ■ ■

The media hype-machine has infected legal proceedings like a dread virus. Journalists get agents before they call rewrite, signing book and movie deals that tempt them to pump up the stories they're covering and nearly require them to withhold revelatory information for their later hardcovers. So-called "serious" journalists become indistinguishable from their racy tabloid colleagues, sitting side by side.

—Jon Katz, Media Rant

One January morning in 1995 soon after the Simpson trial had gotten under way, the Los Angeles Superior Court's new presiding judge, Gary Klausner, asked what the reaction would be if courtroom-camera coverage were banned.[1]

"There would be a huge legal fight," I replied and described the intense media hearing two months earlier in the *Simpson* proceedings.

"Well, judges find cameras intrusive and affecting the outcome of trials," he said. "Specifically, they believe that cameras alter the behavior of jurors and witnesses."

Klausner seemed surprised when I told him about the relative unobtrusiveness of the remote cameras mounted behind the jury box in Ito's courtroom and the one that had been installed on the back wall of the courtroom for the Menendez brothers' first trial a year and a half earlier. "Well," he countered, "in the next high-profile case, you shouldn't be surprised to see cameras banned." A lot of judges were upset about the Simpson trial, he added, and he thought there would be a backlash.[2]

Klausner's prediction was echoed a few months later by one from a broadcaster. "There's nothing typical about this trial," Court TV's Fred Graham said about *Simpson,* "but it will set precedents for years to come that will affect other cases."[3]

Less than seven months after Graham's observation, on the very day of the October 3 *Simpson* verdicts, then-governor Pete Wilson sent a letter to California's chief justice asking for a statewide electronic media-coverage ban in criminal trials.[4]

Although television-camera coverage bore the brunt of the blame for media excesses and the Simpson trial's circus-like atmosphere, Wilson's request included audio recording and radio transmission. It would also have covered laptop computers, which were then just starting to replace reporters' pens and notebooks. Laptops are now routinely used for taking notes in courtroom proceedings. He also wanted the state's Standards of Judicial Administration to dictate "the appropriate length of a trial day where a jury is sequestered" and to bar trial attorneys from making "political appeals" in their closing arguments.[5]

All three ideas were ludicrous, so far as I was concerned, and displayed a degree of gubernatorial naïveté. Whether cameras substantially affect trial participants' behavior remains open to debate. Certainly some of the Simpson trial lawyers preened and pranced, and at least one witness, Kato Kaelin, appeared to treat his turn on the witness stand like an audition. But would their behavior have been any different had a TV camera not been present?

Some say that Cochran's conduct in *Simpson* was no different from that in any other case, and I know of a number of trials that had no camera coverage in which the parties and/or their lawyers acted out. One case involved a defense attorney, known in the Los Angeles legal community for his courtroom caterwauling and cavorting, who used a hamburger bun as a prop during his closing arguments. In an attempt to convince the jury that the prosecution had no case, he dramatically pulled the bun open and asked, "Where's the beef?" Another was a death-by-dog-mauling case moved from

San Francisco to Los Angeles in which a defense lawyer's antics included falling down and writhing on the floor while court was in session. The high-profile trials of Scott Peterson, Michael Jackson, and Martha Stewart had no camera coverage yet were called media circuses. Similarly, says now-retired radio and television broadcaster David Dow, who covered the Simpson trial for CBS radio, the absence of courtroom cameras would not have kept the Simpson trial from becoming the media spectacle it was.

Dow observes,

> There had never before been a trial like this one. An internationally rec-ognized celebrity defendant, a "dream team" of high-profile defense attorneys—some already famous for [their] courtroom theatrics—and a stream of more than a hundred witnesses, including veteran television and trial performers such as forensic expert Henry Lee [later alleged to have contaminated crime-scene evidence in record producer Phil Spec-tor's murder case] and former New York City chief medical examiner Michael Baden.
>
> Throw in an exploding race card and an incredible three—*three*—sets of DNA evidence and testimony, and you've got an unprecedented mix and more than enough to fill three circus rings, camera or no camera.

Like other broadcasters, Dow believes much of that circus occurred out-side of the courtroom.

"The heavily covered arrival and departure interviews of defense lawyers, the ever-rising superstructure of 'O. J. City' and teeming press community across [the street] from the court building" all contributed, Dow says. So, too, did the prime-time television interviews of bit players such as Simpson girlfriend Paula Barbieri, Nicole Brown Simpson pal Faye Resnick, and peripheral grand jury witness Jill Shively.[6]

Despite some judges' and lawyers' assertions that camera coverage does affect the outcome of cases, the media point out that no court has made such a finding since the 1965 U.S. Supreme Court ruling in the fraud verdict of Texas financier Billie Sol Estes. The Court overturned his conviction on grounds that television coverage deprived him of a fair trial.[7]

But, while some critics might have rational arguments for opposing cam-eras, banning microphones seemed laughable and smacked of just another way to shroud court proceedings from the public. I'm not aware of any lawyer, witness, defendant, juror, or judge in modern times who has pandered to a microphone or gained fame via voice recordings. In fact, I often wonder why the media, if they are indeed serious about wanting to gain access in order to inform the public, don't counter camera-coverage denials with requests to air audio only.

Mandating the length of a trial day when juries are sequestered, as Wilson suggested, would hobble the ability of any judge faced with the kinds of unforeseen and convoluted circumstances that proliferated in the Simpson trial. And a prohibition on "political appeals" in closing arguments would have stumbled quickly on First Amendment challenges.

Rather than complying with the governor's proposals, however, the California Judicial Council conducted an extensive investigation and held a series of public hearings. Based on its findings, the council decided against a camera ban, but it did give judges complete discretion over whether to allow cameras in their courtrooms. That effectively negated the need for hearings on camera-access requests and doomed the possibility that any denials would be reversed on appeal.

Although not an official ban, to hear the media talk, the revised rule might as well have been. Judges were denying camera requests left and right, the media said, particularly in Los Angeles County. First Amendment attorneys who represent the media, such as Ted Boutrous and Kelli Sager, both based in Los Angeles, say California courtroom-camera access dropped dramatically in the wake of the Simpson trial. While some in the media are finding that the clampdown has begun to ease in recent years, Sager says that "post-O. J., it was very, very difficult to get a camera in any court."[8]

The Los Angeles Criminal Courts Building media center offers silent proof. With the dearth of camera approvals after the Simpson trial, the center fell into such disuse that it took on the look of an abandoned tenement, and more than once I chased out squatters from the district attorney's office, which was desperate to find more courthouse space.

Hoping to get an accurate picture of the camera-access situation, California's Administrative Office of the Courts conducted a three-year survey in which courts were asked to tabulate electronic-coverage requests. The results seemed to contradict media claims. Judges had granted 81 percent of all television and still camera and audio-recording requests, according to the report issued in 2000.

"However, as the study itself notes," California Chief Justice Ronald M. George says, "the data does not constitute a precise accounting of all media activity in California courts. Only thirty-two of the fifty-eight counties submitted media requests and other responses at the [Administrative Office of the Courts], which means that nearly half of the counties did not participate in the study."

The survey also relied on self-reporting by judges and their staffs. In Los Angeles, for example, after advising its nearly three hundred judges and commissioners about the survey, the court's leadership left to them whether to participate. It's impossible to know how many did. My guess, however, is that most ignored it, and that the bulk of the data came from my office based on media requests I learned about and followed up on. Consequently, Los Angeles County data was spotty and incomplete.

The judicial council's effort, however, is more than the media appear to have done. None of the approximately eighteen national and state media advocacy and support organizations, such as the Radio-Television News Directors Association in Washington, D.C., the Media Law Resource Center in New York, and the First Amendment Center at Vanderbilt University, or major media law firms maintain specific access data. That leaves the media with little to go on except for anecdotal information.

Tim Sullivan, senior vice president of Court TV, attributes the near shutdown of camera access in the states of New York and Texas in addition to Los Angeles County, if not all of California, to *Simpson,* although, he says, most judges won't admit it. His company's records, however, provide interesting evidence.

In the four years after Court TV was launched in 1991, the network televised sixteen Texas trials, Sullivan says. In the seven years immediately following the Simpson criminal trial, Court TV got into only eleven trials. Before New York State banned camera coverage in the wake of *Simpson,* Court TV broadcast thirty-three criminal trials and "dozens of civil trials" from New York courtrooms.[10]

On the federal level, a three-year experiment begun in 1991 and limited to civil cases in six district and two appellate courts wasn't expanded or renewed. Sullivan feels certain that was because of *Simpson.* As chair of the federal Judicial Conference Committee on Court Administration and Case Management, U.S. District Court Judge John R. Tunheim testified before a Senate Judiciary Committee on September 2007 in favor of continuing the camera ban. Based on the three-year project, he said, the conference concluded that cameras had a potentially intimidating effect on some witnesses and jurors and that it was not in the interest of justice to permit cameras in federal trial courts.[11]

Sullivan says Court TV televised "dozens of federal trials during that experiment," and in a survey conducted after the project ended, a large percentage of the judges who had allowed cameras said they would do it again.[12]

His Court TV colleague Fred Graham says courts have to go back more than forty years to find a case on record for supporting proof that cameras have an adverse effect. "We at Court TV do not know of a single case since *Billie Sol Estes versus United States* in 1965 that has been overturned due to television coverage of the trial," Graham told a gathering of chief justices in 2003, "but in extremely important cases judges with unbridled discretion to ban cameras have tended to do so, just to take no chances."[13]

Radio-Television News Directors Association president Barbara Cochran says states with liberal access have good track records. "We can point to more than twenty-five years of experience in numerous states such as Florida, Iowa and Washington where cameras in court are commonplace and where not one case has ever been reversed because of the presence of a camera," she says.[14]

Florida, where even jurors can be photographed, has the most liberal camera-access rules in the country. Yet, the state's supreme court communications counsel, Craig Waters, says he knows of no significant problems during the nearly twenty-year history cameras have had court access.

"In Florida, cameras in the courtroom are now so ubiquitous that few even pay attention to them," says Waters, who has served as both court staff attorney and information officer. "In our [Supreme Court] courtroom, the cameras are so well recessed into the architecture that they are hard to notice."[15]

Waters, who was court spokesman during the 2000 Gore versus Bush presidential election lawsuit, says cameras are just part of the courtroom landscape. "I have not seen a single document in my twenty years here suggesting that the cameras themselves, operating under our rules, have any negative impact on witnesses."[16]

But, he cautions, "I think cameras could have a negative impact if not managed properly, as has amply been demonstrated in cases like the Lindbergh baby murder trial and the Billie Sol Estes trial. However, Florida has taken great care to fashion a rule that provides for strict management of cameras in the courtroom."[17]

But do people in the U.S. really care if court proceedings can be televised or photographed? With no outcry from the public demanding courtroom-camera coverage, the media seem to be the only ones who favor and are fighting for it—until you consider viewer ratings. The ACNielsen Company, which tracks television viewing, reported that virtually all of the television sets in Los Angeles–area homes and 91 percent of those nationwide that were turned on the morning the *Simpson* verdicts were announced were tuned to the trial.[18] Also, as the media and their attorneys point out time and again, if viewership of televised trials weren't so high, the broadcast media wouldn't air them.

The huge public appetite for watching trials is not only indisputable, cultural anthropologist Karen Stephenson noted at a 2005 national conference on high-profile trials, it's historic. The difference, she says, is that the venue is now the television screen instead of the town square where people used to overflow courtroom galleries.[19]

The value of television coverage goes beyond prurient interest radio reporter Gail Eichenthal pointed out at a media roundtable discussion a few weeks after the *Simpson* verdicts. Eichenthal anchored coverage of the case from preliminary hearing to the verdicts for KNX's radio station. She watched televised coverage and read newspaper and wire accounts. On one occasion she saw a wire report that said something had occurred in the courtroom that Eichenthal hadn't noticed.

"I thought, my gosh, did that really happen?" she told the roundtable gathering. "I didn't see it that way. Where was I? Did I miss something?" Later, the report was corrected, she said, indicating that the wire reporter had made a mistake.[20]

Ito related a similar experience to me. He had seen a program on courtroom-camera coverage in which *New York Times* and *Los Angeles Times* reporters wrote about an exchange in the Simpson trial involving prosecutor Clark. One story had described her as snapping and sarcastic. The other had characterized her differently. But a review of video footage of the exchange showed that both of the reports were wrong.[21]

One Los Angeles judge in the camera-ban camp, who chafed at the California Judicial Council's failure to oust cameras, launched her own campaign to keep the pesky things out of, if not courtrooms, then all other areas of Los Angeles County's twenty-three superior court buildings, a number that nearly doubled when the superior court and twenty-four municipal courts merged in 2000. The rule she fashioned won court leadership approval and went so far as to require photographers and camera crews to keep lens caps on their cameras in hallways and all other courthouse areas while going to and from courtrooms where their requests had been granted.[22]

The result was disarray, vitriol, and even silliness. That was because each courthouse was left to come up with its own way of interpreting and enforcing the rule, which at times resulted in the media not getting into courtrooms despite having received judicial approval. In one courthouse, for instance, even if photographers got the requisite permission from a judge, they still couldn't take their cameras through the courthouse to get to the courtroom because security personnel said they might take pictures along the way. That, I told the supervising sheriff's sergeant at that courthouse, was akin to saying nobody should be issued a driver's license because they might run a red light or drive drunk.

Another problem was lens caps. Television cameras aren't equipped with them. So camera crews resorted to wrapping their cameras with such things as newspapers, plastic bags, and jackets to avoid violating the rule.

The court's assistant presiding judge at the time, James Bascue, who had been the criminal courts supervising judge during the Simpson trial and exhibited an extraordinarily open mind and even hand in his approach with the media, devised a way to skirt the local-rule problems. He issued court orders for each court building to designate one or more "interview areas" in which cameras could be used. Also, the lens cap requirement was deleted from the local rule. That resolved the situation to almost everyone's satisfaction.

Onerous media restrictions weren't confined to Los Angeles, however. The 2005 Michael Jackson child-molestation trial in the city of Santa Maria, in northern Santa Barbara County, is but one example of how right the prediction of Court TV's Fred Graham was. Santa Barbara Superior Court Judge Rodney Melville said the Jackson case, over which he presided, was the first time in his eighteen years as a judge that he had denied cameras, issued a gag order, or sealed case-file documents that state statute didn't require sealing.[23]

Associated Press legal reporter Deutsch contends that access across the board had worsened in the twelve years after *Simpson.* She says the secrecy in the Jackson case was excessive in the extreme and that Melville violated a major court decision, "which was the *Associated Press vs. U.S. District Court,* which holds that you cannot have prior restraint by sealing documents in advance, before they are filed, [but] he did it anyway."[24]

Melville had explained to me while the trial was still in progress that because of the pervasive pretrial publicity he had to do what he could to prevent the jury pool from becoming polluted to the point that untainted jurors couldn't be found. Once the jury was seated, however, he sealed only documents that required sealing by statute.

Lucy Dalglish, executive director of Reporters Committee for Freedom of the Press, says that based on journalists' contacts with her organization and the cases in which the committee has provided legal assistance, she has seen a definite increase in sealed records, prior restraints, secret proceedings, and gag orders on lawyers, litigants, and witnesses.

"You know there are other ways to ensure a fair trial and they should be used only as an absolute last resort," Dalglish said at the 2005 conference on high-profile trials. "You know, better voir dire, sequestration, jury questionnaires, change of venues, admonitions to the jury to not read them [news reports]. Those I think are tested and true methods. And I really worry about this attitude about, well the only way were going to have a fair trial is if nobody knows anything about it before we actually go to trial. That's troublesome."[25]

At another conference later that year on confidentiality in the courts and media, Dalglish said that gag orders might arguably be justified in a few cases, "But as a result of them, we're limiting information on run-of-the-mill cases out there. And there's no good reason for it."

Gag orders also lead to incomplete, inaccurate, and speculative information, she said. "[R]eporters are going to do a story," she said.

> The question becomes do you want them to do the story with good information or do you want them to find some so-called expert out there and put them on television, or just get them to speculate when the people who actually know what's going on are prevented from even having the slightest conversation with the media about even procedural things. When that happens you have—you are limiting the ability to accurately report on what's going on. Instead, you are forced to go out and find someone to speculate about what is probably going on.[26]

Despite being able to offer a great deal of anecdotal information, though, just as the media and First Amendment advocacy groups can't quote statistics on camera-coverage requests, neither do they keep records on gag orders, sealed documents, or closed proceedings. Nevertheless, they and their attorneys maintain that such measures became commonplace in high-profile cases for years following *Simpson*.[27] Many in the media and some defense attorneys not only question their effectiveness, but also contend that they're counterproductive and generally not enforced, even by the most well-intentioned judges.[28]

Colorado Fifth Judicial District Chief Judge Terry Ruckriegle told conference attendees in 2005 what happened when he issued a gag order in the 2004 Kobe Bryant case in the tiny town of Eagle, Colorado. Although he thought he was prepared to enforce it, as the trial date neared, the "barrage of commentary, including on the national media," from the accuser's attorneys among others, forced him to rethink; he grew concerned about getting caught up in a "sideshow atmosphere" of gag-order side issues. "I really didn't want to do that," Ruckriegle said. "I wanted to get the case to trial, particularly in the last month before. I felt that there were greater issues that I needed to tackle."[29]

Defense attorney Mark Geragos argues in his 2006 *Loyola of Los Angeles Law Review* article that gag orders, also called protective orders, are even prejudicial against defendants. "Although courts originally designed gag orders as a means to protect the defendant from unrelenting prejudicial pretrial publicity, they no longer effectively serve that purpose," Geragos writes. "Instead of acting as a prophylactic shield protecting the defendant, such orders have actually becomes a weapon in the prosecution's arsenal."[30]

Geragos tracks the process that starts with a prosecution press conference announcing that a suspect, whose photograph is generally shown, has been charged with a crime. The announcement describes incriminating evidence, "which," Geragos says, "in my experience is often inadmissible—accompanied by pronouncements that the crime has been solved."[31]

The prosecutor's next step, according to Geragos, is to ask the court for a gag order, which in essence bars the defense from responding to the prosecution's claims. The problem is compounded by others who work with the prosecution, such as law enforcement agencies, who give reporters tips or information, and lawyers whose services are offered to prosecution witnesses. Those lawyers "then parlay their 'representation' into constant media appearances pronouncing the guilt of the accused," Geragos says. "Thus, even though the gag order's intent was to shut down the publicity, as a practical matter it ends up compounding misinformation and rumor."[32]

The specter of *Simpson* continues to haunt courts far and wide. As recently as 2007, nearly twelve years after the *Simpson* verdicts, officials in Canada and in states in this country, such as New York, Connecticut, and Indiana, cited it as a compelling argument for not allowing camera coverage in their courts.

A Connecticut state's attorney voiced his opposition in June 2007 to that state expanding its courtroom-camera rules to include trial courts.

"Eleven years ago, the O. J. Simpson trial in Los Angeles underlined most of these concerns," said Jonathan Benedict. "While courtroom professionals are expected to approach their tasks with professionalism and maturity, being on television inevitably poses a distraction that can interfere with the accomplishment of those tasks."[33]

Despite such opposition, though, Connecticut's new rules, effective January 1, 2008, allow television and print cameras in civil trials and pretrial proceedings. A two-year test program allows camera access to criminal cases in one judicial district, with judges then deciding if that should become the standard statewide. The rules also put conditions on judicial discretion where previously there were none.[34]

Media restrictions are also easing elsewhere. In California, Judge Larry Paul Fidler became a vanguard when he allowed camera coverage of record producer Phil Spector's 2007 trial for murder. In announcing that his decision to permit cameras, Fidler said judges needed to get over the fear that has gripped them since *Simpson*, which he said "made an unwilling celebrity of Ito."[35]

"They don't want what happened to Judge Ito to happen to them," Fidler said. "In essence, what nobody wants is another *Simpson*. . . . In my mind, at some point we have to get past that trial."[36]

Reynolds Center for Courts and Media's Hengstler sees Ito as the third victim in the Simpson case. "Overwhelmingly he was perceived by both the media and the judiciary to have lost control of the trial. Media commentators still refer back to the trial. Judges still say they don't want to be the next Judge Ito."[37]

Los Angeles KNBC-TV news director Bob Long, who represents California on the board of the Radio-Television News Directors Association, is quoted in a *San Francisco Chronicle* article as saying that the consensus among the media is "that enough time has passed since Judge Ito and O. J. Simpson that not every judge wakes up every morning thinking of looking like an idiot on television."[38]

Such statements, however, illustrate the dichotomy of the *Simpson* phenomenon specifically and of courtroom-camera coverage in general. If, in fact, the *Simpson* debacle was rooted in Ito's trial mismanagement and his posturing for the cameras, then why do other judges worry about looking like idiots if they allow camera coverage of their proceedings? If, on the other hand, cameras actually do make judges look like idiots, why do judges blame Ito for the cameras making him look like one?

Legal scholar Erwin Chemerinsky's conclusion probably hits close to the truth. "I think judges would just as soon not have their behavior watched and scrutinized," he says. "I think that is a human tendency."[39]

ABA Journal editor and former court information officer Edward Adams told attendees at the 2005 national conference on high-profile cases that when he served as a federal court public information officer he advised against courtroom-camera coverage to protect judges from themselves.

"Ito is sort of the classic example of how things can go awry," said Adams, who left the U.S. District Court's Eastern Division in 2006 to assume the *Journal* editorship. "[Judges] expound from the bench. They make comments which are unnecessary. They fight with lawyers in a public way." Banning cameras, he says, is "one thing that you can do to try and avoid that problem."[40]

That might be a good argument for more camera coverage, according to legal scholar Laurie Levenson. "I . . . think that in some cases, cameras in the courtroom will actually make the judges and lawyers be on better behavior," Levenson says.[41]

Although it's difficult to quantify the degree to which courts have shunned camera coverage of their proceedings post-*Simpson,* anecdotal evidence abounds.

In a 1997 *NJC Alumni Magazine* article, First Amendment Center founder John Seigenthaler and First Amendment scholar David L. Hudson wrote about the history of courtroom cameras:

> After the O. J. [Simpson] case many judges reacted like Judge Lawrence Antolini, the judge in the child molestation murder trial of convicted Polly Klaus [*sic*] killer Richard Davis, who said 'Nothing like the O. J. Simpson case is going to happen in my courtroom.' . . . The O. J. criminal case caused several states, such as California, New York, and Connecticut, to rethink or amend their rules regarding camera coverage.[42]

Retired jurist Mudd of San Diego thinks judges who are confident of their competency have nothing to worry about. Based on judges he's talked to, he believes their reticence stems not from fear but rather a reluctance to be in a fishbowl.

"When I speak of having 'confidence in your competency,' I mean a willingness to do your job for all to see and comment on, regardless of how critical that commentary may be."[43]

The irony is that's exactly what Ito did. Rather than being unsure of or concerned about his ability or how it might be perceived, he acted on his belief in public access to the courts and was confident enough to put his courtroom and judicial competence on the line for all to see and comment on. While a common perception is that Ito was too aware of the courtroom cameras, the AP's Linda Deutsch disagrees. Ito was the one person in the Simpson trial who didn't play to the cameras, she says. "I remember him in other cases. He was always the same."[44]

While Ito perhaps did not play to the cameras in a conventional way, retired broadcaster David Dow, who covered the Simpson case for CBS radio, believes cameras did affect the manner in which he handled the case. "I did not have the impression Judge Ito 'played' to the camera in the usual sense," says Dow, of the University of Southern California's Annenberg School of Journalism. "But I think the presence of the camera may have prompted Ito to be especially cautious, patient and indulgent in hearing arguments on evidentiary issues, which many mistook for weakness and lack of control. His extreme caution probably helped prolong the trial."[45]

Interestingly, aside from the lawyers in the Simpson case, who were obviously less than objective, those who were in the courtroom every day or who have studied the case transcript have a different view of the trial and all of the attendant ramifications than do people who observed it sporadically or who, because of their day jobs, which includes most if not all judges, had to rely on nightly TV recaps and newspaper accounts, all of which were replete with punditry and speculation.

Some who watched the trial closely, such as AP reporter Deutsch and Irvine law school dean Chemerinsky, think the verdicts were a key factor. Deutsch says people blamed Ito for the acquittals. Chemerinsky thinks another dynamic was also at play. "The country was mesmerized by the trial," he says, "but ashamed of being so obsessed. Lance Ito unfairly got the blame."[46]

A vital question that has yet to be explored, though, is what the consequences would have been had cameras not covered the trial and Simpson had been convicted. That is an especially relevant question in light of the

1992 riots sparked by acquittals in the Rodney King–beating trial, as well as reaction to other trials, not only in Los Angeles but elsewhere, in which African Americans believed justice was not well served. That, as Reginald Denny–beating trial judge John Ouderkirk has said, was his primary reason for allowing the Denny trial to be televised.

Enabling the public to see if justice is being administered fairly and equitably is a major argument for courtroom-camera coverage. People should be able to see for themselves if judges, prosecutors, or defense attorneys are asleep or drunk in court, which has occurred even in death penalty cases.[47] They should also be able to see and assess a judge's behavior for themselves, as they did Florida judge Larry Seidlin's in the 2007 hearing to determine the disposition of Anna Nicole Smith's remains.

While judges cite anomalies like *Simpson* for denying cameras, the public becomes the ultimate loser. With 80 percent of Americans relying on television for news, Court TV's Graham says that people remain largely uninformed about socially significant cases such as that of African American James Byrd Jr. in Jasper, Texas, who was dragged to death behind a pickup truck; the gay-bashing murder in Laramie, Wyoming, of student Matthew Shepard; the Texas insanity-defense trial of Andrea Yates, who drowned her four children; the trial of Richard Allen Davis, whose murder of Polly Klaas prompted California's "three-strikes-you're-out law;" and the Virginia trials of snipers John Allen Muhammad and Lee Boyd Malvo.[48]

Graham gives as an example of such "through the looking-glass" thinking, Fairfax County, Virginia, Circuit Judge J. Howe Brown Jr., who said, "It is the very high-profile nature of this case that makes it unique and makes cameras inappropriate," when he denied cameras in the trial of a Pakistani man accused of killing two CIA employees in Virginia.[49]

Another example is the so-called twentieth hijacker of 9/11, Zacarias Moussaoui. Moussaoui pled guilty then, after receiving a life sentence instead of the death penalty, filed a motion to change his plea. He had pled guilty because he thought a trial would have been a farce. After his experience in the U.S. judicial system, however, he realized that he could, in fact, get a fair trial, which had prompted him to want to change his plea.[50] For the public, particularly for fundamental Islamists, both in the United States and abroad, to be able to witness the proceeding in which Moussaoui's statement was read might have been significant.

Significant trials in other countries that have been televised include the 2007 Spain train bombing in Madrid,[51] the 2002–2006 proceedings of Slobodan Milošević at the UN's International Criminal Tribunal for the Former Yugoslavia in The Hague,[52] Netherlands, and the 2006 trial of Saddam Hussein in Iraq.[53]

Graham points out the irony. "This reasoning produces a perverse result," he told the 2003 meeting of chief judges. "The more important a case is to the public, the less likely the public is to be informed about it."[54]

First Amendment Center executive director Gene Polincinski says while judges might see such restrictions as a way to protect the process in the short term, the overall result is a public that is less informed about the judicial system.[55]

The priority, cultural anthropologist Stephenson says, should be "to continue the dialogue and to remain professional in the treatment of each other not only for the sake of a more workable relationship, but to absorb innovation, which both the courts and the media need to do in order to better understand each other and to better serve the public."[56]

Chapter 14

. . . And Beyond

■ ■ ■

Shortly after the 1997 Simpson wrongful-death civil trial, *Court Manager* magazine ran an article I wrote, titled "What a Difference a Lens Makes." In it I contrasted Simpson's two trials, only one of which was televised, and the Menendez brothers' two trials, of which only one was televised. Of note was the media's reaction to a judge's meeting with a juror.

While they had shown an insatiable appetite for information and tidbits about the *Simpson* criminal jurors, the press demonstrated a marked lack of interest in the civil jury. That was exemplified in an incident near the end of that trial when the judge instructed a juror who had sent him a note to confer with him and the attorneys at sidebar. Court was in session, and the media were present. None, however, asked about the subject of the juror's note or the sidebar conference, and the news carried no reports about it that night or the next day. By contrast, if a juror in the criminal trial so much as burped, the press would have been full of questions. When asked about the media's lack of curiosity about the civil juror's sidebar conference with the judge and lawyers, a print reporter said, "Well, there's no camera in here. No one saw it, so no one asked me about it."[1]

Based on that exchange and the overall premise of the article, readers might conclude that I would argue against courtroom cameras. But I didn't and still don't, although I think there should be conditions. Former California First Amendment Coalition general counsel Terry Francke has it right in saying that cameras should be the norm and should be standard issue in all courtrooms.

"Whether they are taping or not, and I think no one should be told when they are taping," says Francke, now general counsel for the open-government advocacy group Californians Aware. "Make them part of the architecture, as they are so many other places now. But don't call attention to the fact [that they are] taping."[2]

The conditions I would add are that

• each camera be limited to a fixed, medium-wide shot of the courtroom well that shows all of the trial participants, except the jury (only in the state of Florida may jurors be photographed), minors, undercover law enforcement officers, and other individuals on a case-by-case basis in exceptional and rare situations,

• courts, not the media, own the cameras,

• cameras be installed and controlled by the court,

• media be provided immediate and unrestricted access to photographs, footage and/or broadcast signal,

• the coverage be routinely streamed onto the Internet.

Enabling public access that way would help minimize what I consider the biggest bugaboo in courtroom-camera coverage, and that is the way the media use cameras to exaggerate, embellish, and even create drama.

Whether or not Los Angeles Superior Court Judge Larry Paul Fidler knew about my article, he came up with a similar idea four years after its publication. Amid much head-shaking by his judicial colleagues, Fidler said the media could televise the 2001 trial of Sara Jane Olson.

Olson, the exemplary wife of a St. Paul, Minnesota, physician and mother of two, was secretly Kathleen Soliah, a 1970s radical Symbionese Liberation Army member charged with conspiracy to commit murder by planting a bomb under a Los Angeles police car. Fidler was going to let the media install two small cameras on his courtroom wall that could get shots of proceedings without violating prohibitions against showing jurors or spectators. (The ban on photographing spectators was included in the 1997 state electronic-coverage rule revision.)[3]

That trial was aborted, however, when Olson struck a plea deal.[4] A second chance came Fidler's way six years later when the trial of celebrated record producer Phil Spector unfolded in his courtroom. Despite a few unexpected legal grenades and lawyer shenanigans, televising that trial went off without much of a hitch. Granted, it had minuscule onsite media presence during the bulk of the trial compared to the mega-media phenomena that *Simpson* and *Jackson* became. But neither that trial nor subsequent proceedings, when the first one ended with a hung jury,[5] came close to the circus that camera critics had predicted.

Although criminal defense lawyers have historically opposed camera coverage of their clients' trials, some, in the wake of what they say have been media misrepresentations and distortions of nontelevised trials, are reconsidering the drawbacks versus benefits.

Michael Jackson's lawyer, Thomas Mesereau, has talked in favor of a C-Span type of coverage for court proceedings and Scott Peterson's attorney, Mark Geragos, has also revised his thinking. "I think we should have had camera coverage to get the facts out there for people to form opinions for themselves," Geragos said at a high-profile–trial conference in 2005. "The venom the public expressed about Scott Peterson was based on urban legends. It was not based on the evidence presented at trial."[6]

Connecticut defense lawyer Richard Meehan is another camera proponent. "It serves not only to educate the public but really requires both the lawyers and the judge in a case to be as sharp as they can because it would not be just the jurors evaluating them now," Meehan said in 2007 when Connecticut judges approved regulations that expand camera access in courts there.[7]

Stan Levco, an Indiana prosecutor, is among those who favor cameras. "The more the public knows about how we do our jobs, the better off we all are in government," Levco told a New York newspaper soon after his state started allowing limited courtroom-camera coverage. "We have nothing to hide."[8]

Even some law-enforcement officials want cameras. In September 2007, Ron Bolin, who retired as a major from the Minnesota State Patrol, said televising court proceedings is in the public's best interest because it exposes incompetence, bias, and inane rulings. "Over my tenure," the thirty-year police veteran wrote in a letter to the online edition of the *Minneapolis Star Tribune*, "I have had judges take actions that certainly needed some oversight—and not the quasi-secretive methods often in play by the present system."[9]

By 2007, the C-Span approach had begun to gain some traction, but not on television. Free of ratings concerns, commercial breaks, or the intrusion and spin of commentators, a Wisconsin court provided the best-of-all-public-access worlds when it permitted the trial involving a particularly heinous crime with a highly controversial defendant to be streamed onto the Internet.

The accused, Steven Avery, had been exonerated by DNA nearly four years earlier after serving seventeen years of a thirty-two-year prison sentence for assault and rape.[10] A short time after his release, he accepted a $400,000 settlement for wrongful conviction.[11] His arrest for the 2005 mutilation and murder of Teresa Halbach sent shock waves across the state.[12]

The trial, with its lurid details of the crime, the evidence, and the possible involvement of Avery's nephew, who had confessed then recanted,[13] had all the elements for media sensationalism. This seemingly made-for-TV trial was broadcast on local channels in the Green Bay, Wisconsin, area with coverage reaching to the crime-scene town of Gibson. Many people who followed the trial, however, didn't watch it on TV. They turned on their computers for gavel-to-gavel coverage. Both the court and the media gave the coverage high marks.

"We have been broadcasting live video from the courtroom on our Web site (http://www.htrnews.com/)," the *Manitowoc Herald Times* editorialized. "There is no narration or talking heads to tell you what you just saw. Just cameras set up in the courtroom to capture the sights and sounds of the trial as they happen."

"This is not the artificial high drama of television," the editorial continued, "but it is the high drama of real life."[14]

The trial judge, Patrick Willis, said that from his perspective, "the media acted responsibly in following the court's orders relating to courtroom coverage of the trial. I believe the streaming video coverage of the court proceedings was in keeping with both the spirit and the letter of court rules providing that court proceedings be open to the public."[15]

While the word *unfiltered* is generally used pejoratively in Internet lingo—think bloggers, unedited, distorted, uncensored, radical, irresponsible, and wrong—it can be an asset for advocates of public access to the courts.

Fred Graham says Court TV routinely streams "obscure and not-so-obscure trials on the Internet." Interestingly, he adds, while some judges have an aversion to letting trials in their courtrooms be televised, "this distaste doesn't seem to rub off on presenting trials on the Internet, perhaps because the O. J. case was on television, not the Internet."[16]

Graham, who predicted the long-term impact of the Simpson trial, called the shots right again in 2005 with the idea of not only routinely streaming trials gavel to gavel but of another innovation. "Court TV recently created a Website where we simultaneously stream an assortment of trials without commentary or advertising, and we have found almost no resistance from judges and lawyers. . . . Perhaps the Internet is where the C-Span of the Third Branch will eventually find its home."[17]

That has already happened in some European countries. The February 2007 trial in Spain of the 29 defendants accused in the 2004 train bombings that killed 191 people and wounded nearly 2,000 others was streamed onto the Internet. The court arranged with a private legal services technology company, Datadiar, to offer a "courtroom version of C-Span," according to a newspaper account.[18]

The court "has opened the bunker-like courtroom wide to cameras with four posted at different angles in the room and a fifth to show documents presented as evidence," the *International Herald Tribune* reported. "Forty-three microphones are scattered among the tables of the lawyers, permitting instant recordings stored on DVDs."[19]

Although the Datadiar Web site offers primers explaining the legal process, it does not provide chat forums.[20]

The court's presiding judge, Javier Gómez Bermúdez, scoffing at critics citing the Simpson trial in opposing cameras, said he believed coverage would create a closer relationship between the public and legal system.[21]

The Florida Supreme Court system has created its own cable operation. "It had been broadcasting all of its oral arguments live since 1997 using broadcast-quality robotic cameras installed in the courtroom, thereby providing a live and free feed directly over the Web, via cable television, and to any satellite downlink dish anywhere in North America," Florida Supreme Court communications counsel Craig Waters says. "In essence, the Court had three years' experience operating its own 'TV station' before the 2000 presidential election, albeit a TV station that existed solely to feed video and audio to other media."[22]

Internet technology has become an access and communications boon in other ways for both the courts and the media. Thanks to the Web and email, the days of having to deal exclusively in paper are history. Instead of having to individually photocopy, staple, and charge a fee for the file documents made available to each person who requests them, which was the onerous and time-consuming practice up to and including the Simpson criminal and Menendez trials, courts can post them online, where anyone in the world with Internet access can view, download, and print them out. The first iteration of providing electronic access to the media in a high-profile case debuted with the Simpson civil trial (September 1996–February 1997), in which I posted and indexed each filing onto an electronic site made available by a private vendor. To access the documents, news organizations had to subscribe and pay the vendor a fee.

Waters became the true guru of online access in the 2000 Gore versus Bush presidential election controversy. Although his court had been posting documents online for six years, Waters says, the flash flood of hits for Gore versus Bush filings crashed the system. By creating a Web site dedicated exclusively to that case, Waters opened the gates to timely, efficient, inexpensive, and equal-opportunity access to case filings.[23]

The Michael Jackson trial in Santa Barbara County brought a change in California rules that enabled the court to post criminal filings in extraordinary cases online, which previously had been prohibited. In addition to putting documents on the Web site, the court posted media guidelines and advisories, which cut down substantially on phone calls and visits to their and other offices from members of the media seeking information.

Court executive officer Gary Blair's court produced a DVD describing how the Web site was created, which includes perspectives from members of the media and the Santa Barbara legal community. "The reason why we decided to use a Web site is that right after the arrest of the defendant we began to get hundreds of calls from the worldwide media" with all kinds of questions, Blair explains on the DVD. "We then could foresee a huge demand for documents that would ultimately be filed in the case, which would put a huge burden on our clerk's office."[24]

The online postings not only "democratized" the information by making documents available at the same time to everyone, it worked to keep the information accurate. "My belief is that it's better to let the court drive the train of information," Blair said, "rather than let someone else do it and put perhaps all kinds of sensational headlines on it that don't exist."[25]

In the DVD about the Web site creation, Blair lists the benefits both the media and his court derived from it, not the least of which were that it enabled the court to survive the media and public onslaught and that, he estimates, it saved the system more than a million dollars. "We received overwhelming positive feedback from everyone who's accessed our Web site," Blair says, adding that the savings were in not having to hire staff or purchase supplies to deal with the demand.[26]

Although such developments are encouraging, reforms cannot all be technological. They must include a change in philosophy, perhaps even a return to core values, corny as that might sound in this modern, sophisticated era. Retired broadcaster David Dow says that at the risk of sounding naive or arrogant, he believes the media have an educational role to play. "News people should seek out opportunities to sit down with judges and discuss their mutual concerns and dispel some of the myths," Dow says. "For instance, one of the most common criticisms of courtroom television coverage I hear goes something like this: 'But the television stations only show selected snippets of the trial.' Judges need to be reminded that that is exactly what the print media does—uses selected quotes or snippets of testimony."[27]

At the same time, members of the media need to educate themselves by learning about the court systems they cover. Peter Shaplen, who served as the media's pool producer on the Peterson and Jackson trials, agrees. "Reporters and producers must learn the language and know the process," he says. "When a reporter arrives at a court and asks, 'So, in the trial, who speaks first?' It isn't an auspicious start."[28]

Says Dow, "I have heard reporters in the nation's number-two television market [Los Angeles] refer to 'guilty' verdicts in civil trials. A good reporter knows the distinctions between criminal and civil proceedings. If we want access to judicial proceedings we must respect them enough to learn the basics about them."[29]

Failure to do so plays into what cultural anthropologist Karen Stephenson believes is an even greater failure. "If an informed society is important in a democracy," Stephenson said at the 2005 high-profile–trial conference, "then both the media and the courts deserve failing grades so far as public understanding of the judicial system or knowing if fairness is prevailing in the country's courtrooms is concerned."[30]

Education is what Donald W. Reynolds Foundation officials had in mind when they funded, first, a national conference and, second, a permanent institution in response to the Simpson trial.

Through the National Judicial College at the University of Nevada, Reno, the Reynolds Foundation sponsored a conference in 1996, drawing a virtual who's who from judicial and journalism circles concerned with high-profile trials. Four years later the Donald W. Reynolds National Center for Courts and the Media opened. Since then, the center has provided courses for judges, journalists, and court administrators; coordinated regional judge-journalist workshops across the country; and hosted national conferences on topics from high-profile cases to media and court confidentiality.[31]

"The Center owes its existence to the O. J. Simpson criminal trial," the center's director, Gary Hengstler, says. "More to the point, we were started because of the public's dissatisfaction with the way both the courts and the media appeared to have conducted themselves in that trial."

Although *Simpson* was the trigger, the gun had already been loaded by unpopular outcomes in earlier trials of the 1990s. A majority of the public took issue with juries that acquitted four police officers in the 1992 Rodney King–beating case and that hung in the Menendez brothers' first trial in 1994, Hengstler says.

Then came *Simpson* with not only an unpopular outcome, but also unprecedented and unrelenting commentary pounded into the public psyche saying that the verdicts were wrong, and the trial was flawed, and it was the judge's fault.

Fueled by television images, Hengstler says, "This trial was etched into our consciousness like nothing any person had ever experienced before. . . . The net result was that both the courts and media—two fundamental elements of a democracy that must have the public's trust and confidence to succeed— were tarnished."[32]

Despite agreement on all sides that problems abound with high-profile trials and media coverage of them, and the countless symposia, conferences, workshops, and discussions focusing on possible fixes, Hengstler says, "It's still crazy after all these years."[33]

Why is that? Why do media melees erupt anew with court cases such as those that involved Terri Shiavo, Anna Nicole Smith, and Paris Hilton?

Part of the answer is embedded in the overall direction of American media news, a discussion of which could fill an entire book by itself. Briefly, though, news has become increasingly bottom-line–oriented. With news programs evolving from the loss-leaders they were before the mid-1960s to joining the clamber for higher ratings and advertising revenue, television has set the trend of covering what sells rather than what's important. That blurred then nearly obliterated the lines between a serious commitment to inform and dedication to the more profitable business of entertaining. John McManus, director of a California State University, San Jose–based project, www. GradeTheNews.org, has speculated that a factor in erasing those lines comes from the marketing side of news organizations. McManus has cited the Laci Peterson murder as an example of what he calls "market-driven journalism."

"Instead of producing socially responsible journalism, news organizations are increasingly marketing personal tragedies to attract audiences inexpensively," says McManus. "Stories are chosen and reported to maximize return to shareholders rather than maximizing public understanding of the world around them."[34]

In an interview for National Public Radio's "On the Media," McManus said the Peterson case is "a story that the marketers who now run many newsrooms search for. This case had all the elements that promised a tragedy they could really cash in on, and those elements are a handsome suburban couple, adultery, you had a pregnant woman missing on Christmas Eve, you had enormous sentimentality."[35]

In 2004, Drake University journalism professor emeritus Herb Strentz questioned the direction of journalists' ethics when he posted a comment on a journalism ethics listserv. Strentz referenced a quote of fifteen years earlier by veteran journalist and *New Yorker* staff writer Janet Malcolm, who said, "Every journalist who is not too stupid or too full of himself to notice what is going on knows that what he does is morally indefensible. He is a kind of confidence man, preying on people's vanity, ignorance or loneliness, gaining their trust and betraying them without remorse."

"Every journalist . . . morally indefensible," Strentz wrote, "resonates with me today as I try to stomach local and network broadcast news and as newsrooms are decimated by cuts and reductions in order to keep shareholders happy and Wall Street analysts supportive. A commitment to the 'public's right to know' runs a sorry second—at best—to the shareholder's 'right' to a 25 percent return. That does strike me as an ethical issue."[36]

Three years later Strentz says those trends continue, except that the expected return for shareholders is closer to 30 percent.[37]

Another factor in the media melee phenomenon is the proliferation of cable channels since the mid-1990s. That field, dominated by CNN and Court TV during the Simpson case, is now crowded with hundreds of round-the-clock cable channels and has become a $100-billion-a-year business.[38] That has created a nonstop scramble to fill a relentlessly needy twenty-four–hour programming maw.[39] A growing chunk of that hole is being filled with ever more banal, shout-baiting hosts and tag-team pundits, which synergistically reflect and feed an increasingly superficial society.

And if a high-profile case is in the spotlight, defense attorney Mark Geragos says in a *Loyola of Los Angeles Law Review* article, reporters "discuss the case as if they observe minute-by-minute action. The news story begins to take on the ESPN sports model, where journalists report that the prosecution had a good day, the defense is playing catch up, the witness took a beating, etc."[40]

On September 20, 2007, news of a major controversy over American mercenaries in Iraq, busloads of civil rights activists descending on a Georgia town torn apart by a racial incident, and a debate over what constitutes torture in the interrogation of terrorist suspects was shoved aside for wall-to-wall coverage of O. J. Simpson leaving a Las Vegas courthouse after his arraignment on robbery and other charges.

TV Squad blogger Bob Sassone noted the media's goosing of the outsized coverage when he commented on MSNBC anchor Nora O'Donnell repeatedly exclaiming how interesting it was to be watching Simpson once again being driven in a car, reminiscent of the 1994 slow-speed Bronco chase, then asking, "Why is this getting so much media attention?"

"Maybe," Sassone wrote, answering O'Donnell's question, "if the media didn't cover it so much they wouldn't have to ask why it's being covered so much."[41]

The downside of bloggers, however, is that they are among the earthmovers that are altering the news-media landscape.

"The rise of bloggers, many of which are highly partisan and inflammatory [such as] Scottisinnocent.com and the Michael Jackson fan sites also contribute to the noise surrounding the trial," pool producer Shaplen says. "Now that we have seen the rise of attorney-sponsored legal news Web sites in the guise of impartial news gathering but in fact are anything but—I refer to Mark Geragos's own www.thejusticesystem.net—scene becomes evermore clouded."[42]

Retired broadcaster Dow says the educating he would like to see journalists do must reach beyond the judiciary. Journalists' obligation should include educating the public about what they do and how they differ from the rabid and rabble-rousing crowd of cable-television personalities. Even media-savvy judges can become confused, as did retired Rhode Island jurist Robert Pirraglia, who is a staple at National Judicial College media-relations programs, when he referred during a national conference to Nancy Grace, a former prosecutor who's now a CNN talk-show personality, as a journalist.[43]

Journalists need to do a better job of separating themselves from the clamor rather than contributing to it. They need to promote and practice more transparently the commitments cited in the Society of Professional Journalists' mission, which include "stimulating high standards of ethical behavior."[44] They need to start redrawing the line between journalism and entertainment, to find creative ways in this era of media consolidation and corporate-profit bottom lines to distinguish themselves as serious journalists.

The Radio-Television News Directors Association (RTNDA) promotes itself as "the world's largest and only professional organization exclusively serving the electronic news profession" and boasts a membership of more than three thousand.[45] Its code of ethics opens with the preamble, "Professional electronic journalists should operate as trustees of the public, seek the truth, report it fairly and with integrity and independence, and stand accountable for their actions." The first of the code's six basic tenets is public trust. The passage says, "Professional electronic journalists should recognize that their first obligation is to the public."[46]

The RTNDA code is similar to that of the Society of Professional Journalists (SPJ), which, with more than nine thousand members, is the largest organization for both print and broadcast journalists.[47] SPJ Ethics Committee chairman Andy Schotz, in the September 2007 issue of SPJ's magazine, *Quill*, writes:

> We strive to be accurate and fair, of course. We try to be sensitive in telling stories of grief. We don't take sides in news stories.
>
> But are those basics enough?
>
> Don't we have a duty to find stories that matter to our readers, not just stories that fall into our e-mail in-baskets?[48]

While ethical codes are voluntary for members of the news media and constitutionally cannot be mandated by the government, most serious journalists cite them in conferences and grapple with situations that test them.

Concerns raised by Schotz and NBC news producer Nina Zacuto are laudable (see chapter 5), but journalists need to do more to distinguish their profession than preach to the choir at conferences and in their trade and association publications.

Fueling the current crossover between entertainment and news is the confluence of the First Amendment freedom of the press guarantee and the public's right to know. The media seem to equate the two, but they are not the same. It is as if by exercising their First Amendment right the news media are automatically meeting and serving the public's right to know. In acting on that erroneous assumption, the media turn the likes of an O. J. Simpson trial into a burlesque show. Judges, in turn, react by pulling courthouse shutters closed. Neither behavior serves either the public's best interest or the people's right to know.

Lagging behind other courts in the United States is the federal system. Federal courts bar cameras not just from courtrooms, but also from courthouses. As a result, most members of the public cannot observe and determine for themselves if the courts are functioning appropriately.

The value of televising trials has also been demonstrated in the Balkans country of Croatia. A survey commissioned by a Serbia-based nongovernmental organization examined the openness of war-crimes court proceedings in Serbia, Kosovo, Croatia, and Bosnia-Herzegovina. The resulting report found that judges tend to behave more professionally and to respect all of the parties' rights when cameras cover court proceedings. Perhaps more significantly, televising war crimes trials had a profound effect on viewers.[49]

"The living word of victims has more influence than any newspaper story ever could," says report coauthor Milos Milić with the Serbia-based broadcast network B92.[50]

Milić told about a trial in Croatia in which six Serbians were charged with participating in the July 1995 massacre in Srebrenica of more than eighty-three hundred Muslim men and boys. Although Serbian courts didn't permit trials to be televised, Croatia did, and the signal reached into Serbia.

"The shock of seeing that trial completely changed the minds of the people who saw it," Milić says. "More that seventy percent of the people [in Serbia] were in denial about Srebrenica, and that was reduced to forty percent in just a matter of days."[51]

David Souter is not the only Supreme Court justice to reject cameras; opposition has been voiced by Souter's fellow justices Clarence Thomas and vociferously vocal camera critic Antonin Scalia. Thomas, taking the news media to task for what he believes is uninformed coverage, told law school students at Marshall University in Huntington, West Virginia, "Those outside the building have no idea of what goes on inside the court," according to a Huntington News Network report.[52]

By restricting public access to those who can physically attend court sessions, not even making exceptions for lawyers and legal scholars, Thomas will surely help ensure that "those outside the building" will continue to have no idea of what goes on inside the court.

While courtroom-camera coverage remains under discussion at the federal level, some states are easing their restrictions. Nebraska agreed in March 2008 on a pilot project that allows camera access to two courtroom. South Dakota repealed its trial-court camera ban, effective July 2008, although governing rules were yet to be determined when the change was approved in March.[53]

U.S. Senator Arlen Specter (R-Pa.) believes that shutting cameras out of the Supreme Court is counterproductive. Specter, who chaired the Senate Judiciary Committee in 2005, told a committee hearing then that, "opening the Supreme Court to television coverage would be 'an enormously useful tool for public understanding' and would allow the American people to properly evaluate how their government functions," according to a *Los Angeles Times* report.[54]

The media compound their own problems, though, by engaging in what can only be called piling on. Hardly a court proceeding of note since the *Simpson* verdicts goes by that there aren't shots at Ito, each cheaper, nastier, and more outlandish than ever.

Washington Post columnist Charles Krauthamer, for instance, wrote in a December 2005 column about deposed Iraqi dictator Saddam Hussein's trial, "There hasn't been such judicial incompetence since Judge Ito and the O. J. trial."[55]

The whipping-boy specter of Ito and the Simpson trial have so permeated American pop culture that mention of them show up in the most unlikely references. Texas Tech University football coach Mike Leach, discussing his team's abysmal showing in 2007, blamed the problem, in part, on being distracted by media coverage, according to a *Fort Worth Star-Telegram* newspaper story.

> "What happens with players, [it's] just like Judge Lance Ito gets in the middle of a big trial and decides it's more important for him to be a movie star than it is to be a judge," said Leach, referring to the 1995 O. J. Simpson trial.

"He had problems doing his [job] from one snap to the next. So if it can happen to good old Judge Ito, I'm sure it can happen to 18–22-year-olds."[56]

The myths, lore, distortions, and skewed perceptions are not just perpetuated in look-what-a-clever-scribe-am-I columns, they are exaggerated and embellished so that the tale grows taller with each telling. These witticisms are often made by writers and "on-air talent," some of whom hadn't even reached their teens in 1995, as noted by the *Kansan* columnist who was nine years old during the trial. But even those who were adults back then, including one who turned up on occasion in the courtroom, resort to snarky jabs as they display their desperation to be noticed and to find affirmation of their own sense of importance.

"It's O. J. Vu All Over Again with Nutso Judge," read the headline on tabloid columnist Andrea Peyser's February 22, 2007, musings. "The judge who decides tomorrow who gets custody of Anna Nicole Smith's rotting remains," writes Peyser, who attended some *Simpson* proceedings, "is doing to the state of Florida what Lance Ito did to California—turning it into a judicial laughingstock."[57]

So went the first paragraph of Peyser's overreaching comparison of Ito to Florida judge Larry Seidlin, who displayed a penchant during the Smith proceedings for reminiscing about his days as a taxi driver, commenting on the tuna sandwich he had for lunch, and even weeping over his own ruling.

Surely judges are not eager to throw themselves in front of such buzz saws as the Peysers of the world and, therefore, might be excused for wanting to bar cameras and thus spare themselves from being the objects of such vitriol and unwarranted ridicule as Peyser heaped on Ito.

Retired Massachusetts Judge Hiller Zobel, who presided over his own share of high-profile cases and has written for newspapers, summed it up at the 2005 conference on high-profile trials.

"Folks with access to the news media, that is the people who do the writing and the talking, sometimes, to use a presidential phrase, misunderestimate," Zobel quipped. "The effect that nasty words, even unjustified nasty words, have on somebody who may be completely certain that she or he has done the right thing. But here is some uninformed, snide, cynical bastard, to use a technical expression, writing impossible things—lies, vain imaginings. All I'm saying is there is a lot of power. I'm not sure that journalists, and I use that term broadly, quite always recognize how powerful that, not a weapon, but that tool is."[58]

While other factors have contributed to the decline of public access to courts, proceedings, and related information, barring camera coverage tops the list. Keeping them out, however, isn't the answer, so far as Ito is concerned.

"The public has a right to know what goes on in courtrooms," he says. They can't all get in there, so a camera allows that access. Despite what happened [as a result of *Simpson*], I believe the courts are public."[59] Ohio Chief Justice Thomas Moyer agrees. "If we believe in our system and that it's the best system, we have an obligation to let people see it function," he told a gathering of court information officers at their annual meeting in 2007.[60]

Likewise, if the news media have confidence in their ability and believe in their purpose, it will be in their and the public's best interest for the public to see the best they have to offer.

Chapter 15
A Blueprint

■ ■ ■

A few months into the Simpson trial, Ito wanted the media courtroom seating plan revised based on attendance to that point. As expected, the idea created a howl among members of the media. Everyone insisted they had perfect attendance—and even if they didn't, it wasn't their fault. (So goes occasional media logic.) But I had kept score. I had written down who was there and which seats went empty for each court session.

My posting the revised plan and grousing—not for the first time—that I felt like Solomon splitting the proverbial baby, prompted a testy exchange with a reporter.

"You treat us like children," said Jessica Seigel with the *Chicago Tribune* and the Tribune-owned TV station KTLA. "Why don't you let us work out the seating plan for ourselves, one that we can all agree on, and then see what the judge thinks about that."

I laughed.

"If you want to be treated like an adult," I told Seigel, "you should act like an adult."[1]

Boy, I noted in my journal that evening, *everybody in unanimous agreement on a seating plan . . . it would take them 'til way after the trial is over to ever come up with something everyone would agree on.*

Being rather myopic and not exceptionally creative, I didn't realize until later that Seigel might be on to something. When the next big case—*Rufo et al. vs. O. J. Simpson* (commonly called *Simpson* civil)—reared its pretrial head in 1996, I decided to give not only Seigel's idea, but even greater media self-determination, a try.

That is a critical component to a successful high-profile trial blueprint. Include the media in the planning process. I asked the news outlets that had indicated they planned to cover that trial to form a committee with representation from all news-organization categories. The committee's responsibilities included making such media-related decisions as pool-position staffing and media-allocated seating assignments in the Santa Monica courtroom where the case was to be tried. I recounted how well that worked, although no thanks to the trial judge, in the opening sentences of a posttrial article in *California Counties* magazine: "An unusual thing happened after the O. J. Simpson civil trial," I wrote. "Compliments flew."[2]

The media, for the first time since I joined the court, were given the opportunity to provide input at the planning stages of a trial that enabled the court, at no additional cost, to arrange logistics and a communications network that led to a more favorable and satisfying accommodation of their needs.[3]

The benefits included better self-policing. For example, when a Los Angeles TV reporter and producer violated a court order forbidding the media to follow or identify jurors, the district supervising judge, who took over handling media issues when the trial judge refused to deal with them, barred the reporter from the courtroom and ordered him to stay at least five hundred feet away from the courthouse. Instead of flocking to their colleague's defense, as the media had done so often with violations in the criminal trial, other members of the media petitioned the supervising judge to impose even harsher punishment, such as excluding not just the reporter, but everyone with his station from the courtroom. They got their wish a few days later. The entire station lost its seat for the duration of the trial after the reporter came within less than five hundred feet of the courthouse. That came to light when his colleagues ratted on him.

They did that, I think, because by being part of the planning and logistical process, the media felt more responsible and were "able to work more in concert with the court, public-safety agencies and courthouse neighbors," I wrote in the *California Counties* article.[4] That led to better rapport, clearer communication, greater understanding, more cooperation, and improved responsiveness among everyone involved in or affected by the trial. That, in turn, minimized misunderstandings and resulted in a more coordinated process.[5]

Although I had an excellent experience with the committee approach in *Simpson* civil, veteran broadcast producer Peter Shaplen sounds a cautionary note.

"Committees can be very dangerous, depending on when they are formed, who is included and who is excluded." Beyond egos, sensitive feelings, technological know-how and resources, Shaplen says, "The greatest difficulty is that while courts prepare weeks, indeed months in advance, the networks with their greater needs and ability are loathe to commit themselves or their resources of personnel, time and management until it is clear, to them, that the case will proceed in that venue."

The secret to my success was twofold: first, I presented the committee concept to the media early in the process, before the first pretrial hearings were held, in fact; second, the media were to select the committee members themselves, which made any problems with inclusion or exclusion their issue instead of the court's.

Rather than waiting for the storm clouds of a notorious case to gather, though, courts should collaborate now with news organizations that cover them to formulate a high-profile trial plan. Most courts will never need to activate such a plan, but as the tiny communities of Eagle, Colorado, the venue of the Kobe Bryant rape-allegation case, and Union, South Carolina, where Susan Smith was tried for drowning her two little boys, can attest, lightning can and sometimes does strike smaller courts.

A drawback to preparing such plans is that, except in rare circumstances, major media organizations, such as national networks and the largest newspapers, won't participate, yet will insist on inclusion once a case is in progress. The usual modus operandi of those entities is to parachute in, often at the last minute and sometimes with a sense of entitlement that can threaten to torpedo the best-laid plans. There are ways, as this blueprint will show, to bring them into the process even at the eleventh hour. It is a good idea to keep in mind Gary Hengstler's observation that judges value process while the journalists' objective is results. Remembering that will help everyone involved in court-media relations to anticipate and incorporate those dynamics into their planning.

Courts and the media everywhere should also memorialize their relations with each other, whether in a formalized operational plan or jotted on an index card and taped to a Rolodex, with the following bywords:

- Plan
- Prepare
- Coordinate
- Communicate
- Respect
- Remember

Another thought to keep in mind is that courts and the media need each other during calm and routine times as well as during crises and when the TV lights are blazing.

Journalists need the courts as a source of information. Just because courts are "public" with files and information that are, for the most part, public record doesn't mean that the custodians of those records will necessarily be ready and willing to provide them quickly and efficiently enough to suit the media. The fact that courts are posting an increasing number of documents online is helping to ameliorate the problem of overworked or unhurryable court employees. But by no means are all records accessible on the Web. Also, not all information the media seek is contained in documents. Human contact remains vitally important for journalists to do their jobs.

Courts also need the media. Using news outlets is the most effective and efficient means of getting essential information to the public. A good relationship helps smooth the way. It also reduces the odds of conflicts that could lead to what a court might perceive as an attack or negatively slanted coverage. That ultimately contributes to a greater public understanding of the judicial system and court process.[6]

Creating such a relationship has to be an active, not a passive, endeavor. Some courts, such as the Los Angeles Superior Court, have established standing committees composed of judges, members of the media, media attorneys, and court staff who liaison with the media. Monthly or quarterly meetings serve as forums to discuss and resolve issues of mutual concern and ideas that can be mutually beneficial. Other courts and individual judges invite reporters, photographers, news directors, producers, and camera crews from local news outlets to get-acquainted meetings and brown-bag lunches.

Donald W. Reynolds National Center for Courts and Media faculty urge journalists who attend center programs to visit and get to know judges and other officials at courts in their coverage area and to ask for court tours before a pressing occasion arises in which they need to get information from the court.[7] Journalists who do so report myriad advantages, not the least of which are finding good stories and cooperative court staff and judges, scooping their competition on important stories, and knowing who to contact and where to go in breaking-news, emergency, or natural-disaster situations.[8]

This kind of effort can't be just a onetime foray. Courts, like news organizations, can be revolving doors. Reporters, producers, and other members of the media move frequently. That situation is exacerbated by steadily shrinking newsroom budgets and editorial staffs. Judges and court officials who might be perceived as fixtures also come and go. In the few years since I left the Los Angeles Superior Court, probably half of the six hundred bench officers have left. One vehicle media and courts in many areas of the country have developed are bench-bar-media committees or advisory councils. These groups host periodic meetings and other events of interest to inform judges, lawyers, and members of the media.[9] Although such efforts have tended to be local, California Chief Justice Ronald M. George describes a statewide bench-bar-media steering committee appointed in 2008 to improve relationships among journalists, lawyers, and the courts. "The committee most likely will have various working groups," George says, "one of which may focus on high-profile trials and possibly develop a best-practices handbook to guide courts in handling such trials."

Courts are trying to help journalists follow retired broadcaster David Dow's advice to educate themselves and learn about the courts they cover. Many courts at the trial and appellate levels publish media guides that contain everything from directions to the courthouse to structure of the court system to a glossary of legal terms. George of California says the administrative office of the courts there is updating its guide to include a chapter devoted to high-profile trials. Courts' media guides can often be found both in hard copy and on court Web sites. A popular program pioneered in the 1990s by Ron Keefover, public information officer for the Kansas Supreme Court, and emulated by other courts is "Law School for Journalists." In those programs reporters and others with the news media participate in either concentrated daylong sessions or in monthly hour-and-a-half courses, such as the joint Colorado Bar Association/Colorado Judicial Department program.[10]

The Reporters Committee for Freedom of the Press, the First Amendment Center at Vanderbilt University, and the Donald W. Reynolds National Center for Courts and Media at the University of Nevada, Reno, School of Journalism are among institutions with ongoing programs. The Society of Professional Journalists and other media organizations frequently include sessions on court-media relations in their conferences.

But on-site people provide the most effective means of making the most successful links between courts and the media. A growing number of courts are employing full-time professional information officers or appointing an employee already on staff to be trained who can then serve in that capacity in addition to handling his or her primary duties. Florida is leading the country in that area. All of Florida's courts, including its highest court, have trained public information officers on staff, that state's Supreme Court communications counsel Craig Waters says. He attributes the success of Florida's liberal camera access, in part, to that policy. "I think it is no coincidence that every Florida trial court now has a PIO." Waters says. "Part of their jobs is to enforce the camera rule."[11]

Creating information officer positions was among the recommendations of a U.S. Agency for International Development–funded training program conducted in 2003 for Serbia's newly created War Crimes and Organized Crime departments. The courts and news media in that country had a history of enmity, both under the Communist and the Slobodan Milósević regimes. Most upsetting for the judges, so far as news coverage was concerned, were the inaccurate and even slanderously wrong reports. Equally upsetting for journalists was the impenetrability of the courts.

Providing a facilitator to assist journalists seemed a logical move for the courts with the new departments a good starting place. A portion of the USAID-funded project report observes,

> The court system has no mechanism for educating or informing the public about the court system, how it operates or the outcome of cases before it. . . . Secrecy and a closed court system breeds public distrust and lack of confidence. Enabling the public to see and understand how the court system operates and how cases are handled is an effective means for diffusing criticism and distrust, and can lead to the public feeling that it has a vested interest in the system. . . .
>
> The court information officer would interface with the media and assist the court with educating members of the media and the public about the court system and how it operates, serve as the court's official spokesperson and handle all media-related issues, logistics, questions, complaints, concerns and suggestions.[12]

A follow-up report eight months later, after the recruitment and training of information officers had occurred, said,

> Also significant is the improvement of news coverage of their respective areas of responsibility in terms of accuracy, objectivity and balance since the advent of their work, according to each spokesperson and as deduced from interviews with members of the media. Absent in discussions with journalists was a distrust and cynicism that was apparent in my interviews with them in connection with the September 2003 training program and the February 2004 workshop. These factors appear to be contributing to the achievement of the overall objective, which is to affect public opinion.[13]

The media hiring their own liaisons, or pool producers, to assist with prolonged high-profile cases has also proven to be a boon. Broadcast producer Shaplen served in that capacity on both the Scott Peterson and Michael Jackson trials.

Despite not always being in complete agreement with judicial orders, administrative procedures or security tactics in a trial like *Jackson*, Shaplen says, ". . . it was a solid partnership between the court and the media."[14]

Respect, or at least a demonstration of respect, goes a long way to ease tensions and minimize conflicts. Alexander B. Aikman emphasized that in an article in the *Court Manager* magazine about the Stanislaus County, California, court's media coordination on the Peterson case before it was transferred to Redwood City.

"Stanislaus did not see the media as an enemy to be avoided and fought," writes Aikman, a trial and appellate court consultant. "Rather, Stanislaus saw them as professionals who could be treated as adults, as people with a hard and important job to do who would cooperate and assist in the management policies, nonetheless, if treated fairly and given accurate, complete and timely information."[15]

Aikman cites critics who contend that the media can't police themselves.[16] Just as the media covering the Peterson case in Stanislaus defied those contentions, so did the media covering the Simpson civil trial in Santa Monica, as exemplified by their reaction to a colleague's violation there.

A few years later, when paparazzi photographers crashed a line set up for news photographers and camera crews to get shots of the man convicted of killing Bill Cosby's son as he was exiting the courthouse, a television station news assignment manager helped me block the paparazzi's shots. Afterward, photographers and camera crews ganged up on them, physically and verbally.

Essential, in my opinion, are work- and equipment-vehicle parking areas for the media. In my early years with the Los Angeles court, satellite trucks, microwave vans, and other media vehicles ringed the Criminal Courts Building and county courthouse when cases of significant interest were in progress. The media parked in no-parking zones and on sidewalks, blocked bus stops and building connecters for fire department hoses. It was a chaotic situation in which no one was happy, but no one had tried in any concerted and collaborative way to resolve it. For the Reginald Denny–beating trial, space was made available that the media could lease in a parking lot behind the Criminal Courts Building. For the Simpson criminal trial, the county rented the media a portion of a parking lot across the street from the courthouse. In Santa Monica, for the Simpson civil trial, courthouse neighbors, the Rand Corporation and the Santa Monica Civic Auditorium, leased space in their parking lots. Although courts and the media have cooperated in some instances to find mutually workable parking space for media vehicles, in some instances the media have complained about getting gouged.

"Money is a huge issue," Shaplen says. "Some of the greatest challenges have arisen when counties have attempted to inject themselves in the process. San Mateo at one time attempted what the media felt was an extortion of $51,000 per network for space on the public plaza and an additional $48,000 for parking, all demanded up front and prior to the first day of the trial."

Shaplen said an agreement between the media and Santa Barbara County for the Jackson trial was equally egregious. Initially, in exchange for $7,500 a day, the county was to provide "a laundry list of services, which in the final analysis were greatly reduced if ever provided. A protracted four-month renegotiation resulted in an eighty percent decrease in that fee, but it was a faulty agreement that should never have been initiated."

At the same time, he adds, a fee-exemption for local news outlets "on the basis of fear from retribution and negative press coverage" is particularly unfair when local media are part of a decision-making process that leads to passing fees on to nonlocal media. "[It's] an equation that is sure to result in conflict of interest and self-serving decisions to say the least."[17]

Work space for the media can be more problematic. In the days before laptops and cell phones proliferated, out-of-town journalists or those with offices more than walking distance from the courthouse lived a hellish nomadic existence. Finding no vacancy in the Criminal Courts Building media center by the time he arrived, one writer, now with CNN and a frequent legal analyst on other network shows, asked several times for space in my already cramped county courthouse office.

The degree of angst that permeated the media was captured in a nightmare described by AP correspondent Linda Deutsch, who was on constant deadline during the Simpson criminal trial and forever rushing for one of the few pay phones in the criminal courthouse hallways. She said, "I dreamed that Judge Ito had taken the witness stand and I couldn't find a telephone."[18]

Few courthouses have large spaces that can be converted to media centers for a once-in-a-lifetime "trial of the century," although that becomes decreasingly necessary as technology advances. As an alternative, courthouse neighbors, including law offices, have rented space to the media.

Refusing to pay the county fee in San Mateo, Shaplen says, the media went elsewhere, "which resulted in a boon for private landlords within a two-block walk from the court house who quickly found themselves renting office space and rooftops to network media."[19]

A church congregation in Florida capitalized on a high-profile trial in the 1980s that came to a court close to them and collected enough rent for space on its property to build a new educational wing for the church.

The Internet has also alleviated the media impact on courthouses and court staff, as described in the previous chapter. Working out a way to maximize Internet use will help the media get the information that is public but that custodians of such records might not be ready, willing, or able to provide as quickly as the media would like. Still helpful, though, is a pretrial orientation organized by the court's media liaison that allows an opportunity for all entities involved in the case, even peripherally, such as security and juror services, to discuss their concerns and expectations with the members of the media and to answer their questions about logistics, but not about the merits of the case.[20]

The press packets I compiled and distributed in the 1990s have morphed into Web-posted decorum orders. These orders, such as one Judge Ruckriegle made for the Kobe Bryant case, primarily address the court's expectations and approved media conduct and logistics.[21]

"The decorum orders and the conduct of the lawyers, the media, the defendants, the families and the fans are all contributing and interlocking attributes to the trial," says *Jackson* and *Peterson* pool producer Shaplen. "Among the very best were drafted by San Mateo Judge Mark Forcum when as [presiding judge], he was responsible for the courthouse following the [*Peterson*] change of venue from Stanislaus County."

Web sites for communicating trial-related information, however, are effective only if they are maintained and updated immediately with the most recent information. An example of a well-done Web site for that purpose is the award-winning one the Santa Barbara court created for the Michael Jackson case. The court also made a video describing the creation and function of the site, which can be seen on the Web site.[22]

In addition to posting guidelines, case filings, and media advisories on the court's Web site, the court spokesperson needs to provide updates in person as often as practicable. If there is breaking news, anticipation of breaking news, or a great clamor for information that can't be or hasn't yet been posted on a Web site, the spokesperson needs to be as visible and as accessible as possible. That might mean making statements at preannounced times and being available at the scheduled times to give the next update. Keeping those appointments even when the spokesperson doesn't have anything new to say is important, says Waters with the Florida Supreme Court. It helps calm the fears of members of the media who otherwise speculate and agitate that the reason the spokesperson didn't appear with an update is because something is happening that the court isn't telling them about.

Teamwork at the highest levels of the judiciary and administration is crucial when a high-profile case like *Simpson* threatens to overwhelm a court, as Aikman points out in his *Court Manager* article. Sometimes, for various reasons, the trial judge might choose not to take an active part in or make non-courtroom media-related decisions, as did the judge in the Simpson civil case. That led to a "two-judge" concept described in a post-Simpson civil trial report[23] and subsequent California Counties Association magazine article.[24]

Courts and media learn from each other. The media's onsite producer in the Simpson civil trial was able to work more effectively based on what was learned in both the court's and the media's experiences with the criminal trial. Peter Shaplen refined the concept as pool producer on the *Peterson, Jackson,* and other trials. Concurrently, court media-coordination strategies developed for those mid-1990s' trials have been improved and adapted to ever-advancing technology. An interesting study of all aspects of media coverage of high-profile cases, courts' preparation for them, and judges' opinions about public access can be found in two reports with accompanying DVDs funded and distributed by Donald W. Reynolds National Center for Courts and Media.[25]

Although in need of an update, the National Center for State Courts' manual, *Managing Notorious Trials,* while written for those in the court system, can be an informative guide for journalists as well.[26] As the manual demonstrates, high-profile case-media management is not rocket science. The courts, media, and bar associations also collaborate on producing media guides on the legal system and covering the courts. While some are hard copy only, most can be found on and downloaded from court Web sites. Two examples are those of Tennessee and Maryland.[27] Another useful resource is the Conference of Court Public Information Officers. The CCPIO includes members in most states, the federal judiciary, and some courts in other countries. The group's Web site at www.ccpio.org maintains a membership list with contact information.

California Chief Justice George says *Simpson* confirmed what many judges already knew: "[T]he media has a significant impact on our society, not only in terms of public perception of the judicial system but in terms of the increasing requests for access to court records. It has also made courts acutely aware of the careful preparation they must make when faced with high-publicity trials and the need to accomodate national and worldwide media attention."

Nothing about good, cooperative court-media relations is magical or mysterious. For courts as well as for the media, it requires common sense, staying aware of the big picture of media coverage, and keeping in mind the judicial system's capability and legal constraints as well as attending to the minutiae.[28] The media need to self-police, and courts should provide the opportunity and incentive for them to do so. Court officials' and members of the media's willingness to establish and sustain cordial relationships and to maintain a durable sense of humor can provide a good foundation. But all involved need to remember that the public's understanding and support of the judicial system and its respect for a responsible news media are vital to democracy.

Postscript
Where Are They Now?

■ ■ ■

Some of the larger-than-life trial participants and reporters who covered it are no longer among the living. Those who are soldier on. In yet another bizarre twist in the Simpson saga, 2007 found O. J. Simpson once again facing criminal charges, this time in Las Vegas, Nevada, involving the possible robbery of sports memorabilia. Among the hordes of media that flocked to Las Vegas to cover the story was none other than former Los Angeles prosecutor Marcia Clark with *Entertainment Tonight*. Following is a rundown of what has happened to Clark and some of the others associated with the first Simpson trial in the ensuing years, arranged in order of their prominence in the book:

Judge Lance Ito continues to try felony cases—and allow courtroom camera coverage on occasion—in the downtown Los Angeles Criminal Courts Building, which has been renamed the Clara Shortridge Foltz Criminal Justice Center.

Johnnie Cochran wrote a book. He briefly hosted a TV show, while continuing to practice law. He died of brain cancer in 2005.

Marcia Clark, after losing the murder case against Simpson, won a bonus from her boss, Los Angeles District Attorney Gil Garcetti, landed a multi-million-dollar book advance, and left her job as a prosecutor before becoming a legal commentator for the TV tabloid *Entertainment Tonight*.

Robert Shapiro wrote a book and continues to practice law in Los Angeles.

Kristin Jeanette-Meyers got her own show at Court TV before her contract was bought out by CBS where she had a number of assignments.

Roger Sandler reminisced on the *Today* show upon the deaths of Pope John Paul and President Reagan.

Linda Deutsch celebrated forty years with the AP in 2007 and continues to cover high-profile trials, including Simpson's in Las Vegas.

Andrea Ford left the *Los Angeles Times* and moved to Jamaica, where she died in 1999 from apparent heart disease.

Haywood Galbreath chronicled the trial in a book of photographs and still works in Los Angeles.

Dominick Dunne published a novelized version of the trial, still covers high-profile trials, and hosts a show, *Power, Privilege and Justice,* on Court TV, which in 2008 became truTV.

Los Angeles Superior Court Presiding Judge **James Bascue** has retired.

After the trial, **Joseph Bosco** wrote *A Problem of Evidence: How the Prosecution Freed O. J. Simpson.* He teaches writing in China.

Tritia Toyota retired from broadcasting and earned a Ph.D. in anthropology at UCLA, where she now teaches anthropology and Asian American studies.

Dennis Schatzman died in 1997, reportedly from an asthma attack.

Barry Scheck and **Peter Neufeld**, cofounders of the Innocence Project, remain with the project and teach law in New York.

Christopher Darden left the district attorney's office, published a book, dabbled in acting, taught at a Los Angeles law school, then started a law firm, Darden and Associates, Inc. In 2007, he applied to Governor Arnold Schwarzenegger for a judicial appointment.

William Hodgman remains with the district attorney's office.

Robert Kardashian died in 2003 of esophageal cancer.

O. J. Simpson moved to Florida, in part, because of more favorable bankruptcy laws following a $33 million civil lawsuit judgment against him. His Las Vegas robbery trial began a year after his September 2007 arrest.

Joseph McGinniss, instead of writing a book about the trial, went to Europe to write about soccer. In 2007, he published a "true crime" book, *Never Enough.*

Gary Klausner became a U.S. District judge in 2002.

Los Angeles Superior Court Criminal Division Supervising Judge **Cecil Mills** retired and was hired as Los Angeles Superior Court chief of court security.

Paul Flynn retired from Los Angeles Superior Court in 2006 and is a mediator with an alternative dispute-resolution mediation service.

Deirdre Robertson has received several promotions at Los Angeles Superior Court and now serves as administrator of court operations at the renamed Criminal Courts Building.

U.S. District Judge **Edward Rafeedie** died of cancer in March 2008.

Dismissed juror **Tracy Kennedy** moved to Mississippi where he and his wife died in June 2008 of gunshot wounds in an apparent murder-suicide.

Simpson's North Rockingham Avenue house in Brentwood went into foreclosure in 1997 and was bought in 1998 for nearly four million dollars. The new owner had it torn down and replaced with a new house.

Nicole Brown Simpson's Brentwood condo got a frontal makeover by its new owners to make it less identifiable to sightseers. The residences along that stretch of the street have been renumbered so that 875 South Bundy Drive no longer exists.

Mezzaluna Restaurant closed about two years after the Simpson verdicts, reopened and operated for a while as Fuzio, Universal Pasta Company, and is now a Peet's Coffee and Tea Shop.

Ruth Archie's cancer is in remission. She is living in Arizona and sends Ito an hourglass each year for his birthday and Christmas.

Notes

■ ■ ■

Introduction

1. Gary Hengstler (director, Donald W. Reynolds National Center for Courts and Media), interview by author, August 2, 2007; Jon Bruschke and William E. Loges, *Free Press vs. Fair Trials: Examining Publicity's Role in Trial Outcomes* (Philadelphia: Lawrence Erlbaum, 2003).

2. "Simpson's Trial and the Rush to Reform," editorial, *Judicature* 79, no. 2 (September–October 1995): 56, 57; "The Media, the Courts, and the Public," editorial, *Judicature* 83, no. 2 (September–October 1999): 48; "Public Trust and Confidence in the Courts: A National Conference and Beyond," *Court Review* 36, no. 3 (Fall 1999): 4–5, 17, 50; "Public Understanding of and Support for the Courts: 2007 Annenberg Public Policy Center Judicial Survey Results," Annenberg Public Policy Center of the University of Pennsylvania (accessed October 17, 2007) www. annenbergpublicpolicycenter.org; "Perception of the U.S. Justice System," American Bar Association, 1999 (accessed 2007) www.abanet.org/media/perception/perceptions.pdf; Fred Graham (senior editor, Court TV), interview by author, February 23, 2007.

3. Erwin Chemerinsky (Duke University Alston & Bird Professor of Law and Professor of Political Science, founding dean, University of California, Irvine, Law School), interview by author, April 1, 2007.

4. California Rules of Court, Rule 980, July 1, 1984 (revised January 1, 1997, renumbered 1.150 January 1, 2007); Ryan Keith, "Illinois One of Few States to Bar Trial Taping," Associated Press, September 17, 2005; Molly Treadway Johnson and Carol Krafka, "Electronic Media Coverage of Federal Civil Proceedings: An Evaluation of the Pilot Program in Six District Courts and Two Courts of Appeals," United States, Federal Judicial Center, 1994; Fred Graham, Statement before the Conference of Chief Justices, San Juan, Puerto Rico, July 31, 2003; Fred Graham, "Television, Celebrity and the Law" (John Marshall Harlan Lecture, University of Louisville School of Law, Louisville, Kentucky, October 2005); Robert Benzie, "Ontario Court

of Appeal Cameras to Broadcast Live Online," *Star,* Toronto, Canada, September 5, 2007; Joshua Rozenberg, "TV Cameras in Court Start Filming This Week" *Telegraph,* www.telegraph.co.uk, London, England, November 17, 2004; Doreen Carvajal, "Internet Site Provides Access to Inner-sanctum of Spain's 'Trial of the Century,'" *International Herald,* February 18, 2007.

5. Donald W. Reynolds National Center for Courts and the Media, Reynolds School of Journalism, University of Nevada, Reno, www.courtsandmedia.org.

6. Graham, Statement before the Conference of Chief Justices; Graham, "Television, Celebrity and the Law"; Mark Curridan (conference panelist), "From O. J. to Martha to Michael: What Have We Learned about the Conduct and Coverage of Trials?" Donald W. Reynolds Center for Courts and Media, National Judicial College, October 9–11, 2005); Rodney Melville, message to "First Amendment and Media Issues for Judges" class, Donald W. Reynolds National Center for Courts and Media, May 11, 2005.

7. Matt Krasnowski, "Phil Spector Case to Begin Monday," Copley News Service, March 17, 2007.

8. "Famed Rock Producer's Murder Trial to be Televised," Associated Press, February 19, 2007.

9. "Judge Allows Cameras at Phil Spector Trial," Reuters, March 17, 2007.

10. Linda Deutsch (special correspondent, Associated Press), interview by author, July 5, 2007.

11. Larry Elder, "The Good Times of Johnnie Cochran," Creators Syndicate Inc., June 15, 2000.

12. "The O. J. Verdict," *Frontline,* Public Broadcasting Service, October 4, 2005.

13. Ibid.

14. Author's notes, August 9 and 19, 1994.

15. Ray Richmond, "Nearly 100% of TVs Being Used in L.A. Tuned In For Verdict," *Daily News of Los Angeles,* October 5, 1995; Lee Margulies, "Huge TV Audience Saw Trial Climax," *Los Angeles Times,* October 5, 1995; Kathleen Dougherty, "On Just About Every Corner, All Eyes Fixed on Televisions," *Daily Breeze,* Torrance, California, October 4, 1995.

16. Http://workingreporter.com/ojpage.html.

Chapter 1

1. Victor E. Chavez (presiding judge, 1999–2000, Superior Court of California for the County of Los Angeles), interview by author, November 16, 2007.

2. James A. Bascue (presiding judge, 2001–2002, Superior Court of California for the County of Los Angeles), interview by author, November 15, 2007.

3. Nick Sloan, "Memories of the O. J. Simpson Trial," *Kansan,* October 7, 2005.

4. Public Admonishment of Judge Judith C. Chirlin, State of California Commission on Judicial Performance, August 28, 1995.

5. *"Sheppard v. Maxwell, Warden,* 384 U.S. 333 (1966) U.S. Supreme Court, Certiorari to the United States Court of Appeals for the Sixth Circuit, No. 490, argued February 28, 1966, decided June 6, 1966.

6. Lance A. Ito (judge, Superior Court of California for the County of Los Angeles), interview by author, March 24, 2005.

7. Author's notes, September 20, 1994.

8. Ibid., September 19, 22, 1994; Ito, interview, March 24, 2005.

9. Author's notes, September 7, 1994.

10. Governor Pete Wilson, letter to Hon. Malcolm Lucas, Judicial Council of California, October 3, 1995.

11. California Rules of Court, Rule 980.

12. Bob Egelko, "Spector Trial Renews Debate on TV in Courtroom," *San Francisco Chronicle,* April 25, 2007; "From O. J. to Martha to Michael."

13. "Celebrity Trials," *Talk of the City,* KPCC 89.3 FM, Pasadena, California, March 2, 2005.

14. William Mudd (judge [retired] Superior Court of California for San Diego County), interview by author, March 24, 2007.

15. David Dow (broadcast journalist [retired], coauthor, *Cameras in the Courtroom: Television and the Pursuit of Justice;* instructor, University of Southern California Annenberg School for Communication), interview by author, March 14, 2007.

16. Author's notes, September 2, 1994, October 16, 1994.

Chapter 2

1. Robert Shapiro, "How to Deal with the Press," *California Lawyer,* February 1994.

2. Author's notes, January 12, 1995.

3. Court Order, Media Procedures in the Criminal Courts Building during Pendency of the Case of *People v. O. J. Simpson,* Criminal Division Supervising Judges Cecil Mills, Superior Court of the State of California, Veronica McBeth, Municipal Court Los Angeles Judicial District, September 1, 1994; Amended Order, Criminal Division Supervising Judge James A. Bascue, January 27, 1995; Amended Order, Criminal Division Supervising Judges James A. Bascue, Superior Court of the State of California, Veronica McBeth, Municipal Court Los Angeles Judicial District, March 22, 1995; Amended, April 3, 1995.

4. Author's notes, July 13, 1994.

5. Susan McRae, "Is Flynn In?" *Los Angeles Daily Journal,* July 14, 1994.

6. Author's notes, July 13, 1994.

7. Lance A. Ito, "The Media and the Courts," 1994 Criminal Law and Procedure, California Center for Judicial Education and Research Division, California Administrative Office of the Courts, Monterey, California, February 26, 1994.

8. Author's notes, June 19, 1995.

9. Ibid., September 2, 1994.

10. Superior Court of California for the County of Los Angeles, *The People of the State of California vs. Orenthal James Simpson,* Case \#BA097211, trial transcript, p. 1297, September 21, 1994.

11. Author's notes, September 26, 1994.

12. Author's notes, January 25, 1995.

Chapter 3

1. "Judge Lance Ito Face to Face with Tritia Toyota," advertisement, *Los Angeles Times,* November 14, 1994, A21.

2. Ibid.

3. Author's notes, November 29, 1994.

4. Ibid., September 26, 1994.

5. Ibid., August 19, 1994.

6. Ibid., October 20, 1994.

7. "'Lance Ito: Face to Face, An Action News Special Six-Part Series, Debuts Sunday, November 13, at 11pm on KCBS-TV, Channel 2," for release November 10, 1994.

8. Author's notes, November 15, 1994.

9. Howard Rosenberg, "Judge Ito Feeds the Hand He's Bitten," *Los Angeles Times,* November 16, 1994.

10. Robert C. Fellmeth, "Just Another Nice Guy? Phooey!" *Los Angeles Times,* November 16, 1994.

11. Erwin Chemerinsky, "It's Good to Put a Human Face on a God-Like Role," *Los Angeles Times,* November 16, 1994.

12. Author's notes, August 19, September 19, September 27, October 13, 1994.

13. "A Judge's On-Camera Proceeding," editorial, *Los Angeles Times,* November 15, 1994; Bill Boyarsky, "Ito Succumbs to the Sirens of Celebrity," *Los Angeles Times,* November 15, 1994; Jim Newton and Andrea Ford, "Ito's Televised Interview Lands Him in Controversy," *Los Angeles Times,* November 15, 1994.

14. Author's notes, November 19, 1995.

15. "Celebrity Trials," *Talk of the City.*

16. Ibid.

17. Laurie Levenson (professor, Williams M. Rains Fellow, Center for Ethical Advocacy; director, Loyola Law School of Los Angeles), interview by author, April 8, 2007.

18. Leslie Abramson, "The Appearance of Justice: Juries, Judges and the Media" (Blenen Leigh Buchanan Lecture, Northwestern University, School of Law), *Journal of Criminal Law and Criminology, Chicago* 86, no. 3 (Spring 1996): 1096.

19. Don Ray, "Lance A. Ito, Superior Court of California of Los Angeles County: Judicial Profile," *Los Angeles Daily Journal,* June 3, 2005.

Chapter 4

1. Jerrianne Hayslett, *People v. Orenthal James Simpson* haiku, September 22, 1994.
2. *The People of the State of California vs. Orenthal James Simpson,* transcript, p. 1495, September 22, 1994.
3. Ibid., 1496.
4. Ibid.
5. Author's notes, September 27, 1994.
6. Ibid., September 22, 1994.

Chapter 5

1. Author's notes, author's journal, March 1, April 28, 1995.
2. Ibid., August 1, 1995.
3. *The People of the State of California vs. Orenthal James Simpson,* transcript, p. 39235, July 31, 1995.
4. Author's notes, author's journal, July 11 and 13, August 1, 1995.
5. Joe McGinniss, letter to Hon. Lance A. Ito, August 2, 1994.
6. Dominick Dunne, letter to Hon. Lance A. Ito, August 5, 1994.
7. Author's notes, January 27, 1995.
8. Ibid., January 23, 1995.
9. Ibid.
10. Ibid., May 18, 1995.
11. Ibid., June 6, 1995.
12. Author's journal, May 5, 1995.
13. Author's notes, January 26, 1995.
14. Steve Johnson (executive producer, Courtroom Television Network), letter to Jerrianne Hayslett, February 2, 1995.
15. Author's notes, February 2, 1995.
16. Author's journal, May 5, 1995.
17. Author's notes, author's journal, May 19, 1995.
18. Author's notes, author's journal, May 24 and 25, 1995.
19. Author's journal, June 6, 1995.
20. Ibid.
21. Ibid.
22. Author's notes, January 23, 1995.
23. Ibid., September 4, 1995.
24. Ibid., September 4, 1994, January 13, 20, 23, and 26, 1995.
25. Ibid., January 23, 1995.
26. Ibid., August 16, 1994.
27. Kazumoto Ohno (writer, *Bungei Shunju*), letter to Hon. Lance A. Ito, October 9, 1994.
28. Jerrianne Hayslett, letter to Kazumoto Ohno, October 16, 1994.
29. Author's journal, March 9, 1995.

30. Author's notes, author's journal, June 20, 1995.

31. Ibid., August 3, 1995.

32. Author's journal, August 7, 1995.

33. Ibid.

34. Author's notes, August 9, 1995.

35. Author's journal, August 9, 1995.

36. Bob Sassone, "An Open Letter to the Cable News Networks," TV Squad, September 21, 2007, www.tvsquad.com/2007/09/21/an-open-letter-to-the-cable-news-networks.

37. "First Amendment and Media Issues for Judges," "Basic Legal Affairs Reporting for Journalists," "Essential Court Teamwork in Dealing with the Media," courses, all Donald W. Reynolds National Center for Courts and Media, Donald W. Reynolds School of Journalism, University of Nevada, Reno.

38. "From O. J. to Martha to Michael."

Chapter 6

1. Author's notes, September 19, 1994.

2. Ibid., January 25, February 3, 1995.

3. Ibid., February 3, 1995.

4. Ibid., February 8, 1995.

5. Jeffrey Toobin, *Today,* September 10, 1996, www.radicalmedia.com/work/today/trans/1996/sep/960910.txt; Francis X. Archibald, "Toobin Critiques O. J. Simpson Trial," *State* (Columbia, SC), September 29, 1996.

6. Jeffrey Toobin, *The Run of His Life* (New York: Random House, 1996), 229.

7. Ibid., 231.

8. Ibid.

9. Ibid.

10. Author's notes, January 13, 1995.

11. Ibid.

12. Ibid., January 27, 1995.

13. Author's notes, author's journal, September 27, 1995.

14. Author's notes, July 19, 1995.

15. Ibid., April 10, 1995.

16. Paul Tyler, "The Ito I Saw, and the O. J. You Didn't," Citations, Ventura County Bar Association, 1997, http://www.tylerlaw.com/ojisaw.rtf.

17. Author's notes, November 3, 1994.

18. Ibid.

19. Ibid.

20. Ibid.

Chapter 7

1. "On Cameras in Supreme Court, Souter Says, 'Over My Dead Body,'" Associated Press, *New York Times,* March 30, 1996.

2. "Electronic Media Coverage of Federal Civil Proceedings: An Evaluation of the Pilot Program in Six District Courts and Two Courts of Appeals," report, Federal Judicial Center, 1994, 3.

3. Marjorie Cohn and David Dow, *Cameras in the Courtroom: In Pursuit of Justice* (Jefferson, N.C.: McFarland, 1998), 115.

4. Wilson, letter to Lucas.

5. California Rules of Court, Rule 980.

6. Fred Graham, interview.

7. Benzie, "Ontario Court of Appeal Cameras to Broadcast Live Online."

8. *The People v. Orenthal James Simpson,* transcript, 6451–2, November 7, 1994.

9. Ibid., p. 6453.

10. Ibid., pp. 6453–4.

11. *The People v. Orenthal James Simpson,* transcript, p. 11723, January 24, 1995.

12. *The People v. Orenthal James Simpson,* transcript, p. 6452, November 7, 1994.

13. *The People v. Orenthal James Simpson,* transcript, pp. 11723–4, January 24, 1995.

14. Ibid., p. 11724.

15. Ibid., p. 11750.

16. Author's notes, February 8, 1995.

17. Robert W. Bogle (president, National Newspaper Publishers Association, Black Press of America), letter To Whom It May Concern, June 23, 1994.

18. Matt Mahurin, cover photo-illustration, *Time,* June 27, 1994.

19. Author's notes, author's journal, March 3, 1995.

20. Ibid.

21. Ibid., January 23, 1995.

22. Author's notes, October 7, 1994.

23. Author's notes, author's journal, March 8, 1995.

24. Ibid., March 3, 1995.

25. Ibid., March 8, 1995.

26. Author's journal, March 15, 1995.

27. Ibid., May 12, 1995.

28. Ibid., June 12, 1995.

29. Bill Boyarsky, "Photographer Banished from Courthouse Isn't the Only One to Suffer," *Los Angeles Times,* June 21, 1995; author's journal, June 22, 1995.

30. Ibid., July 7–24, 1995.

31. Media Procedures, Amended Order, March 22, 1995.

32. *People v. Orenthal James Simpson* Court Order, March 30, 1995; author's journal, March 23, 1995, and April 6, 1995.

33. Author's journal, June 29, 1995.

34. Ibid., September 20, 1995.

35. Court Order, *People v. Orenthal James Simpson*, April 24, 1995; author Journal, April 25, 1995.

36. *The People v. Orenthal James Simpson*, transcript, pp. 24952–4, April 28, 1995.

37. Ibid.

38. Author's journal, April 28, May 2, 1995.

39. Ibid., July 1995.

40. Ibid., September 28, 1995.

41. Jerrianne Hayslett, "What a Difference a Lens Makes," *Court Manager* 12, no. 3 (Summer 1997) 21.

42. Gary Hengstler, interview by author, June 14, 2007.

43. David Dow, interview by author, March 14, 2007.

44. Barbara Cochran (president, Radio and Television News Directors Association), interview by author, April 8, 2007.

45. William Mudd (judge [retired], Superior Court of California for San Diego County), interview by author, February 23, 2007.

46. Deutsch, interview.

47. Graham, "Television, Celebrity, and the Law."

48. Ito, interview, March 24, 2005.

Chapter 8

1. Ito, interview, March 24, 2005.

2. "Celebrity Trials," *Talk of the City.*

3. *The People v. Orenthal James Simpson*, transcript, p. 8745, December 1, 1994.

4. Ibid., p. 1089, August 31, 1994.

5. Author's notes, October 20, 1994.

6. Lance A. Ito, letter to Los Angeles County Supervisor Michael Antonovich, March 13, 1995, cited in 1995 WL 341571, *1 (O.J.Comm.).

7. Gary Klausner, letter to Los Angeles County Counsel DeWitt W. Clinton, March 15, 1995, cited in 1995 WL 341571 *1 (O.J.Comm.).

8. Author's notes, September 28, 1994.

9. Ibid., October 2, 1994.

10. Ibid., September 28, 1994.

11. Ibid., October 2, 1994.

12. *The People v. Orenthal James Simpson*, transcript, p. 3721, October 18, 1994.

13. Ito, interview, March 24, 2005.

14. Court Order, Media Coverage of the Jury Selection, Lance A. Ito, Judge, Minute Order, D. Robertson, Clerk, August 30, 1994.

15. Author's notes, October 12, 1994.

16. Ibid., October 6, 1994.

17. Court Order, Lance A. Ito, Judge, December 12, 1994.

18. *The People v. Orenthal James Simpson*, transcript, p. 8561, November 30, 1994.

19. Vincent Bugliosi, *Outrage: The Five Reasons Why O. J. Simpson Got Away with Murder* (New York: Norton, 1996), 58–64.

20. "The O. J. Simpson Trial: The Jury," www.law.umkc.edu/faculty/projects/ftrials/Simpson/Jurypage.htm.

21. "The O. J. Simpson Trial: The Jury," http://www.law.umkc.edu/faculty/projects/ftrials/Simpson/finaljury.html.

22. Ibid.

23. Bugliosi, *Outrage*, 91–95.

24. *48 Hours Mystery*, CBS-TV, June 2, 2004.

25. Author's journal, June 1, 1995.

26. Lance A. Ito, interview by author, May 2, 2007.

27. "Shirley Jones to Sing for the OJ Jury," News Release, "News on the March," June 1, 1995.

28. Author's notes, February 12, 1995.

29. *The People v. Orenthal James Simpson*, transcript, pp. 14296–7, February 12, 1995.

30. Author's notes, February 12, 1995.

31. *The People v. Orenthal James Simpson*, transcript, pp. 14300–14323, February 12, 1995; author's notes, February 12, 1995.

32. Author's notes, March 2, 1995.

33. Michael Knox, *The Private Diary of an O. J. Juror* (Los Angeles: Dove Audio, Inc., 1995).

34. Author's journal, March 17, 1995; Tracy Kennedy, Judith Kennedy, Alan Abrahamson, and Judith Spreckels, *Mistrial of the Century* (Los Angeles: Dove Books, 1996).

35. Author's journal, April 7, 1995.

36. Ibid., April 10, 1995.

37. Ibid., April 7 and 10, 1995.

38. Ibid., April 21, 1995.

39. Ibid., May 22, 1995.

40. Ibid., April 13, 1995.

41. Author's notes, April 26, 1995.

42. Author's journal, April 26, 1995.

43. Ibid., May 2, 1995.

44. Ibid., May 4, 1995.

45. Ibid., May 17, 1995.

46. Ibid., May 5, 1995.

47. Ibid., May 17, 1995.

48. *The People v. Orenthal James Simpson*, transcript, p. 27620, May 16, 1995.

49. Author's journal, May 19, 1995.

50. Ibid., May 19 and 20, 1995.

51. Ibid., May 25, 1995.

52. Ibid., May 26, 1995.

53. Author's notes, July 6, 1995.

54. Ibid., June 23, 1995.

55. Ibid., July 26, 1995.

56. Author's journal, June 1, 1995.

57. Ibid., September 14, 1995.

58. Deliberations, Court Order, Lance A. Ito, Judge, September 28, 1995; author's journal, September 28, 1995.

59. Laurie Levenson, interview by author, March 5, 2007.

60. Fred Graham, "Television, Celebrity and the Law."

61. "From O. J. to Martha to Michael."

62. Mark J. Geragos, "The Thirteenth Juror: Media Coverage of Supersized Trials" (symposium: Celebrity Prosecutions), *Loyola of Los Angeles Law Review,* December 2006.

63. "From O. J. to Martha to Michael."

64. Ibid.

Chapter 9

1. *The People v. Orenthal James Simpson,* transcript, p. 8562, November 30, 1994.

2. Author's journal, May 12, 1995.

3. *The People v. Orenthal James Simpson,* transcript, pp. 11107–12, January 18, 1995.

4. Author's journal, May 12, 1995.

5. Author's notes, May 5, 1995.

6. *The People v. Orenthal James Simpson,* transcript, p. 3226, October 14, 1994.

7. *The People v. Orenthal James Simpson,* transcript, p. 953, August 29, 1994.

8. Author's Notes, October 13, 1994.

9. Ibid.

10. Ibid., February 3, 1995.

11. Author's journal, May 2, 1995.

12. *The People v. Orenthal James Simpson,* transcript, p. 22946, April 17, 1995; author's notes, April 17, 1995.

13. Myung J. Chun (pool photographer), *Daily News of Los Angeles, Los Angeles Times,* April 19, 1995.

14. *The People v. Orenthal James Simpson,* transcript, p. 22146, April 17, 1995.

15. Author's notes, April 17, 1995; Court TV Crime Library, Notorious Murders, Most Famous, O. J. Simpson, "Trail of Blood" www.crimelibrary.com/notorious_murders/famous/simpson/blood_12.html.

16. Author's notes, undated.

17. Author's journal, September 19, 1995.

18. Author's notes, March 16, 1995.

19. *The People v. Orenthal James Simpson,* transcript, p. 10506–7, January 9, 1995; author's notes, January 9, 1995.

20. Ibid.

21. Ibid., August 29, 1994.

22. Ibid., January 23, 1995.

23. *The People v. Orenthal James Simpson,* transcript, pp. 11943–12889, January 26, 1995; author's notes, January 26, 1995.

24. Author's notes, author's journal, June 20, 1995.

25. Author's journal, September 13, 1995.

26. Ibid., May 22, 1995.

27. Ibid., June 21, 1995.

28. Ibid., June 28, 1995.

29. Ibid., July 20, 1995.

30. *The People v. Orenthal James Simpson,* transcript, p. 48093, September 29, 1995.

31. Ibid., pp. 13744–55, February 7, 1995.

32. Dow, interview.

33. Author's journal, April 12, August 9, September 7, 1995.

34. Trial transcript, *The People v. Orenthal James Simpson,* No. BAO97211, Dept. 100, James A. Bascue, Judge, California Superior Court, p. 1, February 17, 1995.

35. Author's journal, August 16, 1995.

36. Ibid., August 17, 1995.

37. Lance A. Ito, interview, March 14, 2005.

38. Author's journal, September 11, 1995.

39. Hengstler, interview, June 14, 2007.

Chapter 10

1. www.abanet.org/judicialethics/ABA_MCJC_approved.pdf.

2. California Code of Judicial Ethics, Canon 3(B)(9).

3. California Code of Judicial Ethics, Canon 4(D)(2).

4. "Simpson Judge Has Let Lawyers Take Over Courtroom, Judge Says," Associated Press, October 26, 1994.

5. Author's notes, October 27, 1994.

6. Gary Klausner (presiding judge, Superior Court of California for the County of Los Angeles), memo to All Active and Retired Judges, "Public Comment Re: Judicial Proceedings," February 21, 1995.

7. Author's notes, August 19, 1994.

8. Ibid., December 9, 1994.

9. George W. Trammell III, "Cirque Du O. J," *Court Technology Bulletin* 7, no. 4 (July–August 1995).

10. State of California, before the Commission on Judicial Performance, Inquiry Concerning George W. Trammell III, No. 146, Decision and Order Imposing Public Censure and Order Barring Judge Trammell from Receiving Assignments, January 5, 1999; numerous newspaper and wire reports, including by Associated Press, *Los Angeles Times, Los Angeles Daily Journal, Los Angeles Daily News, Torrance Daily Breeze,* and *Metropolitan News-Enterprise,* 1997–2005.

11. Author's notes, September 28, 1994.

12. Ibid., July 26, 1995.

13. Ibid., February 17, 1995; author's journal, September 13, 1995.

14. Court Order, Superior Court of California for the County of Los Angeles, Case \#BA097211, November 21, 1994.

15. Numerous news reports, including *New York Times,* November 29, December 6, 1994; *Metropolitan News-Enterprise,* November 29, 1994; *Los Angeles Daily Journal,* November 30, December 1, 1994; *Daily News of Los Angeles,* December 3, 1994; *Los Angeles Times,* December 3, 1994.

16. Michael D. Harris, "N. Y. Judge Misled Ito, Neufeld's Lawyers Say," *Los Angeles Daily Journal,* December 5, 1994.

17. Court Order, Superior Court of California for the County of Los Angeles, Case \#BA097211, December 18, 1994.

18. Author's journal, July 19, 1995.

19. Ibid., May 16, 1995.

20. Ibid., September 14, 1995.

21. Ibid.

22. Ibid.

23. Terry Francke (general counsel, Californians Aware: The Center for Public Forum Rights), interview by author, February 23, 2007.

24. "From O. J. to Martha to Michael."

25. Lisa de Moraes, "E!'s Thriller: Floating a Jackson Trial Balloon," *Washington Post,* January 12, 2005; "Michael Jackson Puppet Theater" *Countdown with Keith Olbermann,* MSNBC, January 22, 2005. www.msnbc.msn.com/id/7277380.

26. Mudd, interview, February 23, 2007.

27. Greg Braxton and Jane Hall, "Networks Will Not Cover Case Gavel-to-Gavel," *Los Angeles Times,* November 8, 1994.

28. Hengstler, interview, June 14, 2007.

Chapter 11

1. Author's journal, April 7, 1995.

2. Melinda Henneberger, "D'Amato Gives a New Apology on Ito Remarks," *New York Times,* April 7, 1995.

3. Ibid.

4. Author's notes, April 8; author's journal, April 10, 1995.

5. Author's notes, March 17, 1995.

6. Ibid., July 25, 1995.

7. Ibid.; author's journal, July 26, 1995.

8. Author's notes, September 5, 1995; Jerrianne Hayslett, "*People v. Orenthal James Simpson* haiku," September 5, 1995.

9. "Journalists outside the Criminal Courts Building Downtown Wear Robert Shapiro Masks as They Await the Arrival of O. J. Simpson's Lawyer," Associated Press, *Daily News of Los Angeles,* November 1, 1994.

10. Author's notes, February 8, 1995.

11. Ibid., August 17, 1994.

12. Ibid., October 27, 1994.

13. Ibid., March 16, 1995.

14. Ibid., April 13, 1995.

15. Ibid., October 27, 1994.

16. Author's notes, undated (*Saturday Night Live*, aired September 24, 1994).

17. Author's journal, July 19, 1995.

18. Author's notes, November 16, 1994.

19. Court Ruling, Lance A. Ito, Judge, Superior Court of California in and for the County of Los Angeles, Case \#BA097211, December 15, 1994.

20. Author's journal, May 24, 1995.

21. Ibid.

22. Ibid., May 10, 1995.

23. Ibid.

Chapter 12

1. I marked the conclusion of the trial with another haiku. Jerrianne Hayslett, "*People v. Orenthal James Simpson* haiku," October 4, 1995.

2. Author's journal, October 4, 1995.

3. Howard Rosenberg, "Could Coverage Sink Lower? Don't Even Ask," *Los Angeles Times*, October 4, 1995.

4. Author's journal, September 14, 1995.

5. Ibid., October 3, 1995.

6. Ibid.

7. Ibid., October 6, 1995.

8. "A Judge Shall Perform the Duties of Judicial Office Impartially and Diligently," Canon 3, California Code of Judicial Ethics.

9. Author's journal, October 3, 1995.

10. Author's journal, October 24, 1995.

11. Ibid.

12. "Enough O. J.," editorial, *Daily News of Los Angeles*, October 25, 1995.

13. Susan Goldsmith and Terri Hardy, "Ito Interview Turns Student into Celebrity," *Daily News of Los Angeles*, October 24, 1995.

14. Author's journal, October 25, 1995.

15. Ibid.

16. "Report: Ito, Wife Wept after Trial," *Daily News of Los Angeles*, October 26, 1995.

17. Author's journal, October 26, 1995.

18. "Report: Ito Wept."

19. Deutsch, interview.

20. Sloan, "Memories of the Simpson Trial."

21. Wilson, letter to Lucas.

Chapter 13

1. Jon Katz, "O. J. Simpson and the Death of Justice," Media Rant, January 24, 1997, http://webmonkey.wired.com/netizen/97/04/index0a.html.

2. Author's notes, January 5, 1995.

3. Ibid., March 16, 1995.

4. Wilson, letter to Lucas.

5. Ibid.

6. Dow, interview.

7. United States Supreme Court (*Estes v. Texas,* 381 U.S. 532 [1965]).

8. Egelko, "Spector Trial Renews Debate."

9. "Cameras in the Courtroom: Report on Rule 980," California Administrative Office of the Courts, May 2000.

10. Tim Sullivan (senior vice president, Court TV News), interview by author, October 10, 2007.

11. "Judicial Conference Opposes Use of Cameras in Federal Trial Courts," News Release, Administrative Office of the U. S. Courts, Office of Public Affairs, September 27, 2007.

12. Sullivan, interview.

13. Graham, Conference of Chief Justices.

14. Cochran, interview.

15. Craig Waters (communications counsel, Florida Supreme Court), interview by author, November 11, 2007.

16. Ibid.

17. Ibid.

18. Margulies, "Huge Audience Saw Trial Climax"; Richmond, "Nearly 100% of TVs; Dougherty, "On Just About Every Corner."

19. "From O. J. to Martha to Michael."

20. Author's notes, October 27, 1995.

21. Ibid.

22. "Media Procedure," Los Angeles Superior Court Rules of Court, Rule 4.1 (January 1, 1998, Amended, January 1, 2000).

23. Author's notes, May 11, 2005.

24. "From O. J. to Martha to Michael."

25. Ibid.

26. "Confidentiality in the Courts and Media: The Gathering Storm," National Conference on Courts and the Media, George Washington University School of Media and Public Affairs, Washington, D.C., December 5–6, 2005.

27. "From O. J. to Martha to Michael."

28. Ibid.

29. Ibid.

30. Geragos, "Thirteenth Juror."

31. Ibid.

32. Ibid.

33. Daniel Tepfer, "New Rules to Ease Courtroom Camera Access," *Connecticut Post* Online, June 24, 2007.

34. Paul Janensch, "Cameras a Good Fit in Courtroom," *Connecticut Post* Online, July 14, 2007; Connecticut Practice, Rules of Appellate Procedure, Chapter 70, Arguments and Media Coverage of Court Proceedings, Section 70.9.

35. "Judge Allows Cameras at Phil Spector Trial," Reuters, February 17, 2007.

36. Ibid.

37. Hengstler, interview, June 14, 2007.

38. Egelko, "Spector Trial Renews Debate."

39. Chemerinsky, interview, April 1, 2007.

40. "From O. J. to Martha to Michael."

41. Levenson, interview, March 5, 2007.

42. "Journalism and the Judiciary," by John Seigenthaler, First Amendment Center, Founder, Vanderbilt University, and David L. Hudson, First Amendment Center, Legal Scholar, Vanderbilt University, *NJC Alumni Magazine,* National Judicial College, University of Nevada, Reno, Winter 1997.

43. Mudd, interview, March 24, 2007.

44. Deutsch, interview.

45. Dow, interview.

46. "From O. J. to Martha to Michael."

47. Anthony Lewis, "Texas Executions: GW Bush Has Defined Himself, Unforgettably, as Shallow and Callous," *New York Times,* June 17, 2000; "Death Penalty 101," National Death Penalty Fact Sheet, Capital Punishment Project, American Civil Liberties Union, March 2007.

48. Graham, "Television, Celebrity, and the Law."

49. Graham, Conference of Chief Justices.

50. *United States of America v. Zacarias Moussaoui,* Criminal No. 01-455-A, Document #1857, Motion filed together with Affidavit by Zacarias Moussaoui to Withdraw Guilty Plea (Entered: 05/08/2006).

51. Carvajal, "Internet Site Provides Access."

52. *International Criminal Tribunal for the Former Yugoslavia v. Slobodan Milósević,* Crimes against Humanity and Violations of the Laws or Customs of War, Case No. IT-99-37-PT, The Hague, Netherlands, February 12, 2002–March 11, 2006.

53. *Iraqi Special Tribunal v. Saddam Hussein, Crimes Against Humanity,* October 19, 2005–November 5, 2006.

54. Graham, Conference of Chief Justices.

55. "From O. J. to Martha to Michael."

56. Ibid.

Chapter 14

1. Jerrianne Hayslett, "What a Difference a Lens Makes."

2. Francke, interview.

3. California Rules of Court, Rule 980.

4. Harriet Ryan, "Judge: Olson Plea Will Stand," Court TV News, December 3, 2001.

5. Dan Whitcomb and Dana Ford, "Mistrial Declared in Spector Trial," Reuters, September 27, 2007.

6. "From O. J. to Martha to Michael."

7. Tepfer, "New Rules."

8. Larry Fisher-Hertz, "Court Cameras Pushed in N.Y. Some Say Filing Proceedings Compromises Cases," *Poughkeepsie Journal,* January 31, 2007.

9. Ron Bolin, letter to *StarTribune*.com by, Netlets for Saturday, September 1, 2007, www.startribune.com.

10. "Innocence Project Wins 2nd Exoneration," *Law School News,* University of Wisconsin, Madison, www.law.wisc.edu/news/index.php?ID=663, September 11, 2003.

11. Meg Jones, "Avery Nephew Charged," *Milwaukee Journal Sentinel,* March 2, 2006.

12. Tom Kertscher, "Avery to Be Charged on DNA," *Milwaukee Journal Sentinel,* November 11, 2005.

13. "Dassey Recants ·Confession In Halbach Murder," August 4, 2006, www.wisn.com/dasseytrial/9630177/detail.html.

14. "Avery Trial Is Lesson in Courtroom Reality of Criminal Cases," editorial, *Manitowoc Herald Times Reporter,* February 18, 2007.

15. Patrick Willis, judge, Manitowoc County Circuit Court, interview by author, November 26, 2007.

16. Graham, "Television, Celebrity and the Law."

17. Ibid.

18. Carvajal, "Internet Site Provides Access."

19. Ibid.

20. Ibid.

21. Ibid.

22. Waters, interview.

23. Ibid.

24. "Public Access Web Site for Extraordinary Criminal Cases," DVD, Superior Court of California for the County of Santa Barbara, February 2005.

25. Ibid.

26. Ibid.

27. Dow, interview.

28. Peter Shaplen (owner, Peter Shaplen Productions), interview by author, November 19, 2007.

29. Dow, interview.

30. "From O. J. to Martha to Michael."

31. www.courtsandmedia.org.

32. Gary Hengstler, interview by author, July 6, 2007.

33. Ibid., August 2, 2007.

34. John McManus (director, www.GradeTheNews.org, California State University, San Jose), interview by author, November 15, 2007.

35. John McManus, "The Peterson Circus," interview by Kathy McAnally, *On the Media*, National Public Radio, March 12, 2004.

36. Herb Strentz (professor emeritus, Drake University School of Journalism and Mass Communication), J-Ethics listserv post, Des Moines, Iowa, October 26, 2004.

37. Herb Strentz, interview by author, November 13, 2007.

38. Twelfth Annual Video Competition and Pricing Report, Federal Communications Commission, Statistics, Industry Statistics, March 3, 2006.

39. "From O. J. to Martha to Michael."

40. Geragos, "Thirteenth Juror."

41. Sassone, "An Open Letter."

42. Shaplen, interview.

43. "From O. J. to Martha to Michael."

44. www.spj.org/mission.asp.

45. www.rtnda.org/pages/about-rtnda.php.

46. Ibid.

47. Andy Schotz (chair, Society of Professional Journalists Ethic Committee), interview, November 13, 2007.

48. Andy Schotz, "Easy to Report, Easy to Forget," *Quill: A Magazine by the Society of Professional Journalists* 95, no. 7 (September 2007).

49. Sonja Prostran (judge, Belgrade, Serbia, Municipal Court) and Milos Milić (reporter, B92, Belgrade, Serbia), "Transparency of Trials for Breaches of International Humanitarian Law in the Region of Former Yugoslavia," Report no. 16, March 1, 2006, www.yi.org.yu.

50. Milos Milić, presentation, Nevada Council for International Relations, Las Vegas, Nevada, October 17, 2006.

51. Ibid.

52. Tony Rutherford, "First U.S. Supreme Court Justice Ever to Walk MU's Hallowed Halls," *Huntington News Network*, September 11, 2007.

53. "Court OKs TV Cameras at Trials," KETV-TV 7, Omaha, Nebraska, March 14, 2008; Josh Verges, "Jury Still out on Courtroom Cameras: Justices to Decide How Far New Law Goes," *Argus Leader* (Sioux Falls, South Dakota), March 24, 2008; "Cameras Provide Window for Public: Judges Should Open Courtrooms When Practical, but Exceptions Are Clear," editorial, *Argus Leader*, March 30, 2008.

54. Emma Vaughn, "Cameras Could Get Rolling on High Court Sessions," *Los Angeles Times*, November 10, 2005.

55. Charles Krauthamer, "The Incompetent Trial of Saddam Hussein," *Washington Post*, December 9, 2005.

56. Dwain Price, "Humbled Tech Seeks a Rebound," *Star-Telegram*, October 23, 2007.

57. Andrea Peyser, "It's O. J. Vu All Over Again with Nutso Judge," *New York Post*, February 22, 2007.

58. "From O. J. to Martha to Michael."

59. Ito, interview, May 2, 2007.

60. Thomas Moyer (chief justice, Ohio Supreme Court) presentation, Conference of Court Public Information Officers, Columbus, Ohio, August 3, 2007.

Chapter 15

1. Author's journal, May 5, 1995.

2. Jerrianne Hayslett, "Multiple Agency Planning and Other Useful Strategies for High-Profile Events," *California Counties: Journal of the California State Association of Counties* (September–October 1997), 28.

3. Jerrianne Hayslett, *Sharon Rufo etal vs. Orenthal James Simpson,* Media Management Report, Los Angeles Superior Court Public Information Office, April 1997.

4. Hayslett, "Multiple Agency Planning," 30.

5. Hayslett, *Sharon Rufo etal vs. Orenthal James Simpson,* Media Management Report.

6. Public Trust News, National Center for State Courts (Spring 2003), www.ncsconline.org/projects_Initiatives/PTC/PublicTrustNews4.htm; "The Media, the Courts, and the Public"; "Public Understanding of and Support for the Courts: 2007 Annenberg Public Policy Center Judicial Survey Results; Jerrianne Hayslett, Serbia Special Court Consultant Report, National Center for State Courts, International Division, September 27, 2003.

7. Donald W. Reynolds National Center for Courts and Media, Courses, "First Amendment and Media Issues for Judges," "Basic Legal Affairs Reporting for Journalists," "Essential Court Teamwork in Dealing with the Media," www.judges.org/nccm/courses/courses.htm.

8. Ibid.

9. Bench-Bar-Media Advisory Group Mission Statement, Maryland Judiciary.

10. www.courts.state.co.us/exec/media/lawforjournalists.htm.

11. Craig Waters, interview.

12. Hayslett, Serbia Special Court Consultant Report.

13. Hayslett, Serbia Special Court Consultant Report, National Center for State Courts, International Division, June 10, 2004.

14. Shaplen, interview.

15. Alexander B. Aikman, "From Chaotic to Copesetic: Lessons in Media Relations for Courts from *People vs. Scott Peterson,*" *Court Manager* 19, no. 4, 9.

16. Ibid., 8.

17. Shaplen, interview.

18. Author's notes, November 22, 1994.

19. Ibid.

20. Jerrianne Hayslett, "Court-Media-Community Planning for High-Profile Cases," Library, 2002, 7, www.courtpio.org.

21. District Court Eagle County, Colorado, Plaintiff: People of the State of Colorado, Defendant: Kobe Bean, Case 03 CR 204, Fourth Amended Decorum Order www.courts.state.co.us/exec/media/eagle/07–04/DecorumOrder.pdf

22. View the Video, www.sbscpublicaccess.org.

23. Jerrianne Hayslett, *Rufo etal v. Orenthal James Simpson,* report, Los Angeles Superior Court Public Information Office, March 1998.

24. Hayslett, "Multiple Agency Planning," 8.

25. "From O. J. to Martha to Michael"; "Confidentiality in the Courts and Media."

26. Timothy R. Murphy, Paula L. Hannaford, Genevra Kay Loveland, and G. Thomas Munsterman, *Managing Notorious Trials* (Williamsburg: National Center for State Courts, 1998).

27. *The Journalist's Guide to Maryland's Legal System,* www.courts.state.md.us/journalistguide2003.pdf; *Media Guide to Tennessee's Legal System,* www.tsc.state.tn.us/geninfo/PRESSREL/pressroom.htm.

28. Hayslett, "Court-Media-Community Planning."

Bibliography

■ ■ ■

The following is a list of publications and documents that were among the sources for this book in addition to the trial transcript, court orders, government and news reports, and the author's notes and journal.

Abramson, Leslie. "The Appearance of Justice: Juries, Judges, and the Media," Leigh Buchanan Blenen lecture, Northwestern University, School of Law, *Journal of Criminal Law and Criminology,* Spring 1996.

Aikman, Alexander B. "From Chaotic to Copesetic: Lessons in Media Relations for Courts from *People vs. Scott Peterson,*" *Court Manager* 19, no. 4, 8–9.

Bruschke, Jon, and William E. Loges. *Free Press vs. Fair Trials: Examining Publicity's Role in Trial Outcomes* (Philadelphia: Lawrence Erlbaum, 2003).

Bugliosi, Vincent. *Outrage: The Five Reasons Why O. J. Simpson Got Away with Murder* (New York: Norton, 1996).

Carelli, Richard, and Linda Deutsch. *Covering the Courts: A Manual for the Associated Press Staff* (n.p.: Associated Press, 2002).

Cohn, Marjorie, and David Dow. *Cameras in the Courtroom: Television and the Pursuit of Justice* (Jefferson, N.C.: McFarland, 1998).

Court Review, the Journal of the American Judges Association 36, no. 3.

Donald W. Reynolds National Center for Courts and Media. "From O. J. to Martha to Michael: What Have We Learned about the Conduct and Coverage of Trials?" A Report, National Conference on Courts and Media, Reno, Nevada, 2007; "Confidentiality in the Courts and Media: The

Gathering Storm," National Conference on Courts and Media, A Report, Washington, D.C., 2007; "First Amendment and Media Issues for Judges," "Essential Court Teamwork in Dealing with the Media," "Basic Legal Affairs Reporting for Journalists" course materials, Donald W. Reynolds School of Journalism, University of Nevada, Reno.

Elias, Tom, and Dennis Schatzman. *The Simpson Trial in Black and White* (Toronto: Stoddart, 1996).

Geragos, Mark J. "The Thirteenth Juror: Media Coverage of Supersized Trials," Symposium: Celebrity Prosecutions, *Loyola of Los Angeles Law Review,* December 2006.

Hayslett, Jerrianne. *The People v. Orenthal James Simpson,* Los Angeles Superior Court Public Information Office Staff Report, January 1996; *Rufo et al v. Orenthal James Simpson,* Los Angeles Superior Court Public Information Office Media Management Report, April 1997; *Rufo et al v. Orenthal James Simpson,* Los Angeles Superior Court Public Information Office Staff Report, March 1998; "What A Difference a Lens Makes," *Court Manager* 12, no. 3 (Summer 1997); "Multiple Agency Planning and Other Useful Strategies for High-Profile Events" *California Counties* (September-October 1997); "Court-Media-Community Planning for High-Profile Cases," (2002), www.courtpio.org; Serbia Special Court Consultant Report, National Center for State Courts, International Division, September 27, 2003, June 10, 2004.

Judicature, American Judicature Society magazine 79, no. 2, (September–October 1995); 83, no. 2 (September–October 1999).

Murphy, Timothy R., Paula L. Hannaford, Genevra Kay Loveland, and G. Thomas Munsterman. *Managing Notorious Trials* (Williamsburg: National Center for State Courts, 1998).

Prostran, Sonja (judge, Belgrade, Serbia, Municipal Court) and Milos Milić (reporter, B92, Belgrade, Serbia). "Transparency of Trials for Breaches of International Humanitarian Law in the Region of Former Yugoslavia," Report no. 16, March 1, 2006, www.yi.org.yu.

Public Trust News, National Center for State Courts (spring 2003).

Schotz, Andy. "Easy to Report, Easy to Forget," *Quill: A Magazine by the Society of Professional Journalists* 95, no. 7 (September 2007).

Toobin, Jeffrey. *The Run of His Life: The People vs. O. J. Simpson* (New York: Random House, 1996).

Acknowledgments

■ ■ ■

My deepest appreciation to my former journalism professor Dean Mills for his stellar teaching, mentoring, and fortuitous connections, to University of Missouri Press director and editor in chief Beverly Jarrett for her belief in and enthusiasm for *Anatomy of a Trial,* to UMP assistant managing editor Sara Davis for her invaluable guidance, deft editing, resourcefulness, patience, and wisdom, and to the many other UMP staff who helped with the development and promotion of the book, especially publicity manager Beth Chandler. My eternal gratitude to my forbearing family who lived through the Simpson trial, my postcourt years as a globe-trotting consultant, and the birthing and completion of this book. My special and profound thanks to my husband, Hibbie, for his saintly support, faith, encouragement, and endless reading and rereading, and to my son, Chapen, for his critiques and for his film- and TV-editor's eagle-eyed scrutiny of the final draft. Last, but by far not least, my writers group, who listened to each chapter, offered invaluable observations and suggestions and kept me on track from start to finish. Chief among the group is my longtime friend Michael Szymanski who, like my family, experienced the throes of the trial through my many iterations and served as the most supportive advocate one could ever hope to have.

Index

■ ■ ■